PENGUIN BOOKS

THE NEW PENGUIN FREUD
GENERAL EDITOR: ADAM PHILLIPS

Wild Analysis

Sigmund Freud was born in 1856 in Moravia; between the ages of
four and eighty-two his home was in Vienna; in 1938 Hitler's invasion
of Austria forced him to seek asylum in London, where he died in
the following year. His career began with several years of brilliant
work on the anatomy and physiology of the nervous system. He was
almost thirty when, after a period of study under Charcot in Paris,
his interest first turned to psychology; and after ten years of clinical
work in Vienna (at first in collaboration with Breuer, an older colleague) he invented what was to become psychoanalysis. This began
simply as a method of treating neurotic patients through talking, but
it quickly grew into an accumulation of knowledge about the workings
of the mind in general. Freud was thus able to demonstrate the
development of the sexual instinct in childhood and, largely on
the basis of an examination of dreams, arrived at his fundamental
discovery of the unconscious forces that influence our everyday
thoughts and actions. Freud's life was uneventful, but his ideas
have shaped not only many specialist disciplines, but also the whole
intellectual climate of the twentieth century.

Alan Bance is Research Professor in German at the University of
Southampton. His publications include books on nineteenth- and
twentieth-century literature and many articles on German literature
and culture in a social, political and historical context. Previous
translations include A. M. Vogt's *Art of the Nineteenth Century*.

Adam Phillips was formerly Principal Child Psychotherapist at Char-
ing Cross Hospital in London. He is the author of several books
on psychoanalysis including *On Kissing, Tickling and Being Bored*,
Darwin's Worms, *Promises, Promises* and *Houdini's Box*.

SIGMUND FREUD

Wild Analysis

Translated by Alan Bance
with an Introduction by Adam Phillips

PENGUIN BOOKS

PENGUIN BOOKS

Published by the Penguin Group
Penguin Books Ltd, 80 Strand, London WC2R ORL, England
Penguin Putnam Inc., 375 Hudson Street, New York, New York 10014, USA
Penguin Books Australia Ltd, 250 Camberwell Road, Camberwell, Victoria 3124, Australia
Penguin Books Canada Ltd, 10 Alcorn Avenue, Toronto, Ontario, Canada M4V 3B2
Penguin Books India (P) Ltd, 11, Community Centre, Panchsheel Park, New Delhi – 110 017, India
Penguin Books (NZ) Ltd, Cnr Rosedale and Airborne Roads, Albany, Auckland, New Zealand
Penguin Books (South Africa) (Pty) Ltd, 24 Sturdee Avenue, Rosebank 2196, South Africa

Penguin Books Ltd, Registered Offices: 80 Strand, London WC2R ORL, England

www.penguin.com

'Über "wilde" Psychoanalyse' first published 1910 in *Zentralblatt für Psychoanalyse* 1
(Wiesbaden: Bergmann Publishers)
'Die Handhabung der Traumdeutung in der Psychoanalyse', 'Zur Dynamik der
Übertragung' and 'Ratschläge für den Arzt bei der psychoanalytischen Behandlung' first
published 1912 in *Zentralblatt für Psychoanalyse* 2 (Wiesbaden: Bergmann Publishers)
'Zur Einleitung der Behandlung' first published 1913 in *Internationale Zeitschrift für
ärztliche Psychoanalyse* 1
'Bemerkungen über die Übertragungsliebe' first published 1915 in *Zeitschrift für
Psychoanalyse* 3
'Die Widerstände gegen die Psychoanalyse' first published 1925 in *Imago* 11 (3)
Die Frage der Laienanalyse: Unterredungen mit einem Unparteiischen first published 1926
(Leipzig, Vienna and Zurich: Internationaler Psychoanalytischer Verlag)
'Nachwort zur *Frage der Laienanalyse*' first published 1927 in *Internationale Zeitschrift für
Psychoanalyse* 13 (3)
'Die endliche und die unendliche Analyse' and 'Konstruktionen in der Analyse' first
published 1937 in *Internationale Zeitschrift für Psychoanalyse* 23

This translation published in Penguin Classics 2002

010

Sigmund Freud's German texts collected in *Gesammelte Werke* (1940–52) copyright ©
Imago Publishing Co., Ltd, London, 1943, 1946, 1948, 1950
Translation and editorial matter copyright © Alan Bance, 2002
Introduction copyright © Adam Phillips, 2002
All rights reserved

The moral rights of the translator and author of the Introduction have been asserted

Set in 10/12.5 pt PostScript Adobe New Caledonia
Typeset by Rowland Phototypesetting Ltd, Bury St Edmunds, Suffolk
Printed in England by Clays Ltd, St Ives plc

www.greenpenguin.co.uk

ALWAYS LEARNING   **PEARSON**

Contents

Introduction

> I suspect that one can learn more about the problems of interpretation from the puzzled descriptions of those for whom certain kinds of interpretation are incomprehensible than from the authorized voices of the participants in those interpretive exercises.
>
> (Miguel Tamen, *Friends of Interpretable Objects*)

Freud, who was himself resistant to therapy, invented a form of therapy called psychoanalysis; and it was a therapy based, as these papers show, on understanding the resistance to the therapy he had invented. When it came to writing about the practice of psychoanalysis – both what doing it involved, and just how you could tell that someone hadn't understood it – Freud found himself investigating what it was about the analyst and the patient that made psychoanalysis so impossible. Indeed, in the late paper 'Analysis Terminable and Interminable', published in 1937 (when Freud was eighty-one), Freud goes as far as to suggest that one of the ways the analyst knows that she is practising real psychoanalysis is that real psychoanalysis keeps on not working in the same ways. It is consistent in what it fails to do for people – to free them, for example, from the special attractions of their history, from telling certain kinds of family stories, from the appeal of particular fears. And as a scientist Freud is interested in failure, in how and why his theory and practice don't work: in the heuristic value of anomaly and ignorance.

But also, like many writers of his time, Freud saw something he wanted to call sexuality – a sexuality that people were, by definition, largely unconscious of – as the making and the breaking point of what went on between people. Sexual desire, from childhood on, was the medium of exchange between people. Sexuality was the satisfaction they seemed to suffer, and the suffering that seemed to satisfy them. Sexuality was what there was to be disturbed about. And it was this, specifically, that psychoanalysis addressed: the rationalization of sexuality. Psychoanalytic treatment – as the five 'papers on technique' here show – utilized the patient's capacity to love and desire as a means to an end. The stuff of romance became the stuff of cure. When Freud is writing about technique in psycho-analysis – and these papers represent his most significant contri-butions to the subject over three decades of his work – it is important to remember that he is talking about what a couple, an analyst and a so-called patient, can say and hear in a room together. For better and for worse.

Freud, as we shall see, was always ambivalent about the romance of cure. He was always torn between being a lover of conversation and a lover of being right. As a lover of conversation he just wanted to go on talking (and writing) in his lifelong pursuit of the pleasures that made his life a continual temptation; as a lover of being right he wanted to come to some sort of conclusion about this temptation. About just what it was that made his (and therefore other people's) life worth living. So in these papers we find Freud's wish for definitive formulation of the means and ends of psychoanalysis coming up against something about the subject – the vagaries of unconscious desire – that makes such traditional forms of authority, of closure, seem somehow beside the point. As though there was something about psychoanalysis that made the more assured pronouncements about it sound silly; dogma staving off a sense of the ridiculous. When Freud writes, as he does in these papers, about whether sexuality – in all its unconscious provenance – is subject to what can realistically be called psychoanalytic technique, and, indeed, about why someone would wish that it was, he is writing, unavoidably, as the ironist of his own project. The unconscious spells the death of whole-heartedness. And if the doctor – on his own terms, in the light of his own theory – cannot be whole-hearted about his wish to cure, about his desire to understand, then what is he up to? Unsurprisingly perhaps, Freud was never all that keen about being a therapist. He preferred being a writer, and writing about why he preferred being a writer.

Freud had, in his own words, 'become a therapist against my will'. 'I knew no longing other than that for philosophical insight', he wrote to his friend and colleague Wilhelm Fleiss in 1896, 'and I am now in the process of fulfilling it, as I steer from medicine over to psychology.'[1] This steering that was going on in the 1890s was Freud's invention of what would be called psychoanalysis. It would always be a question for Freud whether psychoanalysis was a branch of medicine (and so a form of treatment and even of cure), or a move over to something else called psychology, which would then free Freud to 'nourish the hope of reaching my original goal, philosophy'.[2] It would not be long, of course, before Freud would be proposing that everyone's original goal was the forbidden object of incestuous desire; psychoanalysis was to be, if nothing else, a radical re-description of original human goals, and of their pursuit. For 'original goals', or 'personal ambitions' – or even for the Sovereign Goods of traditional moral philosophy – Freud would write, objects of (forbidden) desire. And objects of desire would be defined, would be recognized by our indirection in relation to them. And by just how early they turn up in our lives.

'My interest', Freud wrote in 1935 in the 'Postscript to an Autobiographical Study', 'after making a lifelong detour through the natural sciences, medicine and psychotherapy, returned to the cultural problems which had fascinated me long before, when I was a youth scarcely old enough for thinking.'[3] In retrospect a detour is part of the route. It is of interest that Freud considers all the ways in which he actually made a living as possibly a distraction from, or a circuitous way to, his real fascinations. When Freud is writing about psychoanalytic technique he is writing about psychoanalysis as a detour. He is unsure, in other words, as many analysts after him have been, as to whether psychoanalysis is, or even could be, an object of desire, an end in itself. A technique, after all, is a means devised by someone to get what they want. It makes wanting make sense. A technique is not supposed to have an unconscious. The analyst's technique should tell us what the analyst wants, and what the analyst wants from psychoanalysis. It is this that Freud is struggling to work out in the papers in this book.

In 1913 Freud entertained the hope that, 'the time is not far distant when it will be generally recognized that no sort of nervous disturbance can be understood and treated without the help of the line of approach and often of the technique of psycho-analysis'.[4] In these papers – in which Freud asks both what is wild psychoanalysis, and what is wild about psychoanalysis? – these are Freud's haunting and daunting distinctions. What is the link between understanding and treatment, are they the same thing, and if not why not? Which is a version of the question: why would the analyst and the patient, why would anyone, prefer to understand and be understood rather than to desire and be desired? And, is psycho-analysis simply a line of approach, or a technique; an unusual form of curiosity and description, or a transmittable method for the treatment of human unhappiness? Should psychoanalysis best be seen as a contributor to other disciplines, or as a discipline in its own right? This, at least, Freud is prepared to wonder about.

Psychoanalysis is everything that is said and written about psycho-analysis; and no writer is the privileged authority on his own work. Inevitably, Freud was always puzzled about what he was writing about when he was writing about psychoanalysis. His writing – in which he can be so apparently lucid and fair in describing the obscurity and the derangement of what he calls the unconscious – is a performing of this puzzle. There is far more speculation and conjecture in his writing, more theory-making and story-telling, than instruction or even guidelines about the actual practice of psychoanalysis (and his case histories are nothing if not tributes to the cult of his personality; they are not easily replicable or imitable experiments). It was not clear whether psychoanalysis was the opportunity to have a new kind of experience of talking and listening, which was indeterminate in its consequences; or whether, more traditionally, it was a new way of helping people through understanding them. Freud's ambivalence about psychoanalysis as a form of therapy – the senses in which a how-to book about psychoanalysis would miss the point about psychoanalysis – is reflected in how little

Freud wrote, how little he seemed interested in writing about psychoanalytic technique. It is one of the secrets of psychoanalysis that Freud was not overly impressed by its curative powers. Indeed, what Freud never wrote about the teaching and the practice of psychoanalysis was, as several of his followers noticed, the key text in psychoanalysis. And the whole issue was complicated by the apparent discrepancy between Freud's written prescriptions about psychoanalysis and the actualities of his clinical practice. 'There is a very great irony at work here', Freud's recent biographer Louis Breger writes:

Freud's published papers on technique prohibit the very activities – personal support, praise, friendly interactions, the giving of gifts – that were involved in successful therapeutic outcomes, while recommending the methods – abstinence, anonymity, silence – that were unhelpful and damaging. Freud's publications on technique came to define classical psychoanalysis for many years; the effects of his actual behaviour with patients is only known from their scattered memoirs, reports and interviews, none of which had any effect on the rules for how a 'proper analysis' was to be conducted. When commentators note that Freud did not practice analysis in accord with his published recommendations they typically see this as a lapse, forgivable because he was a genius who was free to do as he pleased.[5]

There was, to put it mildly, an uneasy relationship for Freud between theory and practice. But then psychoanalysis was always about the odd connections and disconnections between people's words and their so-called actions. Freud's papers on technique – his ruminations on the teaching, the transmission, the practice of psychoanalysis – take us to the heart of the puzzle that is psychoanalysis; and of Freud's resistance to his own discovery.

Freud, of course, was the first wild analyst in the sense that he was never psychoanalysed by anyone else. Like many of the early analysts he had no psychoanalytic training because there was no psychoanalytic training available. As he evolved his own method he evolved his own definitions of what it was, of what it would be to be a psychoanalyst. Freud knew he was a psychoanalyst because he described himself, he described what he did, as psychoanalysis. Freud, as the founder, seemed uniquely placed to be the legitimator, answerable to no one else, of his own invention. He could, as it were, dispense (and dispense with) qualifications. When his colleague, George Groddeck, asked Freud in a letter, 'What is a psychoanalyst?', Freud was in a position to reply: 'Anyone who has recognized transference and resistance as the focal points of therapy belongs irretrievably to the mad horde.'[6] So being a psychoanalyst simply involves particular recognitions. But having recognized such things as transference and resistance, why is one then 'irretrievably' a psychoanalyst, and why are analysts as a group referred to by Freud as a 'mad horde', rather than, say, a group of like-minded individuals, or indeed some kind of institution? Where in this description is the idea of training? The idea that one could be lost to psychoanalysis; or, indeed, that to acknowledge the power of transference and resistance was akin to joining a cult, suggests a kind of exhilarated fearfulness in Freud about what he might have unleashed through psychoanalysis. The very idea of being self-legitimated, of being free to invent a description of oneself, and confer it on others, was, as it were, unprecedented. In any other profession a person is defined, is qualified, by the institution that trains them. For none of that extraordinary group of early analysts was there a psychoanalytic training, or a psychoanalytic institution available. They had to wait on Freud's word. Until, that is, they grew impatient. And it seemed to be about technique that Freud was at his most reserved.

'I do not share, for instance, your view', his follower Ferenczi was writing to Freud as late as 1930, 'that the therapeutic process is negligible or unimportant, and that simply because it appears less interesting to us we should ignore it.'[7] Replying to a letter of Freud on 27 December 1931, Ferenczi is still harking back to what is in his view Freud's own resistance, Freud's blind spot: 'You'll doubtless recall', he writes, 'that it was I who pointed out the necessity of also publishing details regarding technique, provided it had been applied methodically; you, on the other hand, were inclined to keep communication on technical points to the minimum.'[8] Freud, who writes so insistently in these papers on technique about the founding force of human resistance, seems himself to be resistant about psychoanalytic technique. It was the paradox that Ferenczi was rightly attentive to; and that makes his own *Clinical Diary*, and the book he wrote with another 'heretic', Otto Rank, *The Development of Psychoanalysis*, the essential parallel texts to the papers in this volume.

Freud wrote in his *Autobiographical Study* that he 'felt no particular partiality for the position and activity of a physician in those early years, nor, by the way, later. Rather, I was moved by a sort of greed for knowledge.'[9] The man who wrote to his *fiancée* when he was a young and struggling doctor that he would, 'sit by a sickbed in order to observe . . . I treat human suffering as an object';[10] the man who would warn Ferenczi that he, Ferenczi, was 'too much under the influence of his patients';[11] the man who promoted the idea of 'analytic neutrality' (the analyst's asserting his anonymity for the sake of the treatment) was clearly preoccupied by the forms and the necessities of self-protection. As though when people get together they are contagious, potentially too evocative for each other, and that something needs to be done about this. And one of the things Freud seemed to be doing, wittingly or unwittingly, was trying to describe, through the figure of the psychoanalyst, a new way of being present to another person in a way that freed them – both of them, the analyst and the patient – to think and feel and speak freely. The question for Freud was, what kind of freedom does the analyst need in order to free the patient to speak? The problem, in terms of technique, was that this was not simply or solely a question of technique, of knowing which rules the analyst must abide by.

'There should not be any doubt', Freud apparently replied to Adler in one of the meetings of the first psychoanalytic group, the Wednesday Society, 'that the psychoanalytic method can be learned. It will be possible to learn it once the arbitrariness of individual psychoanalysts is curbed by tested rules.'[12] And yet when it came to the making of rules, not to mention the testing of them, Freud was curiously unforthcoming. To be a science, as Freud knew, psychoanalysis required testable rules; and scientists, by definition, with their shareable procedures, with their capacity to replicate experiments, were not subject to the arbitrariness of individual judgement. And yet psychoanalysis seemed to be a science in which none of the experiments could be easily or obviously replicated. No third party could ever witness a psychoanalytic treatment, and no two analysts or so-called patients could ever be the same. In science, as Freud intimates, you can only have a method – that is, something that can be reproduced – if you have testable rules; a method, like a teaching, must be repeatable (science makes a methodology out of the repetition compulsion). But what the psychoanalysts kept coming up against was what Freud would begin to call the 'personal factor' in psychoanalysis; that the analyst, just like her patient, had an unconscious and a personal history. In other words, did the analyst need to be less unconscious, so to speak, than the patient, in order to do her work? And if this were possible – and the unconscious was in Freud's view glimpsable but unfathomable – how could it be achieved? After all, there is no test for unconsciousness. Psycho-analysis itself may have been the product of the arbitrariness of one individual founding father; but its future depended on the curbing of such arbitrariness. It was one of Freud's great gifts to show us that such contradictions were the sign of conflict; and that signs of conflict were signs of life. A close reading of the papers in this volume reveals Freud at his most seemingly and certainly self-contradictory. There was nothing like writing about psychoanalytic technique to expose Freud's most instructive confusions. Trying to convince other people is always the best cure for self-doubt.

It would make sense that one would not be able to write with conventional coherence about psychoanalysis. The unconscious, as described by Freud, would see to that; because the unconscious, by its very nature, is disruptive. That Freud wished to write with apparent clarity about something of such apparent obscurity as the unconscious is one of the many unremitting ironies he had to contend with in writing about psychoanalysis. And perhaps especially when writing about the implied mastery involved in the whole notion of technique (it is the difference between describing a dream and describing a rule). If the unconscious is amenable to technique – and the whole practice, if not the theorizing of psychoanalysis depends upon it being so – this, in itself, would change our sense of what the unconscious is like. The idea of technique implies that someone knows what they are doing. After the inventions of psychoanalysis, the idea of knowing what you are doing, the idea of a person as an agent of intentions that are transparent to himself, never quite makes sense. Where the ego progresses, Freud suggests, the unconscious digresses (the motto of the ego is: *no links where none intended*). So these papers should be read, among other things, to see what the sentences that are called psychoanalysis do to the whole notion of technique; and, indeed, to our ideas of science, and truth, and love, the other key words in these texts.

❀

Freud's infamous attitude to what he called the 'heresies' in his psychoanalytic 'movement' – the innovations, most notably, of Adler, Jung, Rank and Ferenczi – was itself a sign of just how wild he feared psychoanalysis might be. Other people always represent the parts of one's mind that one has no control over. And these particular people that Freud needed to punish and pathologize and disown – and with whom he is in dialogue in these papers – showed him something that he already knew, and that was integral to psychoanalysis as he had conceived it; and this was, simply, the limits of his own omniscience. To assume that there is an unconscious is to believe that there really are other people, other voices, inside and outside oneself (that if there is a mind it has minds of its own). If you encourage people to speak freely as psychoanalysis does, then you have to encourage people to bear more conflict. Psychoanalysis, like the burgeoning democracies it grew up around, is an experiment in how many voices can be contained without the relief of violence. Freud, as we shall see, is sceptical – and therefore both insistent and often vague – about technique because he senses that it may be a forlorn attempt to contain the uncontainable. We can see Freud in these papers being boldly straightforward in describing what the aspiring psychoanalyst is supposed to do; and then, as he begins to follow his thoughts, his words through, he seems to run out of steam, or into profound doubt. It is often as if he is saying – especially in the late papers: this is what you do, and this is why it doesn't work. But that why psychoanalysis doesn't work tells you more about what modern people are like. As though psychoanalysis is at its most revealing where it fails. Its competence resides in what it can show us about its own incompetence. It cures us of the notion of cure.

To read these papers in the order in which they were written, as they are presented here, is to read the story of Freud's growing disillusionment with psychoanalysis as a treatment; his sense, over time, of the limits of what psychoanalysis can do; of the intractable obstacles to cure. But as the therapy reaches its limits, the theory, in its description of why this is so, grows stronger. As Freud writes his elegies here for the idea of what was once called the perfectibility of man, for our capacity to be happier, freer and more just – and, of course, for psychoanalysis as a means to such ends – he is at the same time at his most startlingly speculative about what was once called the human condition. Freud the writer triumphs where Freud the doctor falters. It is a wonderful piece of extravagant ambition to invent a form of cure, and then to suggest that where it fails reveals not the limits of the treatment, but the limits of life itself.

°

> . . . the myth that rationality consists in being constrained by rule.
> (Richard Rorty, *Consequences of Pragmatism*)

What Freud had realized by 1910, the date of the first paper here, 'On "Wild" Psychoanalysis', was that the resistance to psychoanalysis in his professional world was akin to the resistance of the patient in psychoanalysis. Freud is excessively mindful in all these papers of the critics of psychoanalysis, and of the ways in which his patients are unwilling to hear or accept what he has to say. And yet this embattled Freud – even when he is in calm and reasonable dialogue with himself as critic in 'The Question of Lay Analysis' – is also discovering something very interesting: that you can find out what something is, in this case psychoanalysis, by describing the resistances to it. Freud, in other words uses criticism, indeed needs conflict, to define what he is doing (if there is an unconscious then there is no reason to assume that Freud understands psychoanalysis any better than anyone else does; he too is trying to work out what it might be). If you want to get a sense of what something (or someone) is, Freud seems to say, then find out who resists it and why. Only through conflict can there be sense; only by rejection (or negation, as Freud called it) and an interest in the nature of rejection, are a person's desires revealed. Like the neurotic patients who Freud as a psychoanalyst identifies with – like psychoanalysts 'they' are not taken seriously or properly listened to; 'they' are spurned by the medical profession – Freud exploits in his writing the satisfactions, the benefits of conflict.

'On "Wild" Psychoanalysis' begins with a patient's complaint against a doctor; it is, once again, the traditional story of the helpful person who harms. 'Long experience', Freud writes, 'has taught me, as it might anyone else, not to accept at face value what patients tell me about their doctor, especially if they are neurotic'(p. 3). Just as Freud is suspicious of neurotics – that is to say, he wonders whether they are telling the truth – the public is suspicious about psychoanalysts. And yet Freud uses this truth-telling drama to proffer an account of real psychoanalysis (it is not clear what the opposite of wild analysis is). Freud accepts what the woman says, endorses her criticism of the doctor who uses his smattering of psychoanalytic knowledge so ineptly; and then concludes by saying, 'In the case of the lady whose complaint about the doctor we have heard, I am inclined to think that the wild analyst did more for the patient than any highly rated specialist who would have told her that she was suffering from a "vasomotor neurosis"'(p. 8). Wild analysis is better than no analysis; a little psychoanalytic knowledge can go a long way. Reading books about psychoanalysis, we read here, won't work; but reading books on psychoanalysis can tell us why reading books on psychoanalysis won't work. And the reason for this – the error of technique that this doctor is guilty of, in Freud's view – is that there is no cure by information. '[T]he illness', Freud writes, 'is not located in this ignorance itself [ignorance about psychosexual desire], but in the foundation of ignorance, the *inner resistances* that are the cause of the ignorance and continue to sustain it'(p. 7).

It's not what the patient doesn't know that needs to be addressed, it's why and how they go about not knowing. And the neurotic's art of unknowingness takes long and patient exploration. To call the crass doctor Freud describes in this paper a wild analyst seems unduly glamorous.

The wild psychoanalyst is, according to Freud, someone who has not been 'following the clear rules of psychoanalytic technique'; and these rules can only be learned, 'like other medical techniques, from accomplished practitioners'(p. 8). But, apart from the obvious question about legitimation here – who legitimates the legitimators? – it is not clear whether Freud has provided any clear rules. It is as though he takes for granted what a rule is, and what it is to follow one. He tells us about the 'conditions' for analysis: the preparatory work of interpretation that begins to familiarize the patient with what he might have repressed, the cultivating of an attachment to the analyst, a sufficiently positive transference. And he tells us what the analyst must believe in: the nature of resistance, the (psychoanalytic) facts of psychosexuality, free association, the workings of the unconscious. And then he says that the wild analyst, who followed none of these putative rules, probably did the patient some good. It would not be odd to wonder what the rules are, and why not following them might also work.

These techniques, Freud says, can only be acquired by 'sacrificing much time, effort and success'(p. 8); and yet the wild analyst, who has done none of this bracing and taxing training, has still managed to direct his patient's attention to 'the real cause of her trouble, or at least to the right area, and despite all her resistance his intervention will not lack favourable results'(pp. 8–9). It is a remarkably confident prediction for someone promoting the value of a training that he himself never had. There was, after all, no accomplished practitioner of psychoanalysis for Freud to learn from. It is not surprising, perhaps, that Freud had a certain ambivalence about psychoanalytic training; his 'technique', after all, was something he had to make up, with help from other disciplines, as he went along. Freud's divided loyalty – what in psychoanalytic language would be called a 'split identification' – between the wild analyst and the domesticated analyst is a consistent theme in these papers. He lays down the law with his misgivings shining through. He can't quite bring himself to be too hard on this inept wild analyst; the one who is just trying something out.

So it is an interesting exercise in reading through these papers to make a list of what Freud calls the rules and to see what kind of rules they are. What kind of rule, for example, could there be – and, of course, how would you follow it? – to enable a patient to make what Freud calls in 'On "Wild" Psychoanalysis' an 'attachment to the doctor (through *transference*) [that] has become strong enough to create an emotional relationship that rules out further attempts at flight'(p. 7)? Can trust be created by following a rule? There are very few relationships that can guarantee the ruling out of further attempts at flight. And if there was a technique for creating trust, what would that say about the nature of that trust? The wild analyst that Freud has such mixed feelings about engendered enormous distrust in his patient, and yet Freud still thinks that some good might have come of it. It is around issues of trust and attachment and desire – of the patient for the analyst, and more guardedly of the analyst for the patient – that the question of technique, the issue of the rules, becomes tricky for Freud. It is as though in writing about technique it is implied that what the analyst wants is merely to abide by the rules of psychoanalysis; when Freud knows that, as a person with an unconscious, the analyst is likely to be wanting rather more than that. Given what he thinks of as the nature of unconscious desire, it is not clear or convincing to Freud that there can be techniques or rules for its containment. Psychoanalysis, after all, was doing something horribly disillusioning, if not outright scandalous; it was using the patient's capacity to love and desire as an instrument for a cure. As though there was something better, some other more important need that the patient had than loving his doctor.

Initially the psychoanalyst had to do something to induce what Freud calls an attachment, an emotional relationship that the patient has to have with the analyst as a precondition for the treatment. And then it will be the analysis of that very attachment that will be the cure. The technique is a calling up, an evoking of the patient's desire, and then instead of acting on her desire the patient must be encouraged, against enormous resistance, to understand it. Like the analyst, she must speak but not touch. Psychoanalysis is about what two people can say to each other if they agree not to have sex. The question for Freud was whether the desire that was disclosed in psychoanalytic treatment was amenable to something that could reasonably be called a technique. And if there was no teachable technique – if the success or failure of psychoanalytic treatment depended upon something as indeterminate as 'the personal factor', who the analyst happened to be – then the legitimacy of psychoanalysis as a science was in question. What was wild about the psychoanalysis Freud had invented was the wayward urgencies and enigmas of unconscious desire. If the unconscious was as Freud described it, what made the analyst more stable, more authoritative than the patient? And who was in a position to decide (the unconscious as described by Freud plays havoc with the whole notion of integrity)? After the inventions of psychoanalysis it is not quite clear what it would be to be a realistic person. It was not that Freud wasn't that interested in psychoanalysis as a therapy; it was that he was all too aware that to write about psychoanalysis as a technique – and so, inevitably, to write about the training of analysts – was to write about the conundrums that were constitutive of its theory and practice. To write about technique, in short, was to write about what the analyst was supposed to want.

If the unconscious is rule-bound – as Freud proposes in, among other places, *The Interpretation of Dreams* (1900), and in 'Formulations on the Two Principles of Mental Functioning', written the year after 'On "Wild" Psychoanalysis' – then, by the same token, there could be a rule-bound technique for deciphering its energies and inclinations. But if what he called 'the unconscious' was also, as Freud kept sensing through his sober, tempered prose, something that made a mockery of rules; if indeed unconscious desire was by definition desire for the forbidden, and was therefore by its very nature targeting the rules; then the unconscious was the saboteur of the ego's world of rules and methodical procedures. Indeed, from a psychoanalytic point of view following a rule could be re-described as obsessional neurosis. Dreams may go by the book – maybe constructed along the lines of a book called *The Interpretation of Dreams* – but the forces and meanings, the drifts of desire and attention they dramatize and disguise are cause for disarray. There can be no making of sense without rules for doing so; but by the same token, rules can reassure us that sense can be made (if there are rules we must know what we are doing). When Freud writes about psychoanalytic technique he comes up against the limits, not to mention the anomalies of sense-making (in 'Constructions in Analysis' he notes that a construction can be inaccurate but sufficient: that the histories that work in psychoanalysis are not necessarily the histories that happened). In trying to make sense of the ways in which his patients didn't make sense to themselves – indeed didn't want to make sense, didn't want meaning as an object of desire – he can't help but wonder about the value, for human beings, of their intelligibility to themselves and others. Psychoanalysis may be an epistemological project, a therapy through knowledge of oneself and others; but whether unconscious desire could be an object of knowledge in the same way that other natural phenomena like bodies and planets were, was not quite clear. It is as though Freud is wondering, in his scant writings about the teaching and practice of psychoanalysis, whether it is possible for a person to float free of the reassurance of family stories in all their myriad narrative forms; whether there are other satisfactions than the satisfactions of personal history.

°

> things changed to the names he gave them,
> then lost their names . . .
>
> (Robert Lowell, 'Ulysses and Circe')

In 1908, Ernest Jones tells us, in volume two of his biography of Freud, that Freud was thinking of writing 'A General Account of Psychoanalytic Technique', but it kept being put off. In 1909 Freud told Jones that he wanted to write 'a little memorandum of maxims and rules of technique'. That it would be little, and that it would include maxims and rules – wisdom, and the procedures for its disclosure – an odd mixing of genres for a scientist, is itself telling. And the book was never written. In a paper given at the 1910 Nuremberg Congress of Psychoanalysis, 'The Future Prospects of Psychoanalytic Therapy', Freud announced that he planned, 'in the near future' to write 'A General Methodology of Psychoanalysis'. But this too, another generalizing text, was never written ('a therapeutic procedure', Freud reminds us in this paper, 'cannot be carried out in the same way as a theoretical investigation').[13] And then, between December 1911 and July 1914 he wrote the six 'papers on technique', five of which are published here ('Remembering, Repeating and Working Through' is newly translated, and newly contextualized in the volume entitled *Beyond the Pleasure Principle*). And after these papers Freud's main contributions to the subject are in the other writings re-translated in this volume. Every ten years or so – around 1914, around 1925, and again around 1936/7 – against significant internal resistance (and often provoked by significant others), Freud had a go at writing about the actual practice of psychoanalysis. But as Freud knew, unconscious desire and psychoanalytic technique were uneasy bedfellows. There was nothing more self-revealing, nothing more autobiographical, in its way, than the attempt to prescribe and describe the psychoanalyst's working methods. Because his working methods were the official – and often officious – form his desire took.

When Freud writes about technique, in short, he is writing about truth-telling. In telling the truth or in telling the public truth about what the psychoanalyst is supposed to do, and about how psychoanalysis is supposed to work – we must read his letters for the more unofficial truths – he has to say something about how love works. Because, from a psychoanalytic point of view all truth-telling is about love. What the analyst does is the clue to what he loves and wants. 'Sexual love', Freud writes in 'Observations on Love in Transference', 'undoubtedly has a prime place among life's experiences . . . Everybody knows this, apart from a few weird fanatics, and arranges his life accordingly; only in scientific circles does anyone make a fuss about admitting it' (p. 77). What distinguishes the analyst is that he doesn't fall for, doesn't fall in with, the patient's love for him. 'However highly [the analyst] prizes love', Freud writes, 'he must value more highly still his opportunity to lift the patient over a decisive stage in her life' (p. 77). What the analyst prizes more than love is the patient's development; though why this is so Freud doesn't tell us. In Freud's view there are two kinds of love; the love that thwarts our growing up (transference love), and the love that makes it possible. Our love of the future drains away into our love of the past. Psychoanalysis shows us how we take refuge from the shock of the new.

The analyst, though, has to persuade the patient to believe his progress myth; to live as if there is something better than, something other than transference love (the love that is merely a repetition of past loves). In 'Observations on Love in Transference' – as a title a quite different proposition from Strachey's 'Observations on Trans-ference-Love' – there are two people who resist the distinction: the analyst, in a certain mood, and someone Freud calls 'women of elemental passion, who will not put up with any surrogates' (p. 74). On the one hand this transference love 'destroy[s] the authority of the doctor by reducing him to a mere lover' (p. 70); and yet, Freud writes, this 'love in transference does not seem inferior to any other; you have the impression you could achieve anything by its means' (p. 76). Freud, in other words, is wondering what the phrase 'a mere lover' might mean; and why medical authority would be the preferred (sexual) position. Is transference love the truth of love, or does the analyst's love of truth demand that he should analyse it in his own and the patient's best interests? After all, as Freud himself says, 'that is always the essence of falling in love. Everybody repeats childhood patterns' (p. 75). As in the paper 'On "Wild" Psychoana-lysis', Freud is at once on both sides, and knows which side he is on. The writing itself struggles to keep the differences in play, to sustain the conflict. Is it the analyst or the patient who has 'an overestimation of sexual life' that holds them 'in its grip' (p. 78)? If the analyst resists and analyses the patient's 'infatuation' for him, is that because the doctor is a scientist, or because he is infatuated by psychoanalysis?

Psychoanalysts 'know they are working with the most explosive forces', as Freud says, but they must resist 'fanaticism' (p. 78); as though fanaticism is what can happen when passions are not met. Most of what we call love, Freud proposes, is our resistance to the future, our inability to leave home. Psychoanalysis can free us to be curious about something other than the past. Psychoanalysis is a technique for transforming love into development. Passion must be in the service of growth.

And yet Freud's progressivist ideals – his commitment to the truth of change as opposed to the distortions of desire – are continuously thwarted, as these papers show, by his clinical experience. What is most striking about people is how resistant they are to the self-improvements on offer in psychoanalysis. If there is a pleasure people seek, it is all too often the pleasure of suffering; the only ambition that sustains people is the ambition to repeat the past. What a life of psychoanalysis has revealed to Freud is just how at odds with themselves, just how riddled with contradictions modern people are in their accommodations to and their refusals of contemporary life. A more-or-less secular capitalism produces its counter-culture of symptoms; what the psychoanalyst finds is that, for many people, the future has become a phobic object. Could there be a technique, Freud seems to wonder, for dispelling nostalgia?

That psychoanalysis works, no one for whom it has worked doubts. That there would be people for whom it didn't work – and indeed people for whom it would be utterly spurious – was not surprising for Freud (if psychoanalysis is a theory about anything it is a theory about why people don't like it). What did surprise Freud – and is a persistent theme of the writings in this volume – was something far more important: people's commitment to their own unhappiness. It was as though modern people had, beneath their fashionable hedonisms, a virtually religious devotion to their own misery; that modern people only seemed to be what Nietzsche called 'clever animals' in their quest for suffering. When tragedies are toys what is a cure? What psychoanalysis promised the patient, in Freud's view, were more convincing pleasures. And yet nothing seemed to make his patients more resistant than the possibility of pleasure.

Freud was not a pessimist, but he was a great writer about the nature of dismay. It was the contemporary frustrations that fascinated him, the obstacle course of everyday life. If his writings on the practice of psychoanalysis are as much about what makes the analyst happy as what might do the patient some good it was because psychoanalysis was a new way, a different way of paying tribute to the most ironic, the most characteristically modern of our wishes: the wish to frustrate ourselves. Freud paid tribute to this particular wish by showing how and why it worked; and by asking us to imagine how we would live if we were not so entirely in its grip. What is wild about psychoanalysis is that it reminds us of our unforgettable satisfactions, and of how we can forget them.

Adam Phillips, 2002

Notes

1. Peter Gay, *Freud, A Life for Our Time* (London, J. M. Dent & Sons, 1988), p. 118.
2. Ibid.
3. *SE* XX, p. 72.
4. *SE* XII, p. 346.
5. Louis Breger, *Freud* (New York, John Wiley, 2000), p. 373.
6. Quoted in Grossman and Grossman, *The Wild Analyst* (London, Barrie Books, 1965), p. 73.
7. *The Clinical Diary of Sandor Ferenczi*, edited by Judith Dupont (Cambridge, Harvard University Press, 1988), p. xii.
8. Ibid.
9. *SE* XX, p. 8.
10. Gay, *Freud*, p. 40.
11. Ferenczi, *Clinical Diary*, p. 46.
12. Bernhard Handlbauer, *The Freud–Adler Controversy* (Oxford, One-World Publications, 1998), p. 23.
13. *SE* XI, p. 142.

Translator's Preface

As a monument of modernism, a literary giant, a universal referent in almost any intellectual discourse, and the most household of names, Freud is a daunting prospect for the translator. And yet the brief of this new Penguin venture is exhilarating and liberating. Translators have been encouraged as far as possible to render the texts as though they were being translated for the first time, and primarily to regard them as part of a literary canon. There are productive tensions in this dual objective. A fresh translation has to pay due attention to the writer's literary style and his period flavour, while not being overwhelmed by these requirements and being bold enough to produce a readable and accessible modern version.

Of course, there are terms and concepts that have become so embedded in English terminology since Freud was first translated that it is difficult to avoid using them, and in many cases it would be perverse to do so. But in other cases, the chance to start from scratch is irresistible. In the present volume, a prominent instance is the discarding of the traditional (and completely embedded) 'id' and 'ego' – for Freud's *das Es* and *das Ich* – in favour of 'the It' and 'the I'. Logically speaking, the choice was unavoidable, since within the text of his essay 'The Question of Lay Analysis' Freud makes a point of explaining that he chose to nominalize these plain pronouns, rather than adopt some more fancy Greek or Latin terms, precisely because he wanted to use language accessible to those of his patients who, though intelligent, were not highly educated. 'Ego' may have become completely absorbed into everyday English (although it tends to have connotations of self-centredness), but 'id' remains an educated or inkhorn term, and therefore even today does not meet

Freud's demotic requirements. 'The It' and 'the I' may seem strange at first, but my experience is that they read quite naturally after a while. And we have to bear in mind that Freud and his group were themselves inventing language to express their theories as they evolved (see section II of 'The Question of Lay Analysis'). We are reminded of this by his advocacy of his own term 'paraphrenia' in preference to Bleuler's ultimately more successful suggestion – 'schizophrenia' (see 'On Initiating Treatment').

Faithfulness to the tone of the original is the duty of the translator. But there is no point in a new translation if the language is not updated, refreshed and made more readable for today's audience. One small example: in contrast to the first translators, I have used the 'you' form as often as possible where Freud employs the impersonal 'man' construction (which he does very frequently), instead of the formal 'one'; 'man' in German is not at all formal or strained. This alone creates a different texture in the prose.

Greater familiarity with Freud's writings has made me aware of how colloquial and relaxed an author he can be. The lively and convincing dialogues he concocts in his 'discussions with an impartial listener' (see 'The Question of Lay Analysis') project dramatically and to great effect the situation of the pioneer thinker facing an intelligent but sceptical layman. The Freud who could create such enjoyable exchanges would surely have delighted in the flexibility, economy and inventiveness of our modern idiom.

We have all the linguistic resources of the original translators at our disposal, plus many new formations. For example, Freud refers twice in this collection of essays to the *Zeitlosigkeit* of our unconscious processes. 'Timelessness' will not serve as a translation; the associations are self-evidently wrong. An earlier translator was obliged to resort to the phrase 'inappreciation of time', which is both clumsy and not particularly easy to understand (the contrast with Freud's plain term shows how he has been let down and misrepresented in this instance). But our modern language has evolved hyphened combinations with the adjective 'free', and 'time-free' offered itself as the basis of a rendering of Freud's expression that would not have been available in Freud's lifetime. Other handy expressions we now have at our disposal include, for example, references to 'same-sex' and 'other-sex' parents.

You have to sympathize with the original translators for being deprived of this neat vocabulary. You might recall, for example, that even the word 'drive' was not quite at home in the psychoanalytical lexicon then. The alternatives, 'impulse' or 'instinct', do not quite seem to convey the 'driven', compulsive nature of what is signified by the German *Trieb*, which quite simply had to be adopted into English sooner or later as a loan-translation. It will be a matter of judgement whether 'off-putting' is a modernization too far for what would earlier have had to be rendered as something like 'exerting a deterrent effect', but it is certainly very much closer to the directness of Freud's everyday word *abstossend*. More hesitant was my adoption of the rather awkward modern word 'analysand' for *der Analysierte*. (Freud always uses the masculine form, naturally.) The latter term appears countless times in Freud's texts, and there is no obvious strategy in English for dealing with it – which, no doubt, is why the Latinate form 'analysand' was invented. I have used it as sparingly as possible, and mostly when tiring of the endless repetition of references to 'the patient'.

A related lexical difficulty centred on the term *der/die Kranke*, 'the ill/sick person'. Apart from the point that 'the sick person' is an unwieldy phrase, this particular crux concerns a nagging feeling in the mind of the English speaker that 'sick' or 'ill' are rather drastic ways of referring to somebody suffering from a neurosis – though Freud makes it clear enough that the physical effects of psychological disorders can indeed be fairly drastic. But part of the problem is that Freud himself at some points makes a very clear distinction between neurosis and mental illness, a differentiation that he seems to abandon in his casual usage of *der Kranke*. ('Pathogenic' and 'pathological' are terms that likewise shift between strictly psychiatric and loosely psychoanalytical usage.) Here too, the ubiquitous 'the patient' often had to serve.

English no doubt tends to euphemism. It certainly did not seem quite right – and neither did it to earlier translators – to translate the brutally honest *erraten* literally as 'guess', in contexts that related to the analyst's attempts to put a construction on the meaning of the patient's revelations. 'Conjecture' or 'interpret' seem more respectable terms, offering fewer hostages to fortune. But if the equivalent of 'guess' was good enough for Freud . . . ? It was no use; I simply could not bring myself to deploy it. This is an example of the way the translator can begin to identify with the translatee, even to the point of trying to protect the latter's posthumous interests.

It goes without saying that a translation is an interpretation, and also that dilemmas can result from this fact. For example, there is always a need to interpret wherever the German term *Wissenschaft* occurs. In context, does it mean science in the English sense, or – as it commonly can – academic study that incorporates disciplines we would not include under 'science'? The dilemma here is that while Freud is able to avoid category definitions, and thereby to maintain precisely the ambivalence surrounding psychoanalysis as both science *and* art, English usage requires a distinction between 'knowledge' and 'science', and thus rules out the kind of interdisciplinarity that Freud instinctively embraces (and which puts him about a hundred years ahead of his time). There is a whole debate that Freud is engaging with here, upon which any English translation tends to foreclose. Incidentally, in this connection, Freud the man of (broad) science gives away his attitude to the men of (hard) science in a kind of parapraxis or Freudian slip he would have relished if it had been pointed out to him. In 'Resistance to Psychoanalysis' he says that 'there is plenty in the content of psychoanalytic theory to provoke an impassioned reaction in people, and not just in scientists [*Wissenschaftler*, by which in this context he means 'hard' scientists]' (p. 87). In the text I have intervened and interpreted by adding the parenthetical '[lay]' before the word 'people', to make this otherwise odd sentence read more easily. But the distinction between people and scientists is a telling one. It unconsciously marks off Freud's real allegiances as a humanist and a man of letters.

What is Freud like to translate? Often a joy, especially in his unexpected flashes of humour or dry wit. He can be down to earth, practical (see especially 'On Initiating Treatment'), forensically skilled in arguing a case, but admirably tactful about the claims he makes for his colossal achievements. He writes on the whole a clear and not over-academic prose, though like many writers of German of his day – Thomas Mann, for example – he is much given to long, involved sentences. These can be a pleasure to read, if you take pleasure in the mastery of the complex inflections of the German language. They can of course be a challenge to the translator, who has to unpack these convoluted clauses and yet lose none of the contents. I have to confess that literal faithfulness to the text has been sacrificed on a number of occasions to the convenience of the reader by splitting up such long sentences. But plenty of examples of the latter remain to give the flavour of Freud's style. He does also occasionally present truly cryptic paragraphs that defy translation even after long contemplation. These were the occasions on which I was happy to consult earlier translators in order to resolve a crux of meaning. After all, they enjoyed the benefit of advice from those close to the source. It was equally helpful to return to the work of predecessors when tackling some of Freud's more idiosyncratic usage, such as *Unlust* (unpleasure or dis-pleasure), to which he gives a quite different meaning from that of the standard German idiom, 'lack of enthusiasm'. The, at first sight, baffling use of *Auskunft* is another such case. As any tourist knows, in ordinary German this means 'information (office)', but Freud returns to the root of the word, the verb *auskommen*, meaning 'to escape' or 'to manage', so that for him *Auskunft* means 'way out (of a difficulty)', or 'expedient'.

What in the end grounds Freud in accessible and ordinary language, and thus makes him overwhelmingly a pleasure to translate, is his hypersensitivity to the dangers of arrogant intellectualism. Although he quite likes the analogy, Freud is *not* attempting to replace the priest with the psychoanalyst. For one thing, he is healthily aware that knowledge of the unconscious is not the same as awareness of your own unconscious, and that the psychoanalyst – like the scientist in general? – can be as partial as anyone else. His luminous intelligence is offset by a (perhaps Jewish) aversion to idolatry. For all his ambition and his fierce defence of his intellectual territory, it is far from his purpose to play the part of a new god, or even the new prophet who offers a doctrine to compensate for his modernist displacement of authority figures from their pedestals.

The question remains: why re-translate Freud? Because, for one thing, that same intelligence continues to provide a critique of our own unfinished project of enlightenment. His vision of psychoanalysis extending into all realms of cultural and intellectual life has been realized. It is inconceivable, for example, that without Freud we would have progressed from shooting military victims of 'shell-shock' (war neurosis) for cowardice in the First World War to treating them for Post-Traumatic Stress Disorder today. But how many more such anomalies remain to be overcome? And what better excuse for a new Freud in the new millennium?

On 'Wild' Psychoanalysis

In my consulting room a few days ago there appeared, accompanied by a solicitous friend, a woman of mature years suffering from attacks of anxiety. She was in the second half of her forties, quite well preserved and obviously not past her prime as a woman. The attacks had been brought on by her divorce from her husband, but she said that her anxiety had become considerably more intense since she had consulted a young doctor in her suburban neighbourhood. He had explained to her that the cause of her panic was her sexual deprivation. She could not do without a male partner, and so there were only three routes to health: she could either go back to her husband, or take a lover, or resort to masturbation. Since then she had been convinced she was incurable, for she did not want to go back to her husband, and the other two measures were against her morals and her religion. She had come to me, however, because the doctor had told her that this was a new discovery, for which I bore the credit, and she ought to consult me just to confirm that what he had said was true. Her friend, an older woman, rather faded and unhealthy-looking, then implored me to assure the patient that the doctor was wrong. What he said must be untrue, for she herself had been a widow for many years and had remained respectable without suffering from any anxiety.

I do not wish to dwell on the difficult situation that this visit placed me in, but to highlight the conduct of the colleague who had sent this patient to me. But first I want to sound a note of caution, which I hope is not redundant. Long experience had taught me, as it might anyone else, not to accept at face value what patients tell me about their doctor, especially if they are neurotic. A neurologist not only

3

all too easily becomes the target for many a hostile impulse on the part of the patient; he must also at times be prepared to take upon himself, by a kind of projection, responsibility for the secret, repressed desires of the neurotic. It is a sad but telling fact that such accusations most readily find credence among other physicians.

I am entitled to hope, then, that the lady who consulted me gave me a distorted version of her doctor's statements, and that I am doing him (someone I have not met) an injustice if I attach my remarks about 'wild' psychoanalysis to this case in particular. In doing so, however, I may prevent other doctors from doing an injustice to their patients.

Let us assume, therefore, that the doctor did say exactly what this patient reported to me.

Everybody will then be ready to criticize him for lacking the tact and delicacy a doctor ought to show if he decides that he must raise the topic of sexuality with a woman. These requirements also coincide with certain rules of technique to be followed in analysis, and furthermore the doctor would have to have misjudged or misunderstood a whole series of *scientific* principles of psychoanalysis, and thereby to have demonstrated very little prowess in understanding its essence and intentions.

Let us begin with the latter type of mistake, the scientific errors. The advice given by the doctor clearly indicates how he conceives of 'sexual life'. This amounts in fact to nothing more than the popular conception that sexual needs merely consist of the urge to coitus, or analogous measures for procuring an orgasm or voiding sexual fluids. But the doctor cannot be unaware that psychoanalysis is commonly criticized for stretching the concept of sexuality far beyond its usual confines. It is true that it does so, although whether this fact justifies the criticism is another matter. In psychoanalysis, the concept of sexuality certainly embraces much more; in both higher and lower senses it reaches beyond the popular meaning. This extension is justified in terms of the human genetic heritage; for us, 'sexual life' includes everything that prompts those tender feelings deriving from the original source of primitive sexual impulses, even if those impulses have been subjected to inhibitions placed upon their original sexual aims, or if they have exchanged these aims for others that are no longer sexual. That is why we prefer to talk about *psychosexuality*, and thus stress the importance of not overlooking or underestimating the emotional factor in sexual life. We employ the word 'sexuality' in the same broad sense as the German language uses the word 'lieben' [to love]. We have also known for some time that emotional frustration, with all its consequences, can persist even where there is no lack of normal sexual intercourse. And, as therapists, we never forget that the unsatisfied sexual desires that find pseudo-gratification in the neurotic symptoms we grapple with, often hardly lend themselves at all to being channelled off into coitus or other sexual acts.

A practitioner who does not subscribe to this conception of psychosexuality has no right to invoke those principles of psychoanalysis that deal with the causal significance of sexuality. Stressing exclusively the physical factors of sexuality no doubt greatly simplifies the problem, but anyone who proceeds on this basis will have to answer for the consequences.

The doctor's advice exposes another, equally dire misconception. It is correct to say that psychoanalysis claims that sexual dissatisfaction is the cause of nervous ailments. But does it not go further? Is it too complicated to bear in mind the psychoanalytical tenet that neurotic symptoms arise from a conflict between two forces, a libido (usually unduly enlarged), and an over-powerful sexual denial or repression? If you remember this second factor, which is by no means secondary in importance, you will never be able to believe that satisfying sexual desires is, by itself, a universally reliable remedy for those suffering from nervous disorders. A large number of these people are incapable of sexual satisfaction under the prevailing circumstances, or not capable at all. If they *were* capable, if they did not have their inner resistances, then the strength of their sex drive would show them the way to satisfaction, even without their doctor's encouragement. In that case, what is the point of such advice as the doctor is supposed to have given to the lady in question?

Even if it could be scientifically justified, it is not something she could act on. If she had no inner resistance to masturbation or a love affair, she would long ago have resorted to one of these means. Perhaps the doctor thinks a woman of over forty does not know about taking a lover; or does he so overestimate his influence that he thinks she could never bring herself to take this step without his medical blessing?

All this seems very clear, and yet one must admit that there is one element that makes it difficult to form a judgement. Many nervous conditions, the so-called 'actual' neuroses such as the typical neurasthenia and pure anxiety neurosis, clearly do hinge on the physical element of sexual life; but as yet we have no reliable idea of the role played in these states by mental factors and by repression. In such cases the course of action that suggests itself to the doctor is a therapy of immediate steps to alter physical sexual activity, and this is perfectly justified as long as his diagnosis is correct. The lady who consulted the young doctor was complaining above all of panic attacks, and so he probably assumed she was suffering from anxiety neurosis, and felt justified in prescribing a physical therapy. Yet another lazy-minded misconception! Somebody suffering from anxiety does not necessarily therefore have an anxiety *neurosis*; the diagnosis cannot be derived from the name. You need to know what phenomena constitute an anxiety neurosis, and distinguish them from other pathological conditions that manifest themselves through anxiety. I have the impression that the lady in question suffered from anxiety *hysteria*, and the only – though perfectly adequate – value of such descriptive distinctions between disorders is that they indicate different causation and different therapies. Anyone bearing in mind the possibility of such an anxiety hysteria, could not neglect the mental factors in the way demonstrated by the options the doctor advised.

Strangely enough, the therapeutic options offered by the would-be psychoanalyst leave no room for psychoanalysis itself! Supposedly, the woman could only be cured of her anxiety if she returned to her husband or gratified herself by means of masturbation or a lover. Where would analytical treatment come in – something we regard as the chief remedy for states of anxiety?

This brings us to the errors of technique that the doctor is guilty of in the case in question. There is an outdated idea, based on superficial appearances, that a patient's sufferings result from a kind of ignorance, and that if only this ignorance could be overcome by effective communication (about the causal links between the illness and the patient's life, about his childhood experience, etc.), a recovery must follow. But the illness is not located in this ignorance itself, but in the foundation of ignorance, the *inner resistances* that are the cause of the ignorance and continue to sustain it. Combating these resistances is the task of therapy. Explaining what the patient does not know, because he has repressed it, is only one of the steps necessary in preparation for therapy. If knowledge of the unconscious were as important as those inexperienced in psychoanalysis believe it to be, then all you would need for a cure would be for the sufferer to listen to lectures or read books. However, that would have about as much impact on neurotic symptoms as distributing menus would have on hunger during a famine. The analogy is even more appropriate than it looks at first sight, because explaining what is unconscious for the patient generally results in exacerbating the conflict in him and making his suffering more acute.

However, since psychoanalysis cannot manage without such an explanation, it lays down two conditions that must be met before it can take place. First, that through preparatory work the patient has moved closer to what he has repressed; and, second, that his attachment to the doctor (through *transference*) has become strong enough to create an emotional relationship that rules out further attempts at flight.

It is only when these conditions have been fulfilled that it is possible to recognize and master the resistances that have led to repression and ignorance. So psychoanalytical intervention absolutely presupposes prolonged contact with the patient. Any attempt to bowl the patient over at his first consultation by suddenly revealing to him the secrets interpreted by the doctor is reprehensible in terms of technique, and usually punished by deep hostility on the part of the patient and an end to any further chance of influencing him.

Quite aside from all this, one often advises wrongly, and one's conjectures can never cover everything. Following the clear rules of psychoanalytic technique is a substitute for that mysterious 'medical tact' that is demanded of the practitioner but for which he needs some special gift.

It is not enough for the physician to know a few of the results of psychoanalysis; you also have to be familiar with its techniques if you wish your medical practice to be guided by its way of thinking. These techniques cannot yet be learned from books, and you can only acquire them yourself by sacrificing much time, effort and success. You learn them, like other medical techniques, from accomplished practitioners. Hence, in assessing the case I am linking with these observations, it is not insignificant that I do not know the doctor who is supposed to have issued the advice, and have never heard of him.

Neither my friends and colleagues nor I feel comfortable about claiming a monopoly over the practice of this medical technique. But in view of the dangers for patients and the cause of psychoanalysis that one can see resulting from the practice of 'wild' psychoanalysis, we were left with no option. In the spring of 1910 we founded an international psychoanalytical society, the names of whose members are published, in order to protect our reputation from the activities of all those who do not belong to our group but who call their medical procedure 'psychoanalysis'. For the truth is that these wild analysts do more harm to the cause than to individual patients. It has frequently been my experience that such clumsy treatment, although at first making the condition of the patient worse, has ultimately been beneficial to him. Not always, but often. After the patient has fulminated about the doctor for a good while, and when he feels himself sufficiently removed from his influence, his symptoms improve, or he decides to take a step on the road that will lead to recovery. The eventual improvement comes about 'by itself', or the credit for it is given to the distinctly mediocre treatment of a doctor the patient subsequently consults. In the case of the lady whose complaint about the doctor we have heard, I am inclined to think that the wild analyst did more for the patient than any highly rated specialist who would have told her that she was suffering from a 'vasomotor neurosis'. He directed her attention to the real cause of her trouble, or at least to the right area, and despite all her resistance his intervention will not lack favourable results. But he did harm to himself, and helped to increase the prejudice against the activity of the psychoanalyst that results from the patient's understandable emotional resistance. And this can be avoided.

(1910)

*On the Uses of Dream
Interpretation in
Psychoanalysis*

The *Zentralblatt für Psychoanalyse* [Central Journal for Psychoanalysis] sets out not only to provide news about advances in psychoanalysis, and even to publish its own short contributions to them; it also aims to fulfil other objectives, such as presenting established knowledge in a clear format to students of the subject, and saving beginners in analytical treatment time and effort by offering them suitable instruction. Thus, whether or not they convey anything new will not be the essential point about the didactic and technical essays that will appear in this journal from now on.

The question I want to deal with today does not concern the technique of interpreting dreams. I will not be discussing how to interpret dreams and how to apply the interpretation, but only the right way to make use of the art of dream interpretation in psychoanalytical treatment. No doubt there are various ways of proceeding, but in psychoanalysis there is never one obvious answer to technical questions. There may be more than one good way, but there are very many bad ones, and comparing various techniques can only be enlightening, even if it does not lead to a decision to choose one particular method.

Anyone starting out from a theoretical approach to dream interpretation and coming into analytical practice will want to maintain his interest in the content of dreams, and as far as possible perfect his interpretation of every dream the patient recounts to him. But he will soon find out that he is working under completely different conditions now, and that pursuing his original intention will clash with the most immediate requirements of the therapy. It may be that the first dream serves superbly well to link up with the first explanations offered to the patient, but dreams soon crop up that are so long and obscure that interpretation cannot be completed within the limits of one day's session. If the doctor continues the work of interpretation over the next few days, he will be told about fresh dreams, which have to be put aside until he considers he has resolved the first dream. The quantity of dreams produced is sometimes so great, while the patient makes such slow progress in understanding them, that the analyst is bound to think that all this material is simply an expression of the patient's resistance, which has discovered how to present him with more matter than the therapy can master. Meanwhile, however, a good deal of slippage has occurred between the treatment and the present, and the therapy has lost touch with the current situation. This technique of dream interpretation is up against the rule that it is extremely important for the therapist to know the surface state of mind of the patient at any one time, to be informed about what complexes and what resistances are active within him, and what conscious reaction to them will direct his behaviour. It is hardly ever right to neglect this therapeutic aim in favour of an interest in dream interpretation.

How is it possible to continue with dream interpretation in analysis while bearing this rule in mind? Roughly as follows: always accept the interpretative results that you can obtain in an hour, and do not regard something less than a full insight into the content of the dream as a loss. The next day, do not as a matter of course continue to work on the interpretation, but only do so if you observe that nothing else has moved into the forefront of the patient's conscious-ness. In other words, do not allow the pursuit of an interrupted dream-analysis to form an exception to the rule of always dealing with whatever first comes into the patient's mind. If new dreams have cropped up before you have finished with the earlier ones, just concentrate on this new output and do not reproach yourself for neglecting its predecessors. If the dreams have become altogether too expansive and prolix, then tell yourself to give up from the outset any idea of resolving them completely. In general, you should avoid showing any special interest in dreams, or giving the patient the impression that the analysis will come to a halt if he does not produce any. Otherwise, you run the risk of concentrating his resistance on his output of dreams, thus causing the supply of dreams to run out. You should rather aim to convince the patient that the analysis will always find something to work on whether he brings his dreams into it or not, and regardless of the time spent on them.

The question then arises: don't you have to renounce too much material that is valuable for exploring the unconscious, if you impose these methodological restrictions on your interpretation of dreams? The answer is that the loss is not nearly as great as a superficial view of the matter would suggest. For one thing, you should realize that some of the elaborate dreams produced in severe neurotic cases must be regarded as basically beyond resolution. Such a dream is often constructed above the whole pathogenic material of the case, still unknown to the doctor and patient (so-called programmatic or biographical dreams); sometimes it can be equated with a translation of the whole content of the neurosis into the language of dream. When you attempt to interpret such a dream, all the resistances that are present, but have so far not been touched upon, will be activated, and quickly curtail any insight. The complete interpretation of such a dream is simply coextensive with carrying out the whole of the analysis. If you have made a note of it at the beginning of the analysis, then you may come to understand it by the end, several months later. Much the same is true of gaining full comprehension of a single symptom (the main symptom, for instance). The whole analysis serves the purpose of explaining it; during the treatment you have to try to build up the interpretation of the symptom bit by bit, until you can put all these bits together. Likewise, no more is to be expected from a dream that occurs at the beginning of the analysis, either; you have to be content if your attempt at an interpretation leads you to deduce a single pathogenic wish-motive.

You are therefore not renouncing anything that is within your capacity when you give up your aim of a total dream interpretation. But neither are you forfeiting anything, as a rule, if you discontinue your interpretation of an older dream to devote yourself to a more recent one. A number of fine examples of completed dream interpretations have shown us that a series of scenes from the same dream can have the same content, perhaps asserting itself with increasing clarity as the scenes go on. We have also learnt that multiple dreams occurring in the same night need not amount to any more than attempts to express the same content in different forms. Generally speaking, we can be certain that every wish-motive that presently gives rise to a dream will reappear in a different dream, as long as it has not yet been deciphered and removed from the domination of the unconscious. Thus the best way to complete the interpreting of a dream may be to abandon it in favour of the new dream, which recasts the same material in a form which may be more accessible. I know it is asking a lot of the doctor, as well as the patient, to give up the conscious aims of the treatment and to abandon oneself to a direction that we can only see as 'random'. But I can assure you that you will always gain by deciding to give credence to your own theoretical assertions and letting yourself be guided by the unconscious towards constructing a coherent whole.

What I am advocating, therefore, is that the interpretation of dreams in analytical practice should not be conducted as an art for its own sake, but that its uses should be subordinate to the technical rules governing treatment as a whole. Of course you can occasionally deviate and follow up your theoretical interests for a while. But if so, you must always know what you are doing. There is another case to be considered that has arisen since we developed a greater confidence in our ability to understand the symbolism of dreams, and have felt less dependent upon the patients' own associations. A particularly skilful interpreter of dreams, say, may find himself in the position of understanding all his patient's dreams, without needing to impose upon him the strenuous and time-consuming task of processing them. None of the conflicts between the demands of dream interpretation and those of therapy applies to such an analyst. What is more, he will feel tempted to use his dream interpretation to the full and tell the patient everything he has deduced from his dreams. This methodological tendency represents a considerable deviation from the standard treatment, as I shall explain in another context. Beginners in psychoanalysis are advised against adopting this exceptional case as a model.

The approach of any analyst to the very first dreams that the patient recounts, before the latter has himself learned anything about the technique of dream interpretation, is like that of the superior interpreter of dreams we put forward above. These initial dreams are naïve, so to speak; they give a good deal away to the listener, like the dreams of so-called healthy people. The question then arises as to whether or not the doctor should translate for the patient everything he has gleaned from the dream. This is not the place to answer this question, for it is obviously subservient to the more comprehensive question of which stages of the treatment are the appropriate ones, and what is the right pace for the doctor's initiation of the patient into what has been psychologically concealed from him. And the better informed the patient is about the practice of interpreting dreams, the more obscure his later dreams will generally be. All acquired knowledge about dreams serves as a warning hint when it comes to dream formation.

Time and again in 'scientific' work on dreams, which despite rejecting our analytical interpretation of dreams has received a new impetus from psychoanalysis, you find a completely redundant concern about preserving an accurate record of the dream-text, which supposedly needs protecting from the distortions and the routine occurrences of the next day. It seems that many psychoanalysts likewise are making less than consistent use of their own insight into the conditions of dream formation when they require their clients to write down every dream the moment they wake up. This measure is superfluous in therapy; and patients tend to use this prescription to disturb their own sleep and exhibit great keenness in a sphere where it cannot be useful. For if you yourself have ever struggled successfully to save a dream-text that otherwise would have been consigned to oblivion, it will not take much to convince you that the patient gets nothing out of this. His associations will not match the text, and the effect is the same as if the dream had not been preserved. Certainly the doctor may gain in one case something that would escape his attention in another. But it is one thing for the doctor to know something, and another for the patient to do so; we will consider elsewhere the significance of this distinction for the technique of psychoanalysis.

Finally, I want to mention a particular kind of dream, which, in the nature of things, can only occur in the course of psychoanalysis, and which can be disturbing and misleading for the beginner. These are the so-called retarded or corroborating dreams; they are easily accessible to interpretation, and when translated they yield nothing more than what has been revealed by the material of daytime associations during recent sessions. It then looks as though the patient has been kind enough to produce in dream form precisely what has been 'suggested' to him immediately beforehand. However, the more practised analyst will be hard-pressed to see this as a kindness on the part of his patient; he accepts such dreams as welcome confirmations, and notes that they only occur under certain conditions which are influenced by the therapy.

By far the most numerous kind of dream is one that rushes ahead of the treatment, so that, after everything that is already known and understood is abstracted from it, the dream provides a more or less clear indication of something that was previously hidden.

(1912)

On the Dynamics of
Transference

The almost inexhaustible topic of 'transference' was recently described in this [journal], the *Zentralblatt*, by W. Stekel.[1] I would like to add here a few remarks to show how transference comes about during psychoanalytical therapy, and how it acquires its well-known role in the course of treatment.

Let us be clear that every individual has his own distinct character, the combined result of innate predisposition and childhood influences. His character expresses itself in the form of his erotic life, the drives that it satisfies and the goals he sets himself.[2] This gives rise to a cliché or stereotype, so to speak (or perhaps several), that is regularly reproduced over a lifetime – external circumstances and the nature of the available erotic objects permitting – but is certainly not completely impervious to change in response to new impressions. Our experience shows that not all the impulses that determine erotic life have undergone a complete psychological development; the portion that has, is aligned towards reality, is available to the conscious personality and constitutes a part of it. Another portion of these libidinous impulses has been arrested in its development; it is removed both from the conscious personality and from reality, and has either been unable to create a space for itself anywhere but in the imagination, or has remained in the unconscious and thus unknown to the individual's consciousness. If somebody's erotic needs are not completely gratified by reality, he is obliged to project his libidinous expectations on to every new person he meets, and it is very likely that both parts of his libido, conscious and unconscious, are involved in this projection.

It is therefore completely normal and understandable that the receptive libido of somebody who is not wholly fulfilled should be drawn to the person of the doctor. According to our theory, this receptivity will relate to certain models and be linked with one of the clichés already present in the person concerned, or, to put it another way, it will fit the doctor into one of the 'series' the sufferer has previously formed in his mind. If the father imago (to use Jung's felicitous term)[3] is decisive in the process of accommodating the physician to this series, it will correspond to his real relationship with the doctor. But the transference is not tied to this model; it can be built upon the mother or brother imago, etc. The specific features of transference on to the doctor, which enable it to exceed by far the bounds of what is justifiable when viewed soberly and rationally, are comprehensible when you consider that the transference arises not just from conscious expectations but from repressed or unconscious ones.

There would be nothing more to say or to worry us about this topic of the manner in which transference takes place, if it were not that two points of special interest to the psychoanalyst remain unexplained. First, we cannot understand why the transference expresses itself so much more intensely in neurotic people undergoing analysis than in those who are not; and, second, it is a puzzle to us why transference represents the most powerful kind of resistance that treatment is faced with, while outside analysis it has to be seen as a healing force and a prerequisite for success. But time and again practice will confirm that if the patient runs out of free associations,[4] you can remove the blockage by assuring him that what is dominating his mind is some idea that has to do with the doctor personally, or something connected with him. No sooner has this explanation been put forward than the block is removed, or you have transformed a situation where the patient has dried up, into one where he is deliberately withholding his associations.

At first sight it appears to be a massive methodological disadvantage for psychoanalysis that it transforms transference, otherwise the mightiest instrument of success, into the most powerful means of resistance. But on a closer look at least we can dispose of the first of these two problems. It is not true to say that transference makes its presence felt more intensely and less controllably in psychoanalysis than outside of it. In institutions where analysis is not the treatment on offer for neurotics, you can observe the most intense and degrading form of transference, verging on sexual dependence, and taking on the most overtly erotic coloration. At a time when psychoanalysis hardly existed as yet, a sensitive observer such as Gabriele Reuter described this in a remarkable book, which offers the best possible insights into the nature and origins of the neuroses.[5] These characteristics of transference should not therefore be laid at the door of psychoanalysis, but attributed to the neurosis itself. The second problem has not previously been tackled.

We must now move closer to this problem of why transference opposes itself as a resistance to psychoanalysis. Let us reconstruct the psychological situation of treatment: a regular and essential precondition for every psycho-neurotic illness is the process aptly called by Jung 'introversion of the libido'.[6] That is to say, there is a decrease in the portion of the libido that can be raised to the conscious level and is aligned with reality, while there is a corresponding increase in the portion that is unconscious, turned away from reality, and able to nourish the fantasies of the individual while remaining in the unconscious. The libido has retreated – in whole or in part – into regression and reactivated the childhood imagos.[7] The analytical cure pursues it to the same place, with the aim of seeking out the libido and making it accessible to consciousness and eventually amenable to reality. A conflict is guaranteed whenever analytical inquiries locate a libido that has withdrawn to its hiding places. All the energies released by the libido's regression will rise up as 'resistances' against the analyst's efforts, in order to preserve this new *status quo*. For if the introversion or regression of the libido had not been justified by a particular relationship with the external world (in the broadest sense, by some failure to achieve gratification) and had not been expedient even at that time, it would not have come about in the first place. But resistances arising from this quarter are not the only ones, nor even the strongest. The libido available to the individual's personality had always been subject to the attraction of unconscious complexes (or, properly speaking, the parts of these complexes belonging to the unconscious), and succumbed to regression because the attraction of reality had waned. In order to liberate the libido, this attraction of the unconscious must now be overcome, by removing the repression of unconscious drives and their derivatives that has developed in the individual. It is from this attraction that the most imposing part of the resistance arises, often causing the illness to persist even when the original grounds for turning away from reality have disappeared. The analysis has to combat resistances from both these sources. Resistance dogs every step of the treatment; every single association, every move by the patient has to take the resistance into account, and represents a compromise between the forces seeking recovery and those we have mentioned that oppose it.

If we trace a pathogenic complex from its presence (either as a noticeable symptom, or completely inconspicuous) in the conscious mind back to its roots in the unconscious, we soon find ourselves in territory where the resistance asserts itself so forcibly that the next association that occurs to the patient is bound to deal with it, and will appear to be a compromise between the demands of the resistance and those of the analytical inquiry. Experience tells us that this is the point at which transference occurs. If anything contained in the material or content of the complex lends itself to being transferred on to the person of the doctor, then this transference will take place, provoke the next association, and announce its presence by some indication of a resistance, perhaps by means of a block. We deduce from this experience that the reason why this idea of transference succeeds in reaching the conscious level, where other thoughts do not, is that it also satisfies the needs of the resistance. Such processes are repeated countless times in the course of the analysis. Time and again, when you approach a pathogenic complex, it is the part of the complex capable of transference that is pushed forward into consciousness and defended with extreme stubbornness.[8]

Once this is overcome, the other elements of the complex will present little difficulty. The longer the analytical treatment lasts, and the more clearly the patient recognizes that simply distorting the pathogenic material offers no protection against exposure, the more consistently he will resort to a type of distortion that appears to offer him most advantage, distortion by means of transference. The situation that shapes these circumstances is one in which all conflicts must eventually be fought out on the territory of the transference.

In analytical treatment, then, we always perceive the transference at first simply as the most powerful weapon of resistance, and we are entitled to deduce that the intensity and persistence of the transference are a result and expression of the resistance. The question of the mechanism of the resistance is settled by relating it back to the willingness of a libido that has retained its infantile imagos. But its role in treatment can only be explained by exploring its relationship with the resistance.

Why should transference be such a suitable medium of resistance? The answer seems straightforward. For it is clear that confessing any disreputable wish-impulse is made especially difficult when the recipient of the confession is the person who is the object of the impulse. This compulsion gives rise to situations that seem almost impossible to resolve. That is exactly what the analysand is trying to achieve by merging the object of his emotional impulses with the person of the doctor. But further reflection reveals that this apparent gain cannot provide the solution to the problem. On the other hand, a relationship of affectionate and devoted attachment can help to surmount all the difficulties of confessing. In a similar situation in normal life people often say 'With you I don't feel ashamed – I can tell you everything.' Transference on to the doctor might therefore equally well serve to make confession easier; it is not clear why it should make it harder.

The answer to this recurrent question will not come from further reflection, but from the experience gained by examining individual transference-resistances in the course of treatment. In the end you discover that you cannot understand the use of transference in resistance while you still think in terms of 'transference' pure and simple. You have to decide to distinguish a 'positive' from a 'negative' transference, the transfer of affectionate feelings from hostile ones, and to deal separately with both kinds of transference on to the doctor. Positive transference then divides either into the type derived from friendly or affectionate feelings which are accessible to consciousness, or the type that comes from those that remain unconscious. Analysis has shown that the latter kind often originate in erotic sources. Thus we are obliged to recognize that all the emotional relationships we draw upon in life, such as liking, friendship, trust and so forth – however pure and un-sensual they seem to our conscious self-perception – are genetically related to sexuality, and have developed out of purely sexual desires through the modifying of sexual aims. Originally, sexual objects were all that we knew, and psychoanalysis has shown us that the people we merely esteem or respect in our real lives can still be sexual objects for our unconscious.

The solution to the puzzle, therefore, is that transference on to the doctor is only suited to the formation of a resistance in treatment if it is a negative transference, or a positive one composed of repressed erotic impulses. If we 'remove' the transference by making it conscious, all we are doing is detaching these two components of the emotional transaction from the person of the doctor. The other component, which is inoffensive and accessible to consciousness, will remain in existence, and in psychoanalysis the success of the cure rests upon it as much as it does in any other form of treatment. To that extent we readily agree that the results of psychoanalysis depend upon suggestion. But 'suggestion' must be understood in the sense that we and Ferenczi[9] are agreed upon: influencing an individual by means of whichever transference-phenomena are possible in his case. Our concern is to create independence in the patient by using suggestion to permit him to complete a psychological operation that will necessarily result in a permanent improvement in his psychological condition.

Another question that might arise is why the phenomena of resistance-transference only appear in psychoanalysis, and not in other kinds of treatment, e.g. in institutions. The answer is that they do occur there, but they need to be recognized as such. Negative transference actually comes to the fore quite regularly in institutions. In so far as the patient comes under the influence of a negative transference, he leaves the institution either unchanged or in a state of relapse. Erotic transference has a less inhibiting effect in institutions, because it is glossed over there instead of being laid bare. But it expresses itself very clearly as a resistance to recovery – not, however, by driving the patient away from the institution (on the contrary, it serves to keep him there), but by keeping him at some distance from life. For his recovery it is completely unimportant whether the patient overcomes this or that fear or inhibition inside the institution; what is important is that he should also be free of them in the reality of his life.

Negative transference deserves a fuller discussion than is possible within the limits of these remarks. In the treatable form of psychoneurosis it occurs alongside affectionate transference, and is often focused upon the same person. This is a state of affairs for which Bleuler coined the nice term *ambivalence*.[10] To a certain extent, ambivalent feelings seem to be normal, but without doubt a high degree of emotional ambivalence is peculiar to neurotics. In obsessional neurosis a premature 'splitting of pairs of opposites' seems to characterize the instinctual life of patients and to represent one of its constituent conditions. The ambivalence of their emotional tendencies is the best explanation we have for the ability of neurotics to place their transferences at the service of resistance. With patients whose capacity for transference has become essentially negative, as with paranoiacs, all chances of influencing and curing them vanish.

In all this discussion so far we have devoted our attention to just one feature of the phenomenon of transference; we now need to turn it upon another aspect of the same topic. If you have formed an accurate impression of the way the patient is cast out of his real relationship with the doctor as soon as he is dominated by a substantial transference-resistance; the way he then takes the liberty of neglecting the basic rule of psychoanalysis, which says that you are supposed to communicate uncritically everything that comes into your mind; the way he forgets the intentions with which he entered upon analysis; and the way he now becomes indifferent to logical connections and conclusions which had deeply impressed him shortly before – then you will feel the need for some explanation

27

for this impression other than the factors put forward so far. And indeed, such explanations are not hard to find; once again, they arise out of the psychological situation in which the treatment has placed the patient.

On the trail of a libido that has broken away from consciousness, you have penetrated into the realm of the unconscious. The reactions you aim to provoke bring with them out into the light of day much of the character of unconscious processes, as we have got to know them through the study of dreams. The unconscious impulses do not wish to be recalled, as the cure requires, but seek to go on reproducing themselves, in keeping with the 'time-free' nature and the hallucinatory power of the unconscious. As he would in a dream, the patient treats the results of the awakening of his unconscious impulses as though they were real and present; he wants to act out his passions regardless of the real situation. The doctor wants to make him fit these emotional impulses into the context of the treatment and that of his life history, to subordinate them to intellectual reflection and recognize them for their psychological value. It is almost entirely within the phenomenon of transference that this battle between doctor and patient, between intellect and instinctual life, between recognition and the desire to act out is conducted. It is on this battleground that the victory must be won, whose expression will be a permanent recovery from the neurosis. It is undeniable that getting the phenomena of transference under control is enormously difficult for the psychoanalyst, but it must be remembered that it is precisely these phenomena that do us the invaluable service of making the patient's hidden and forgotten erotic impulses present and manifest; for after all, nobody can be slain *in absentia* or *in effigie* [in their absence or in effigy].

(1912)

Notes

1. *Zentralblatt für Psychoanalyse*, Vol. II, No. II, p. 26.

2. We must protest at this point against the misleading accusation that we have denied the significance of innate (congenital) factors because we have emphasized the role of infantile impressions. Such an accusation is a product of the narrow human need for causal connections, which runs counter to the usual way that reality is formed, and is content to accept a single causative factor. Certainly, psychoanalysis has had much to say about contingent factors as a source of mental disturbance, and not very much about congenital ones. But this is merely because it can bring new information to bear on the former, but knows no more about the latter factors than is known generally. We decline to lay down some kind of difference in principle between the two series of causal factors. Rather, we presume that the two are regularly combined to produce the effects we observe. Δαιμων και Τυχη [spirit and chance] determine the fate of the individual, but rarely, perhaps never, just one of these forces alone. How their respective shares in this causality are divided up can only be a singular and individual matter. The sequence in which varying quantities of the two factors combine will no doubt produce extreme cases, too. We will estimate the part played by constitution or experience respectively according to the state of our knowledge, and reserve the right to modify our judgement as our insights develop. Moreover, we might risk observing that individual constitutions themselves can be seen as the outcome of contingent influences upon an endless series of ancestors.

3. 'Symbole und Wandlungen der Libido', *Jahrbuch für Psychoanalyse*, Vol. III, p. 164.

4. I mean when they really fail him, not when they are suppressed by him out of some trivial feeling of unwillingness.

5. *Aus guter Familie* [*A Woman of Good Family*], 1895.

6. Although many of Jung's pronouncements give the impression that this introversion characterizes dementia praecox, and does not occur in other neuroses.

7. It would be too easy to say that it has reoccupied the childhood 'complexes'. That would not be right, however; the only correct way of putting it would be 'the unconscious portions of these complexes'. The extraordinary complexity of my present topic tempts me to go into a number of related problems that would actually need to be cleared up before I could talk in

unambiguous terms about the psychological processes I am describing here. The problems in question are: distinguishing between introversion and regression; fitting the theory of complexes into that of the libido; identifying the relationship of fantasizing to the conscious and the unconscious as well as to reality, etc. I do not need to make any excuses for resisting these temptations at this point.

8. However, this should not lead us to attribute some special pathogenic significance to the elements selected to form the resistance involved in the transference. When there is an especially fierce struggle over possession of some small church or a particular farmyard, we do not have to assume that the church is a national treasure, nor that the farmhouse contains the Army's war-chest. The objects involved may have merely tactical value, only coming into play in this one battle.

9. Ferenczi, 'Introjektion und Übertragung' ['Introjection and Transference'], *Jahrbuch für Psychoanalyse*, Vol. I, 1909.

10. E. Bleuler, 'Dementia praecox oder Gruppe der Schizophreneien' ['Dementia Praecox and the Schizophrenia Group'], *Aschaffenburgs Handbuch der Schizophrenie*, 1911. – Lecture on ambivalence in Bern 1910, noted in the *Zentralblatt für Psychoanalyse*, Vol. I, p. 266. – W. Stekel had previously suggested the term 'bipolarity' for the same phenomena.

Advice to Doctors on Psychoanalytic Treatment

The rules concerning technique that I am putting forward here are the result of many years of experience, after I had abandoned other approaches that proved to be troublesome for me. It is not hard to see that they, or at least many of them, combine to form a single prescription. My hope is that, by following them, doctors practising analysis may be spared much unnecessary effort and prevented from overlooking certain factors. But I must stress that this technique has proved to be the only effective one for me personally; I would not dare to deny that another individual with a completely different personality might be drawn towards a different attitude to patients and the task in hand.

a) The first task facing any analyst who sees more than one patient a day will also seem to him the most daunting. For it consists of holding in his head all the countless names, dates and details of recall, associations and output produced by the patient during the months and years of the treatment, and not mixing them up with similar material derived from other patients analysed at the same time or earlier. If you are obliged daily to conduct a clinic for seven, eight or even more patients in analysis, the feats of memory required to do so successfully will inspire disbelief, admiration or even pity among outsiders. Invariably people will be curious to know what technique you use to master such a wealth of detail, and will assume that you make use of some special aids in the process.

Actually, the technique is a simple one. As will become clear, it rejects all aids, even note-taking, and consists simply of not focusing on anything in particular, but giving everything the same kind of 'impartially suspended attention', as I have called it elsewhere. In this way you save yourself the effort of maintaining concentrated attention every day for hours on end, which is impossible, and you avoid a danger that is inseparable from deliberately focused attention. For as soon as you deliberately raise your attention to a certain pitch of concentration, you begin to be selective about the material available. You direct a particularly intense gaze at one element, but then eliminate something else, and you select according to your expectations or inclinations. But this is precisely what you must not do; if you follow your expectations, you run the risk of never finding out anything you do not know already; if you follow your inclinations, then you are bound to distort whatever you perceive. Furthermore, you have to bear in mind that it is only in retrospect that you will recognize the significance of most of the things you hear.

As you can see, the instruction to notice everything impartially is the necessary corollary to the demand that the analysand should relate uncritically and unselectively everything that occurs to him. If the doctor behaves otherwise, he will largely destroy the potential gains when his patient conforms to the 'basic rule of psychoanalysis'. We can express the rule for the doctor as follows: in exercising your powers of observation, you have to exclude all conscious impressions and rely completely on your 'unconscious memory'. Or, purely in terms of technique: you should listen and not worry whether you notice anything or not.

What you can achieve in this way will equip you to cope with all the demands of the treatment. Those parts of the material that have already coalesced to form a coherent whole will become accessible to the doctor at the conscious level. The other part, still disconnected and inchoate, at first appears deeply buried, but readily springs to mind as soon as the patient produces something that connects with it and can develop it further. You then accept with a smile the patient's compliments upon your 'particularly good memory', when you have produced a detail from years ago that would probably have been lost if you had tried consciously to fix it in your memory.

In this process of recall, mistakes only happen at times and at junctures when you are distracted by something relating to yourself (see below), in other words, where you fail badly to live up to the psychoanalytic ideal. Very rarely are matters related to one patient confused with others. In any dispute with the patient about a particular thing he said and how he said it, the doctor is usually in the right.[1]

b) I cannot recommend making copious notes or a transcript etc. during sessions with the patient. Apart from the unfavourable impression this makes on many patients, the same points apply as in our discussion of mental note-taking. Your selection of the material while you write notes or shorthand will inevitably be harmful to the analysis, and you tie up a part of your thinking capacity that would be better employed in interpreting what you have heard. You may by all means make an exception to this rule and note down facts, the contents of dreams, or interesting individual conclusions that can easily be detached from their context and used in a free-standing way as examples. But I tend not even to do this. I write down examples from memory in the evening after my day's work, and I get my patients to write down their dreams after they have told me about them.

c) Writing notes during a session with a patient might be justified if you plan to make the case in question the subject of an academic publication. In principle, one can hardly object to that. But you should not lose sight of the fact that precise records of an analytical case history are less productive than one might expect. Viewed critically, they represent that kind of pseudo-precision of which 'modern' psychiatry affords us a number of striking examples. As a rule they are tedious for the reader, and yet they are no substitute for actually being present at an analysis. And in general our experience is that, where the reader is prepared to believe in the analyst, he will also be prepared to concede to him the small amount of processing he carries out on his material; but if he is not inclined to take the analysis and the analyst seriously, he will disregard even a faithful record of the treatment. This does not seem to be the way to overcome objections to the lack of evidence in psychoanalysis.

d) Analytical work certainly has a name for combining research with treatment. But beyond a certain point, the technique used by the former is in conflict with the latter. It is not a good thing to carry out scientific work on a case before completion of the treatment, acting in the service of science by piecing together its structure, trying to predict the course it will take, or reviewing from time to time what stage the case has reached. The treatment's prospects will be harmed by a process designed to be useful to science and shaped by its requirements. By contrast, the most successful cases are those in which you proceed as though you have no plan, allowing yourself to be taken by surprise at every turn, and constantly maintaining an open mind, free of presuppositions. The proper attitude of the analyst is to be prepared where necessary to shift from one frame of mind to another, not to speculate or fret too much while analysing, and not to attempt to draw up a unified theory about his body of material until the analysis is complete. The difference between one frame of mind and the other would be insignificant if we already possessed all the knowledge that we can obtain through psychoanalytical work about everything – or at least the most essential things – to do with the psychology of the unconscious and the structure of the neuroses. At the moment this is still a distant goal, and we must not close off the channels open to us for re-examining what we know so far and of adding to it.

e) I cannot urge colleagues emphatically enough to take a leaf out of the surgeon's book during psychoanalytic treatment and, like him, put to one side all your emotions and even your human sympathies in order to concentrate your mental powers on a single aim: carrying out the operation as skilfully as possible. The most dangerous emotional motivation for a psychoanalyst working under today's conditions is the therapeutic ambition to achieve something with his new and highly controversial methods that will convince others. This not only puts him in the wrong state of mind for his work, but renders him defenceless against the patient's resistances, the play of whose forces after all contains the key to recovery. The emotional coolness demanded of the analyst is justified by the optimum conditions it ensures for both parties; for the physician, the desirable safeguarding of his own emotional life, and for the patient the best help we can currently provide him with. One venerable surgeon chose for his motto 'Je le pansai, Dieu le guérit' [I dressed the wound, but God healed it]. Something like this should be good enough for the analyst.

f) It is not hard to see the point upon which all these individual rules converge. They are all intended to create for the physician the counterpart of the 'basic rule of analysis' drawn up for the patient. Just as the analysand is required to relate everything he has picked up in the course of his self-observation, overcoming all the logical and emotional reservations that dispose him to be selective, so the doctor should enable himself to use everything he hears for the purpose of interpreting and recognizing what is hidden in the unconscious, without introducing his own kind of censorship to replace the selectivity the patient forgoes. Expressed in a single formula: he should orientate his own unconscious, as a kind of receptive organ, towards the communicative unconscious of the patient, attuning himself to the analysand as the receiver of a telephone is attuned to the disc. Just as the receiver transforms back into sound-waves the electrical oscillations in the line that have been set off by sound-waves, so, from the derivatives of the patient's unconscious which are communicated to him, the unconscious of the doctor is enabled to re-create the unconscious that has conditioned the patient's associations.

But for the doctor to be able to use his unconscious like this as an instrument in analysis, he must very largely fulfil one psychological precondition. He must not tolerate any resistances in himself that would deny to his conscious mind what his unconscious has registered. Otherwise he would simply be introducing a new kind of selection and distortion into the analysis, something much more harmful than his sharply focused conscious attention would have produced. For these purposes it is not enough that he himself should be a more or less normal person. We are entitled to demand that he should have submitted to purification by psychoanalysis and taken note of those complexes of his own that were likely to hamper his reception of the patient's offerings. The disabling impact of such defects on him is beyond reasonable doubt. Every unresolved repression on his part corresponds, as W. Stekel accurately puts it, to a 'blind spot' in his analytical perceptions.

Years ago my answer to the question of how you become an analyst was 'by analysing your own dreams'. This is certainly sufficient preparation for many people, but not for everybody who would like to be proficient in analysis. And not everybody can interpret their own dreams without external help. Among the many merits of the Zurich school of analysis I include the precondition which they have tightened up and laid down as a requirement: that everybody who sets out to analyse others should first have undergone analysis himself at the hands of an expert. Anyone who is serious about the enterprise should take this path, which offers more than one advantage. The self-sacrifice entailed in opening yourself up to a stranger, in the absence of any compulsion by illness, is richly rewarding. Not only will you realize, in a much shorter time and at less emotional cost, your intention of learning about your own hidden depths, but gain at first hand impressions and convictions that you would strive in vain to acquire from books and lectures. Furthermore, one should not underestimate the gain to be made from the lasting psychological relationship that usually arises between the analyst and his mentor.

Understandably, such an analysis of a practically healthy person will remain incomplete. Anyone who appreciates the great value of the self-knowledge and increase in self-control thus achieved will continue subsequently to explore his own psyche through self-analysis, and accept that he must expect constantly to find out something new both about himself and the external world. But any analyst who has spurned the precaution of having himself analysed will not only be punished by his inability, beyond a certain point, to learn from his patients' cases, but will also be subject to a more serious danger, which can become a danger for others. He can easily be tempted to project his knowledge of his own characteristics, derived from a vague self-perception, on to science as a generally valid theory, thus bringing the psychoanalytic method into disrepute and misleading inexperienced people.

g) I will add a few more rules, which will take us from the attitude of the physician to the treatment of the patient.

It is surely an enticing prospect for the young, keen psychoanalyst to deploy a good deal of his own individuality in order to carry the patient along with him and create a momentum that will raise him above the bounds of his narrow personality. You might think it perfectly acceptable, indeed useful for the purpose of overcoming the patient's resistances, for the doctor to allow him a glimpse of his own psychological defects and conflicts and, by confiding in him about his own life, enable him to enjoy parity. One confidence is worth another, and if you want intimate details from somebody else, you must tell him some of yours as well.

However, in psychoanalytic dealings many things take a different course from what we would expect according to the theories of the psychology of consciousness. Experience does not favour this emotive technique. And it is not hard to see that it moves us away from psychoanalysis, and closer to treatments based on suggestion. More or less all you achieve is that the patient feels more relaxed and more ready to tell you what he knows himself, and what he has held back for a while because of conventional resistances. But the technique contributes nothing to revealing what is not consciously known to the patient. It simply makes it harder for him to overcome deeper resistances, and in severe cases it fails because of the insatiable appetite for information it arouses in the patient, who would then like to reverse the doctor–patient relationship, since he finds analysing the doctor more interesting than himself. The resolution of the transference, one of the main tasks of the therapy, is also made more difficult by the doctor's intimate approach, so that whatever gains have been made originally are more than negated in the end. I do not hesitate to reject this kind of technique as defective. For the patient the doctor should remain opaque, and, like a mirror surface, should show nothing but what is shown to him. It is true that, in practical terms, there is nothing wrong with the psychotherapist mixing a little analysis with a quantity of suggestive influence, as is sometimes necessary in institutions, in order to achieve visible results more quickly. But we can ask him to be aware of what he is doing, and to know that his method does not belong to psychoanalysis proper.

h) A further temptation arises out of the educative role that falls to the physician in psychoanalytic treatment, without any particular intention on his part. In resolving the inhibitions in development it happens naturally that the doctor finds himself well placed to set new goals for the impulses that have been set free. It is then just a matter of understandable ambition if, by setting his sights high for him, he tries to make something exceptional out of the person whose liberation from neurosis has cost the analyst so much effort. But here too the doctor should exercise restraint, and be guided more by the inclinations of the analysand than by his own desires. Not all neurotics have much innate talent for sublimation; in many cases you can assume they would not have become ill in the first place if they had known how to sublimate their drives. If you push them too hard towards sublimation and cut them off from the easiest and most accessible kinds of gratification of their drives, you will most often make their lives even harder than they already feel them to be. As a doctor you must above all be tolerant of your patient's weakness, and settle for restoring a degree of pleasure in achievement and appetite for life even in an inadequate person. Educational ambitions are as inappropriate as therapeutic ones. One also has to consider that many people become ill precisely because they try to sublimate their drives beyond the point their constitutions will support, and that among those who are capable of sublimation, this process tends to take place automatically once their inhibitions have been overcome. My view, then, is that the effort to use analytic treatment regularly to achieve sublimation of drives is always praiseworthy, but not to be recommended in all cases.

i) To what extent should one enlist the intellectual cooperation of the patient in the treatment? It is difficult to make valid generalizations about this. It is first and foremost the personality of the patient that is decisive. However, caution and restraint should always be exercised in this regard. It is wrong to give the analysand tasks to do, such as concentrating his memory, thinking about a particular period of his life, etc. What he needs to learn above all is something that everyone finds hard to accept: that none of the puzzles of a neurosis can be solved by an effort of will or concentration, but only by patiently following the rule of psychoanalysis, which demands an uncritical attitude to the unconscious and its derivatives. You should be particularly relentless in your insistence on this rule when dealing with those patients who are adept at escaping into intellectualism during treatment. They reflect frequently and often wisely on their condition, and by doing so they avoid doing anything about dealing with it. For the same reason, I am also reluctant to resort to recommending psychoanalytical reading to aid my patients. I require that they should learn personally, at first hand, and I assure them that the breadth and depth of insight they will gain in this way will outweigh the whole of the psychoanalytical literature. But I recognize that under the conditions of institutional treatment it can be very advantageous to use reading-matter to prepare patients for analysis and to establish an atmosphere favourable to influence.

Most emphatically of all, I would warn against courting the approval and support of parents or relatives by giving them something to read – whether introductory or more advanced – from our literature. Usually this well-intentioned step prematurely provokes an outbreak of the inevitable natural opposition of relatives to psychoanalytic treatment; the result is that treatment never even gets under way.

My hope is that, as psychoanalysts become more experienced, there will soon be agreement on questions concerning the most effective technique for treating neurotics. As regards treatment of 'relatives', I must confess I am totally at a loss, and have little faith in treating them individually.

(1912)

Note

1. The patient often asserts that a certain remark of his was made earlier, while you are able to assure him with calm superiority that he has only just uttered it. It then transpires that the analysand had intended at an earlier point to say something like this, but was prevented from doing so by the continuing presence of a resistance. For him the memory of the intention is indistinguishable from a memory of having carried it out.

On Initiating Treatment

Anyone who sets out to learn the noble game of chess from a book will soon discover that only opening moves and endgames lend themselves to an exhaustive systematic account, while the immense variety of games following the opening move allows no such thing. Only the keen study of matches fought out by master players can fill the gaps in the instruction manual. Similar limitations apply to the rules that can be supplied for the practice of psychoanalytic treatment.

In the following paper I will attempt, for the benefit of practising analysts, to put together a few of these rules as they apply to initiating the treatment. There will be prescriptions among them that may appear petty, and no doubt they are. The excuse for them is that they *are* just rules of the game, which gain their meaning within the context of the game plan as a whole. But it is just as well if I offer these rules as 'advice' and make no binding claims for them. The great variety of psychological configurations, the plasticity of all mental processes and the wealth of determining factors, all offer resistance to the mechanical application of technique, and make it possible for a proven method to fail, and for one that is usually unreliable to succeed. However, this does not mean we cannot establish a procedure that suits the average needs of the physician.

I published some years ago in another place the most important criteria to apply when deciding whether to take on particular patients;[1] I will not repeat them here. In the meantime, they have found favour with other psychoanalysts. I will add that since that time it has become my practice to accept only provisionally, for a period of three to four weeks, patients I do not know well. If you break off the sessions within this period, you save the patient the painful impression that the attempted cure is a disaster. All you have done is take soundings to get to know the case and see whether it is suitable for psychoanalysis. There is no other test available; no amount of conversation and questioning in the consulting room would substitute for it. However, these trial sessions are already the beginnings of an analysis and should follow the rules for treatment. You can assert its special nature by, for example, letting the patient do most of the talking, and not offering him any explanations other than what is required to induce him to continue his narrative.

There is also a diagnostic reason for initiating the treatment with a trial period of a few weeks. Quite often, when confronted with a neurosis displaying hysterical or obsessive symptoms, but not excessively marked and of recent provenance – in other words, exactly of the kind that is suitable for treatment – you have to allow for the suspicion that the case represents an early stage of so-called dementia praecox (schizophrenia, according to Bleuler, paraphrenia according to my suggestion), and that sooner or later it will clearly exhibit the profile of this complaint. I would argue that it is not always so easy to make out the difference. I am aware that there are psychiatrists who are less hesitant about differential diagnosis, but I am convinced that they are no less often wrong. It is just that a mistake is more serious for the psychoanalyst than for the so-called clinical psychiatrist. For the latter does not take any beneficial steps in either case; he merely runs the risk of making a theoretical mistake, and his diagnosis is only of academic interest. But the psychoanalyst in an unfavourable case will have made a practical error, wasted his efforts and discredited his therapeutic method. He cannot fulfil his undertaking to effect a cure if the patient is suffering not from hysteria or obsessional neurosis, but from paraphrenia, and he therefore has a particularly powerful motive for avoiding a mistake in diagnosis. During a trial treatment lasting a few weeks he will often make suspicious observations, which may induce him to discontinue the trial. Unfortunately, I cannot claim that such a trial regularly enables a safe decision to be made; it is just one more good precaution.[2]

Long preparatory discussions before the start of the analytical treatment, a different kind of therapy undertaken earlier, and a previous acquaintance between the doctor and the would-be analys- and, have certain unfavourable consequences for which you should be prepared. For they lead to the patient facing the doctor in a ready-made state of transference, which the doctor must first of all gradually uncover, instead of having the opportunity to observe the growth and development of the transference from the beginning. Thus for a while the patient has a lead one does not like to see him enjoy during therapy.

You should be wary of anybody who wishes to begin the treatment with a postponement. Experience tells us that after the lapse of the agreed period they will not show up, even if their motive for postponement, that is to say their rationalization of their intention, appears impeccable to the uninitiated.

There are particular difficulties when the doctor has enjoyed friendly or sociable relations with new patients or their families. A psychoanalyst who is asked to treat the wife or child of a friend should be prepared to lose the friendship. But this is a sacrifice he will have to make, if he cannot find anyone reliable to substitute for him.

Both lay people and doctors who confuse psychoanalysis with a treatment based on suggestion are inclined to value highly the expectations the patient brings to his new treatment. They often believe that a particular patient will present few problems, since he has great trust in psychoanalysis and is convinced of its truth and its effectiveness. With another patient, they believe there will be more difficulty, because of his sceptical attitude and unwillingness to believe anything until the treatment delivers results for him person-ally. In reality, the attitude of the patient matters very little: com-pared to the inner resistances in which his neurosis is embedded, his initial confidence or distrust are hardly worth considering. The patient's trustfulness certainly makes for very pleasant initial con-tacts with him. You thank him for it, but you must prepare him for the collapse of his positive predisposition when it encounters the first difficulty of the treatment. What you tell the sceptic is that the analysis does not depend on trust, that he can be as critical and untrusting as he likes, and that you will not blame his judgement for this attitude, because he is in no position to form a judgement on these issues. His mistrust is just a symptom like other symptoms, and it will not cause any trouble as long as he conscientiously follows what is prescribed by the rules of treatment.

Anyone well acquainted with the nature of neurosis will not be surprised to hear that even somebody highly competent to analyse other people is capable of behaving like other mortals and producing the most intense resistances as soon as he himself becomes the subject of psychoanalysis. Once again one has a sense of the depth of the unconscious mind, and is not surprised that the neurosis is rooted in layers of the psyche not accessible to analytical training.

Settling questions of time and payment is important at the beginning of treatment. As regards time, I never vary from the principle of charging for a fixed time. Every patient is allocated a certain hour in my working day; that is his appointment, and he remains liable for it even if he makes no use of it. This requirement, self-evidently applying to music or language tutors in our social circle, may seem harsh in the case of a doctor, or even unworthy of a professional man. You might be inclined to point out the many chance occurrences that may prevent the patient from appearing regularly at the same time, and you may ask that allowance should be made for the many intervening illnesses that can occur in the course of a lengthy analytical treatment. But my answer is that there is no alternative. With a lenient regime, the number of 'occasional' cancellations mounts up to the point of endangering the doctor's livelihood. If, by contrast, you strictly enforce your rule, it transpires that troublesome chance events never occur at all, and intervening illnesses hardly ever. You then very seldom find yourself enjoying the kind of leisure that is embarrassing to a breadwinner. You can carry on working undisturbed, and you escape the trying and distracting situation of always having to suspend your work, through no fault of your own, just at what promises to be an important and meaningful point. Practising psychoanalysis for a few years while strictly maintaining the principle of hourly charges is the best way to acquire a proper conviction of the importance of psychogenetic motives in people's daily lives, of the frequency of 'school-phobic illnesses' and of the invalidity of chance. With complaints that are clearly physical, for all their psychological interest, I interrupt the treatment, feel justified in reallocating the appointment that has been released, and take the patient back again as soon as he has recovered and I have another free appointment.

I work with my patients every day except Sundays and public holidays; that is to say, usually six days a week. For minor cases, or in continuing treatment that is already well advanced, three hours a week are enough. Otherwise, there is no advantage either for the doctor or the patient in imposing time-restrictions, and at the beginning they are completely undesirable. Even short interruptions are enough to overlay the work a little; we used to speak jocularly of a 'Monday layer' when we started again after the day of rest. If there are long intervals in the work, there is a danger of not keeping up with the actual experience of the patient, so that the treatment loses contact with the present and becomes side-tracked. Occasionally, too, one comes across patients to whom one must devote more than the standard period of one hour because they need the best part of an hour just to thaw out and to begin to communicate at all.

There is one question that is unwelcome to the doctor, but is raised by the patient right at the beginning: 'How long will the treatment take? How much time do you need to cure my disorder?' By suggesting a trial period of a few weeks, you avoid the need to answer this question directly; you can promise to give a more reliable view by the end of the trial period. Your answer is like that of Aesop in the fable to the traveller inquiring how long the path is. 'Walk!', he tells him, and explains his reasoning thus: you must know the pace of a traveller before you can work out the time needed for his journey. This expedient will help you over the early difficulty, but the analogy is not a good one, for the neurotic person can easily alter his pace, and at times makes only very slow progress. In reality, questions about the prospective length of treatment are almost unanswerable.

Because patients are ingenuous and doctors are not forthright enough, together they place the most excessive demands on the analysis, while granting it the shortest possible time-scale. As an example, let me relate a few data from a letter that reached me some days ago from a lady in Russia. She is fifty-three years old, has been suffering for twenty-three years and has not been capable of sustained work for ten years. 'Treatment in various clinics for nervous disorders' has not enabled her to lead an 'active life'. She has read about psychoanalysis and hopes it can cure her completely. But her treatment has already cost her family so much that she cannot afford to stay in Vienna for longer than six weeks or two months. A further complication is that all she wants to do is 'explain herself' in writing, for to touch upon her complexes would cause an explosion in her or strike her 'temporarily dumb'. In other contexts, nobody would expect you to lift a heavy table with two fingers as though it were a light stool, nor to build a big house in the same time as it takes to put up a small wooden hut. But when it comes to the neuroses, which do not yet seem to have found a place in normal human thinking, even intelligent people seem to forget the necessary correlation between time, work and successful outcome. Incidentally, this is an understandable result of profound ignorance about the origins of neuroses. Thanks to this ignorance, people view the neurosis as a kind of 'strange girl from far away'. Nobody knows where she comes from, and so people expect that she will disappear one day.

Doctors reinforce this trustfulness; even the more informed among them do not properly appreciate the severity of neurotic illnesses. One colleague who is a friend of mine, and whom I greatly respect for his conversion to psychoanalysis after working for decades on the basis of different scientific theories, wrote to me once: what we need is a short, convenient, out-patient treatment for obsessional neuroses. This was something I could not deliver; I was ashamed about it and tried to excuse myself by remarking that probably the relevant specialists would be very happy to have therapies for tuberculosis or carcinomas that combined these advantages.

To put it bluntly, psychoanalysis always involves long stretches of time, six-month periods or whole years; longer than most sufferers expect. You therefore have a duty to inform the patient about this state of affairs before he finally opts for treatment. In general I think it is more honourable, but also more expedient, to be open with him – short of deliberately trying to deter him – about the difficulties and sacrifices entailed in analytic therapy, thus depriving him of any justification for claiming later that he had been enticed into a treatment whose scope and significance he had not realized. Anybody deterred by such statements would later have shown himself to be unsuitable for treatment anyway. It is a good thing to operate this kind of selectivity before beginning treatment. However, as sufferers become progressively more enlightened, the number of those passing this initial test is increasing.

I decline to commit patients to persisting with the treatment for a stated length of time, and I allow everybody to break off the therapy whenever they like. But I do not conceal from them that if they give up at an early point in the work they will have no success to show for it, and, as with an unfinished surgical operation, they could well be left in an unsatisfactory condition. In the earliest years of my psychoanalytic practice I found that the greatest difficulty was persuading patients to continue. This difficulty was overcome long ago; nowadays I anxiously try to persuade them to stop.

It is still reasonable to wish to reduce the length of analytical therapy, an aim that, as we shall see, has been pursued in a variety of ways. Unfortunately, one very important factor works against it: the slow pace at which profound mental changes take place; ultimately, no doubt, the 'time-free' nature of our unconscious processes. When patients are faced with the problem of the very time-consuming nature of analysis, they quite often think they know a way out. They propose to divide their symptoms into those they class as unbearable, and others that they describe as secondary, and say: 'If you can rid me of this (for example a headache, or a particular anxiety), I can cope with the rest by myself.' But they overestimate the degree of control that analysis can exercise. The analyst can do a great deal, but he cannot determine the outcome precisely in advance. He initiates a process, the resolution of existing repressions; he can supervise it, promote the process, remove obstacles from its path – and he can do much to ruin it. On the whole, though, once under way, the process takes its own course, and neither its direction, nor the sequence of points at which it will assert pressure can be prescribed.

The power of the analyst over the symptoms of illness can be compared with male sexual potency. Although he can father a *whole* child, even the strongest man cannot inseminate the female reproductive organism just with a head, an arm or a leg. He cannot even determine the sex of the child. All he does is initiate a highly complex process predetermined by events in the distant past, which ends with the separation of the baby from the mother. A neurosis, too, has the character of an organism, whose individual manifestations are not independent of each other, but mutually condition and support each other. One always suffers from a single neurosis, not a whole collection of them that happen to be concentrated in one individual. The sufferer delivered at his own request from one unbearable symptom can easily find that a previously mild symptom now becomes intensified to the point of unbearableness. In any case, if you want to divorce a successful outcome as far as possible from factors caused by suggestion (that is to say, by transference), it is better to renounce such vestiges of power as a doctor could retain over the outcome of treatment. The psychoanalyst's favourite patients will of course be those who require him to restore them to full health, as far as that is achievable, and grant him as much time as they need for recovery. Naturally, such favourable conditions are rarely met with.

The next point to be settled at the beginning of a treatment concerns money, the doctor's fee. The analyst does not deny that money must be seen first and foremost as a means of self-preservation and of gaining power, but he maintains that powerful sexual factors are also at work in the way we value money. He is able to cite the similarity in the attitudes of civilized people to sex and to money matters; there is the same ambivalence, prudishness and hypocrisy. He is therefore determined in advance not to lend himself to all this, but to treat financial relations with the patient in the same natural and candid manner as he employs in attempting to educate him in sexual matters. By announcing unbidden the value he places on his time, he demonstrates to him that he has cast off any false shame. Common sense then dictates that he does not ask for any large sums all at once, but for payment at shorter, regular (perhaps monthly) intervals. (It is well known that you do not make the patient value a treatment more by underselling it.) We know that this is not the usual practice of neurologists and other specialists in our European society. But a psychoanalyst is entitled to place himself on a par with a surgeon, who is forthright and expensive because he offers treatments that can help. I believe it is more honourable and ethically more defensible to declare your own claims and needs, rather than, as doctors still tend to do at the moment, to play the part of a selfless philanthropist when you are in no position to do so, and then to fret silently or complain openly about how thoughtless and exploitative the patient is. What helps to validate an analyst's claim to payment is that all his hard work will not earn him as much as other medical specialists can command.

For the same reasons, he is justified in refusing to practise without a fee, or to make any exceptions, even for colleagues or their relatives. This last demand seems to offend against medical collegiality. But we must remember that offering free treatment has far greater implications for a psychoanalyst than for anyone else; that is, forgoing a substantial fraction of the working time he has available for monetary gain (an eighth, a seventh, etc.) over many months. A second free course of treatment offered at the same time will deprive him of a full third or quarter of his earning capacity. The effect is comparable with that of serious injury from an accident.

Then the question arises as to whether the patient's advantage to some extent outweighs the doctor's sacrifice. I feel justified in offering my opinion on this, since for about ten years I gave free consultations for an hour a day, sometimes two, because, for the sake of familiarizing myself with the neurosis in question, I wanted to work with as few resistances as possible. It did not yield the advantages I was looking for. A number of the resistances of neurotic people are intensified enormously by free treatment: for example, the increased temptations of the transference relationship for a young woman; or for a young man, his resistance, arising out of the father-complex, to the obligation to be grateful. The latter is among the most adverse of circumstances for the doctor attempting to help a patient. The lapse of the regulatory mechanism provided by paying the doctor becomes painfully apparent; the whole relationship is removed from the real world, and a good motive for working towards the completion of the cure is denied to the patient.

You can distance yourself from the ascetic condemnation of money and yet still regret that analysis is almost completely unavailable for poor people, for both external and internal reasons. Not much can be done about this. Perhaps the widely held belief is true, that people forced by poverty into a life of hard work are less prone to neurosis. But another observation is beyond dispute, that once a poor person has developed a neurosis he will have great difficulty in ridding himself of it. It is too useful to him in his struggle for self-assertion, and the secondary gain of his illness for him is all too important. In the name of his neurosis he can now lay claim to the pity that people denied him for his material deprivation, and can absolve himself from the demand that he should struggle against his poverty by working. Anyone who tackles a poor person's neurosis with psychotherapeutic methods will therefore usually find that in this case he needs a completely different, material kind of therapy, such as used to be dispensed by Emperor Joseph II, according to legend in this country. Naturally, one occasionally comes across worthwhile people, made dependent through no fault of their own, to whom the above-mentioned obstacles associated with free consultations do not apply, and who respond very well to treatment.

For the middle class, the costs entailed in psychoanalysis only appear exorbitant. Quite apart from the fact that health and fitness for living are incompatible with a modest outlay; if you add up the endless expenditure for sanatoriums and medical treatment, and compare the increase in efficiency and earning-power bestowed by a successful analytical cure, you might say that the patient has struck a good bargain. There is nothing more expensive in life than illness – and stupidity.

Before concluding these remarks about initiating analytic treatment, I would like to say a word about the formal staging of the setting in which the therapy is carried out. I strongly advise positioning the patient on a couch, while you seat yourself behind him, out of his sight. This arrangement has a historical dimension: it is a relic of the hypnotherapy out of which psychoanalysis developed. But there are many reasons for keeping it. First, there is a personal motive, which others may share with me. I cannot bear to be stared at for eight hours a day or longer. Since I like to give myself over to my own unconscious thoughts while I listen, I do not want the patient trying to interpret my expression, nor do I want to influence what he is telling me. The patient usually feels deprived of something by being forced into this situation, and resists it, particularly if voyeurism plays an important part in his neurosis. But I insist on this measure, which intends and achieves the prevention of an imperceptible merging of the transference with the patient's associations. It isolates the transference and allows it to stand out clearly as a resistance at the moment it occurs. I know that many analysts do things differently, but I don't know whether their deviation is more to do with some advantage they have discovered, or the desire to do things differently.

With the conditions of the therapy having been thus settled, the question arises: where and with what material should you begin the treatment?

In general it is unimportant what material you use to begin a treatment, whether it be the life story, the case history or the childhood memories of the patient. The point is that you should let the patient tell you something and allow him the choice of where to start. Thus you say to him, 'Before I can say anything to you, I must learn a good deal about you; please tell me what you know about yourself.'

You make an exception only for the basic rule of psychoanalytic technique that the patient must observe. You make him aware of it right from the beginning: 'Just one thing, before you start. Your narrative should be different in one respect from ordinary conversation. Quite rightly, you would normally try to hang on to the threads which hold your account together, and avoid being distracted by intrusive notions and irrelevant thoughts, so that you don't get carried away, as they say. But here you are meant to proceed differently. You will notice that during your narrative a number of thoughts will occur to you, which you would like to reject because of certain critical objections. You will be tempted to say that this or that does not fit in here, or it's completely unimportant, or it's pointless, therefore you don't need to say it. Don't give in to this criticism, but say it anyway, precisely because you are averse to doing so. You will learn and appreciate the reason for this prescription later; it is in fact the only one you have to follow. So you should say everything that comes into your head. Behave like a traveller, for example, sitting in the window seat of a railway carriage and describing to a companion with an inside seat the changing view he is seeing. And finally, don't forget that you have promised to be completely honest, and don't gloss over something because for some reason you feel uncomfortable talking about it.'[3]

Patients who date their illness from a certain time usually concentrate on its immediate causes; others, who have themselves recognized a link between the neurosis and their childhood, often begin by telling their whole life-story. You should certainly not expect a coherent narrative, nor do anything to encourage it. Every part of the story will have to be told again later, and only with such repetitions will the added details emerge that carry the important connections unknown to the patient himself.

There are patients who conscientiously prepare their story in advance, supposedly in order to make the most of their consultation time. What is thus disguised as eagerness, is in fact resistance. Patients should be advised against such preparation, which is only employed to prevent unwelcome associations from cropping up.[4] However sincerely the sufferer believes in his praiseworthy objective, the resistance will insist on playing its part in these deliberate preparations and ensure that the most valuable information escapes mention. You will soon notice the patient devising other ways as well to withhold what is needed by the treatment. Perhaps he will talk over the therapy every day with a confidant, producing for him all the thoughts that should be crowding in upon him in the presence of the therapist. The treatment then suffers from a leak where all the best material seeps away. Sooner rather than later, the patient will have to be advised that the therapy is a matter between the doctor and himself only; and no one else, however intimate or however curious, should be taken into his confidence. In the later stages of the treatment the patient is not usually subject to such temptations.

I do not make difficulties for patients who want to keep their treatment a secret, which they often do because they have kept their neurosis a secret. It does not matter that, as a result of their reserve, some of the finest achievements of therapy will be lost to the wider world. The very fact that the patient elects for secrecy means that a part of his secret history is immediately spotlighted.

Impressing upon patients that, at the beginning of their treatment, they should limit as far as possible the number of people who know about it, serves to protect them to some extent from the many hostile influences that will try to turn them away from analysis. At the beginning of the treatment, such influences can be pernicious. Later on they are irrelevant, or even useful in bringing to the fore resistances that attempt concealment.

If in the course of the analytic treatment the patient should need other, short-term specialist therapy, it is much more appropriate to call in a non-analyst colleague rather than undertake this kind of care oneself. Combined treatments for a neurotic complaint that has a strong physical component are for the most part unworkable. Patients lose interest in the analysis once they are shown more than one route to a cure. It is preferable to postpone the physical treatment until the psychoanalysis has been completed: if the former were to take precedence, it would mostly fail.

Let us return to the initiating of the treatment. Occasionally you encounter patients who begin their therapy with the negative assurance that they cannot think of anything to tell you, although the whole domain of their life-story and case history lies fallow at their disposal. Do not give in to their request to tell them what to talk about, neither on this first occasion nor later. Remember what you are up against in such cases. A strong resistance has taken up a front-line position in order to defend the neurosis; accept the challenge immediately and move in for close combat. Repeating the emphatic assertion that a complete dearth of associations right at the beginning just never occurs, and that what we have here is resistance to the analysis, soon forces the expected confession out of the patient, or begins to reveal his complexes. It is bad if he has to admit that while he was being told the basic rule he had resolved to keep certain things to himself. It is less irksome if all he needs to do is describe the mistrust he feels towards analysis, or the discouraging things he has heard about it. If he denies these and other possibilities that you confront him with, you can still put pressure on him to confess that he has neglected to mention certain thoughts that preoccupy him. For example, he was thinking about the course of treatment itself, though not about anything specific to do with it; or about the appearance of the room he is sitting in; or he can't help thinking about the objects in the consulting room, and that he is lying on a couch here; all of which he has replaced by the evasive word 'Nothing'. These allusions are easy to understand; everything related to his current situation corresponds to a transference on to the doctor, which is a suitable basis for resistance. Thus you are obliged to begin the treatment by revealing this transference; starting from here, it does not take long to find your way into the patient's pathogenic material. The people most likely to preface the analysis with a denial that they have any associations at all are women whose life-experience has prepared them for sexual aggression, or men whose homosexuality is especially heavily suppressed.

Like their first resistance, the first symptoms or chance actions of patients can command particular interest and betray the complex that controls their neurosis. An intelligent young philosopher, with exquisite aesthetic sensibilities, hurriedly tugs the stripe on his trousers into place before he lies down for his first consultation; he turns out to be a former coprophiliac of the greatest refinement, as might be expected of the aesthete he later became. In the same situation, a young woman hastens to cover a glimpse of ankle with her skirt; with this she has already pre-empted the later analysis by giving away its best results: her narcissistic pride in her physical beauty and her exhibitionist tendencies.

Patients often object particularly to the recommended arrangement whereby the doctor sits out of sight behind them; they beg to be allowed to take up a different position for the session, mainly because they cannot bear not to have the doctor in full view. This is regularly denied to them, but they cannot be prevented from so arranging things that they utter a few sentences before the beginning of the session, or after it has been declared closed and they have already got up from the couch. Thus they divide the consultation into an official part, during which they mostly behave in a very inhibited way, and a 'cosy' part, where they speak really freely and talk about all sorts of things that they believe are not part of the treatment. The doctor does not put up with this division for long. He notes what is said before or after the session, and by using it at the first opportunity he demolishes the dividing wall the patient was trying to build. It will have been built out of the material of a transference-resistance.

As long as the patient continues to communicate and to associate freely, the topic of transference should not be raised. You should hold back this most delicate of procedures until the transference has become a resistance.

The next question to confront us is one of principle: when should we start communicating to the analysand? When is the right time to reveal the secret meaning of his associations, to initiate him into the theory and technical procedures of analysis?

The only possible answer is: not until the patient has established a usable transference, a proper rapport. The first objective of the treatment remains to attach him to the therapy and the person of the doctor. You do not need to do anything extra, beyond giving him time. If you show real interest in him, carefully neutralizing resistances as they arise and avoiding certain errors, the patient produces such an attachment of his own accord, and inserts the doctor into a series of imagos of people from whom he has been accustomed to receive affection. It is, however, easy to forfeit this early success if from the very beginning you take up any standpoint other than that of empathy, such as a moralizing one; or if you act as though you were the representative or agent of another party, such as a married partner etc.

This answer of course entails condemning any procedure that would involve translating the patient's symptoms for him the moment you have interpreted them yourself, or even perceiving a special kind of triumph in throwing these 'solutions' into his face at the first meeting. It is not difficult for a practised analyst to identify clearly the suppressed wishes of a patient, even from the nature of his complaints and his case history. But what degree of self-satisfaction and recklessness does it take to reveal to a stranger totally ignorant of analytical theory, upon the briefest possible acquaintance, that he has an incestuous desire for his mother, harbours a death-wish towards the wife he supposedly loves, is contemplating cheating on his boss, etc! I have heard that there are analysts who brag about such instant diagnoses and rapid treatments, but I would warn everyone against following such examples. You will totally discredit yourself and your cause and provoke the most vehement denials, whether you have interpreted correctly or not. The more correctly you have interpreted, in fact, the stronger the resistance will be. The therapeutic effect will usually at first be practically nil, but the deterrent effect for the analysis will be final. Even in the later stages of the treatment you must be careful not to communicate the explanation of a symptom or the interpretation of a desire until the patient has reached the point where he is only a short step away from seizing upon this explanation for himself. In earlier years I had plenty of opportunity to discover that communicating an explanation prematurely put a premature end to the therapy, both because of the resistances it suddenly aroused, and because of the relief the explanation brought with it.

Here you will object: is it really our job to prolong the treatment, rather than completing it as quickly as possible? Doesn't the patient suffer on account of his ignorance and incomprehension, and isn't it our duty to let him know our findings as soon as possible, that is, as soon as the doctor himself knows them?

Answering this question requires a brief excursus, about what it means to know and about the mechanism of healing in psycho-analysis.

I admit that in the earliest days of analytical technique, with our over-intellectualized way of thinking, we rated the patients' knowledge very highly, hardly distinguishing it from our own. We felt particularly lucky if we managed to obtain information from third parties about a forgotten childhood trauma, for example from parents, carers or the seducer himself, as was possible in individual cases. We then lost no time in imparting the message and the proof of its veracity to the patient, in the firm expectation of bringing the neurosis and the treatment swiftly to an end. It was a bitter disappointment when the anticipated success did not follow. How could it be that the patient, who now knew about his traumatic experience, went on behaving as though he knew no more about it than before? And even after we had reported and described it, the patient still could not recall the repressed trauma.

In one particular case, the mother of a hysterical girl revealed to me the homosexual experience that had had a great influence in fixating the girl's attacks. The mother herself had been shocked by the scene, but the daughter had completely forgotten it, although she was already in the preliminary stages of puberty. I now made an interesting discovery. Every time I repeated the mother's story in the girl's presence, the latter would react with a fit of hysteria, and afterwards once more forgot all about what she had heard. There was no doubt that the sufferer was expressing the most violent resistance to the knowledge being forced upon her. In the end, she would feign feeble-mindedness and complete amnesia to protect herself from what I was telling her. The only thing to do was to remove from this knowledge in itself the meaning it was preordained to bear, and to lay the emphasis on the resistances that had caused the failure of knowledge in the first place and were still prepared to defend it. Conscious knowledge, even if not rejected again, was powerless to deal with these resistances.

The disturbing ability of sufferers to combine a certain amount of conscious knowledge with a lack of knowledge, remains inexplicable for so-called standard psychology. Because of its recognition of the unconscious, psychoanalysis has no difficulty with this; moreover, the phenomenon in question provides some of the best evidence in support of a conception that is deepening its grasp of mental processes as localized in different parts of the psyche. The patient's thought-processes are aware of the repressed experience, but they cannot make a link with that place where the repressed memory is stored in one form or another. Change can only occur when conscious thought-processes have penetrated as far as this place and have overcome the repressive resistances there. It is just as though the Ministry of Justice has issued an order to deal with juvenile transgressions in a particular, lenient way. Until this order comes to the attention of individual local courts, or if local magistrates have no intention of obeying the order but just go on dispensing justice as they see fit, then there can be no change in the treatment of individual juvenile delinquents. We should add, by way of correction, that consciously transmitting to the patient what he has repressed does in fact have some effect. It will not achieve the desired effect of putting an end to the symptoms, but it will have other consequences. At first it will arouse resistances, and then, once these have been overcome, it will provoke a thought process that, in due course, finally produces its anticipated influence upon the unconscious memory.

At this point we should review the play of forces activated by the treatment. The primary driving-force behind the therapy is the suffering of the patient and the desire to be cured that it gives rise to. The magnitude of this driving force is reduced by a number of factors that only come to light in the course of the analysis, above all the secondary gain the patient enjoys from his illness. The driving force itself, however, must be maintained until the end of the treatment; every improvement in the patient's condition decreases it. But it is incapable of overcoming the illness on its own. It lacks two prerequisites: it does not know the route to follow to this goal, and it cannot summon up the energy necessary to combat the resistances. Analysis helps with both these shortcomings. It supplies the emotive dynamic needed to overcome the resistances, by mobilizing the energies that lie ready to be used in transference; and with some timely explanations it shows the patient the paths down which to direct these energies. A transference alone can quite often overcome the symptoms of the disorder, but only temporarily, just as long as the transference itself lasts. This then represents treatment by suggestion, not psychoanalysis. A treatment only deserves the latter description when the transference has applied its intensity to overcoming the resistances. Only then does sickness become no longer sustainable, even when the transference has been dissolved again, as it is meant to be.

In the course of the treatment another helpful factor is brought to life, the intellectual interest and understanding of the patient. However, this is insignificant compared with the other forces engaged in the conflict; it is constantly threatened with subversion by the clouding of judgement due to the resistances. This leaves transference and instruction (by explanation) as the new sources of strength called upon by the analyst on behalf of the patient. However, the analyst will only make use of instruction in so far as he is induced to by the transference. For that reason, he should hold back his first explanation until a strong transference is established – and, in addition, should withhold every later explanation until the disturbance of the transference by a succession of resistances has been removed.

(1913)

Notes

1. 'Über Psychotherapie' ['On Psychotherapy'], 1905 (*Ges. Werke*, Vol. 5).
2. There is more to be said than I can develop here about the topic of this diagnostic uncertainty, the prospects of analysis in less severe cases of paraphrenia, and the basis of similarity between the two complaints. I would gladly follow Jung's procedure of opposing hysteria and obsessional neurosis, as 'neuroses of transference', to the paraphrenic complaints as 'neuroses of introversion', if it were not that by doing so the concept of 'introversion' (of the libido) would be deprived of its only proper meaning.
3. Much more might be said about our experience concerning the basic rule of psychoanalysis. You sometimes meet people who act as though they invented it themselves. Others transgress against it from the very beginning. It is imperative to relay it to the patient at the start of the treatment; it is also useful to do so. Later, under the influence of the resistances, patients

withdraw their allegiance to it, and there comes a moment when everybody disregards it. You have to remind yourself how irresistibly tempting it was during your self-analysis to yield to those critical reasons for rejecting associations. You can find regular confirmation of the ineffectiveness of contracts such as this agreement with the patient on the basic rule of psychoanalysis, the first time that intimate details about third parties enter into the discourse. The patient knows he is supposed to tell all, but he turns discretion about other people into a new reason for reserve. 'Am I really meant to tell everything? I thought that only applied to things that concerned me personally.' Naturally, it is impossible to carry out an analytical treatment where the patient's relationships with other people and his thoughts about them are not mentioned. *Pour faire une omelette il faut casser des oeufs* [You can't make an omelette without breaking eggs]. A decent person readily forgets what seems to him not worth knowing about other people's secrets. It is also not possible to avoid naming names, otherwise the patient's narrative has something shadowy about it, like something out of Goethe's *Natural Daughter*, and will leave no lasting impression on the analyst's memory. And the non-disclosure of names closes off access to all sorts of important relationships. Naming of names can perhaps be kept in reserve until the analysand becomes more familiar with the doctor and the process. It is very strange how the whole objective of the analysis becomes unattainable once you have made a single concession about naming. But if, for example, just one place in a city were to be covered by right of sanctuary, you can imagine how quickly the whole underworld element of the city would forgather there. A high-ranking official who was once a patient of mine was obliged by his public-service oath to treat certain matters as state secrets. The treatment failed because of this restriction. Psychoanalytic treatment must be ruthless, because the neurosis and its resistances are ruthless.

4. Exceptions should only be made for facts such as family trees, journeys, operations, etc.

*Observations on Love in
Transference*

Anyone practising analysis for the first time no doubt worries about the difficulties he will face in interpreting the patient's associations and the task of re-creating the repressed. What he will learn in due course, however, is that while he need not take these particular difficulties too seriously, he will instead have really serious problems coping with transference.

From among the situations of this kind that arise, I am going to select a single, very sharply delineated one, chosen both because of its frequent recurrence and its significance in reality, and because of its interest to theory. The case I have in mind is that of the female patient who lets it be known, either by dropping hints or by direct confession, that, like any other woman, she is only human and has fallen in love with the analyst. This situation has its embarrassing and its comic sides as well as its serious one. It is also so complex and determined by so many factors, so unavoidable and so difficult to resolve that discussion of it has for some time been a vital need of analytical technique. But as we who mock others' mistakes are not always free of them ourselves, we have not exactly pushed ourselves to meet this challenge. Time and again here we come up against the obligation to medical discretion, indispensable in life but of no use in our science. Since writing about psychoanalysis is also a part of real life, there is a genuine contradiction here. I recently took up a position beyond discretion and suggested that this precise situation of transference held back the progress of psychoanalysis for its first decade.[1]

For a cultivated layman – the ideal civilized interlocutor for psychoanalysis – affairs of the heart are of a different order of magnitude from everything else; they are, so to speak, inscribed on a special parchment unsuitable for any other form of inscription. Thus, when a female patient falls in love with the doctor, our layman will assume that there can only be two outcomes: the rare one where circumstances permit the legitimate and lasting union of the two, and the commoner one where doctor and patient go their own ways and the work that has been initiated, meant to lead to her recovery, has to be abandoned as though spoilt by an elemental event. Of course, a third outcome is conceivable, apparently even compatible with continuing the therapy; that of starting an illicit love affair not destined to be permanent. But this is surely ruled out as much by bourgeois morality as by the dignity of the medical profession. All the same, our layman would want to be reassured as plainly as possible that the analyst excludes this third option.

Clearly, the psychoanalyst's standpoint has to be different.

Let us take the case of the second outcome of the situation we are discussing: doctor and patient part after the woman has fallen in love with the doctor, and the course of therapy is abandoned. But the condition of the patient necessitates a second attempt at analysis, with a different doctor. It then transpires that the woman feels she has fallen in love with this second doctor, too, and likewise with a third, after she has once again terminated the treatment and then started afresh, and so on. This commonly occurring state of affairs is well known as one of the bases of psychoanalytical theory, and it can be put to use in two ways, one by the doctor conducting the analysis, the other by the patient in need of analysis.

For the doctor it represents a valuable lesson and a good warning about any temptation to counter-transference on his side. He has to be clear that the patient's infatuation is induced by the analytical situation and is not due to his personal attractions, and that he therefore has no reason to be proud of his 'conquest', as it would be called outside the analytical context. And it is always good to be reminded of this. The patient, however, is faced with a choice of alternatives: either she has to renounce psychoanalytical treatment, or she has to accept falling in love with the doctor as her inevitable fate.[2]

I have no doubt that the patient's closest family will declare as decisively in favour of the first of these options as the analysing doctor will for the second. But I think this is a case where the tender – or rather self-centredly jealous – concern of the family should not be allowed to decide. Only the interests of the patient should be conclusive. And her relations' love cannot cure a neurosis. The psychoanalyst does not need to impose himself, but he can put himself forward as indispensable for certain purposes. Any close family member who adopts Tolstoy's position on this problem can continue to enjoy undisturbed possession of his wife or daughter, but will have to try to learn to live with her continuing neurosis and the accompanying problems concerning her ability to love. In the end the case is similar to that of gynaecological treatment. At any rate, the jealous father or husband is greatly mistaken in thinking that the patient can escape falling in love with the doctor if he elects for her to take a non-analytical course of treatment. Rather, the only difference will be that such an infatuation, destined to go unspoken and unanalysed, will never make the contribution to her recovery that analysis would have extracted from it.

It has come to my attention that there are a few doctors practising analysis who often prepare a female patient for the occurrence of love in transference, or even encourage them 'only to fall in love with the doctor in order to move the analysis forward'. I find it hard to think of a more absurd approach. The analyst thereby robs the phenomenon of its convincing spontaneous character and creates for himself many problems that will be hard to overcome.

At first sight, infatuation in transference seems unlikely to bring anything of benefit to the course of therapy. Even the most cooperative patient suddenly no longer understands the treatment and takes no further interest in it, and does not want to talk or hear about anything apart from her love, to which she demands a response. Having given up her symptoms or neglected them, she even declares herself healthy. The scene changes completely, as though a game has suddenly been replaced by the sudden eruption of reality, or the fire alarm sounded in the middle of a theatre performance. When you experience this for the first time as a doctor, it is hard to hold on to the analytical situation and escape the delusion that the treatment really is over.

After some reflection you get your bearings. First and foremost you remember the suspicion that everything that interferes with the progress of the treatment may be an expression of resistance. Resistance undoubtedly has a good deal to do with the outbreak of tempestuous demands for love. For some time you had noticed that the patient was showing signs of an affectionate transference, and you were surely justified in thinking that her feelings for the doctor were responsible for her cooperativeness, her receptiveness to his analytical explanations, and the high level of intelligence she displayed at the time. But now it is as though all of that has been swept away; the patient completely lacks insight; she seems to be lost in her infatuation. And this change happens, with some regularity, just at the point where you had to require her to admit or recall a particularly painful and heavily repressed part of her life. She had thus been in love for some time, but now the resistance begins to make use of her love to prevent the therapy from continuing, completely distracting her interest from the task in hand and causing the medical analyst some painful embarrassment.

On closer inspection it is possible to recognize the influence of complicating motives on the situation; some connected with being in love, but others particularly expressing the resistance. The first type includes the efforts of the patient to convince herself she is irresistible, to destroy the authority of the doctor by reducing him to a mere lover, and whatever else promises to result as a by-product of gratifying her love. You can surmise that the resistance occasionally uses professions of love as a means of putting the strait-laced analyst to the test; should he succumb, his advances would then be turned down. But above all you have the impression that the resistance, acting like an *agent provocateur*, intensifies the state of being in love and exaggerates her willingness to surrender sexually, just in order to vindicate all the more emphatically the effect of the repression by invoking the dangers of such loose behaviour. It is well known that Alfred Adler saw all this by-play, often absent altogether from purer examples of the phenomenon, as the essence of the whole process.

How should the analyst behave in order to avert failure in this situation, if he is still convinced that the therapy ought to continue right through the effects of the love-transference and in spite of it?

It would be easy for me to lay heavy stress on conventional morality and insist that the analyst should never accept or respond to the affection held out to him. I could say that he should consider that the time has come to represent to the infatuated woman the demands of morality and the need for self-denial, to persuade her to renounce her desires and overcome the animal part of her nature so as to continue the work of analysis.

But I am not going to fulfil these expectations, neither the first nor the second part of them. Not the first, because I am not writing for our clientele, but for doctors who have serious problems to wrestle with, and because I can trace the moral prescription here back to its origins, that is to say to expediency. On this occasion I am in the happy position of being able to substitute the requirements of analytical technique for a moral dictate, without altering the result.

I am going to reject even more decisively the second part of the expectation I mentioned. It would be pointless, and not the action of an analyst, to demand that she should repress, renounce and sublimate her instinct as soon as the patient confesses her love-transference. It would be like elaborately summoning up a spirit from the underworld only in order to send him away to the depths again without asking him any questions. This would amount to calling the repressed up to the conscious level and then repressing it again out of fright. And you need not delude yourself about the prospects of success from this procedure. Elevated rhetoric notoriously achieves little against passion. The patient will simply feel she has been spurned, and will not waste any time before seeking vengeance.

Neither am I prepared to recommend a middle course – though it would appeal to many people as being particularly clever – which consists of claiming to reciprocate the patient's affection but avoiding all physical expression of this affection, until you can steer the relationship into calmer waters and raise it to a higher level. My objection to this expedient is that psychoanalytical treatment is built on truthfulness. That is the basis of a fair amount of its educational effect and its ethical value. It is dangerous to abandon these fundamentals. If you have become well used to analytical techniques, you no longer encounter the lies and deceptions that doctors otherwise find indispensable, and when, with the best of intentions, you try to make use of them just for once, you tend to give yourself away. Since you demand that the patient should be strictly truthful, you risk forfeiting the whole of your authority if you yourself are caught out departing from the truth. Moreover, there are dangers in the attempt to let yourself drift into feelings of affection for the patient. Self-control is never so good that you might not find yourself going further than you intended. So I believe you should stay true to the disinterest you have acquired, by suppressing any counter-transference.

I have already indicated that analytical technique commands the doctor to deny the infatuated patient the satisfaction she desires. The course of therapy must be conducted on terms of abstinence. By this I do not just mean physical self-denial, nor do I mean blocking all desire, which might be more than any unwell person could bear. What I want to do is to establish the principle that you tolerate the existence of needs and longings on the patient's part as dynamic factors in treatment and change, and you should be careful not to appease these feelings by means of surrogates. And you could not offer anything but surrogates, since the patient's condition makes her incapable of genuine satisfaction, until her repressions have been removed.

We must admit that the principle of conducting therapy abstemiously takes us far beyond the present individual case, and needs more detailed discussion to map out the limits of its feasibility. But we do not propose to have this discussion here, preferring to keep as close as possible to the situation we began with. What would happen if the doctor acted differently and exploited what freedom there was on both sides to requite the patient's love and satisfy her need for affection?

If he did so as a result of calculating that such compliance would secure him control over the patient and so induce her to bring the business of the therapy to a resolution by achieving lasting freedom from her neurosis, then experience would show him to have miscalculated. The patient would achieve her aims, but the same would not apply to him. All you would have is a recapitulation of the amusing story about the pastor and the insurance agent. At the behest of his relatives, a priest is brought in to convert this seriously ill unbeliever before he dies. The conversation goes on for so long that the waiting relatives begin to be hopeful. Finally the door of the sickroom opens. The atheist has not been converted, but the pastor goes away insured.

It would be a great triumph for the patient to have her offer of love requited, and a total defeat for the therapy. She would have achieved what all patients strive for in analysis, activating and acting out in actual life something that she ought simply to remember, reproduce as mental content and confine within the mental sphere.[3] In the course of the love affair she would display all the inhibitions and unhealthy reactions of her erotic life, with no chance of correcting them, and it would end in regret and a greatly reinforced tendency to repression. The love relationship simply closes off any chance of influencing her through therapy. Any thought of uniting the two is ridiculous.

Satisfying the patient's craving for love is therefore just as disastrous for the analysis as repressing it. The analyst's path is a different one, and there is no pattern for it in real life. You take care not to distract her from the love-transference, to frighten it away, or ruin it for the patient; but just as steadfastly you refrain from reciprocating. You hold on to the love-transference, but you treat it as something unreal, as a situation that has to be worked through in the therapy, taken back to its unconscious origins and made to help bring the most deeply buried aspects of her erotic life up into the patient's consciousness, and therefore under her control. The more you give the impression of being immune to all temptation, the more easily will you be able to extract the psychoanalytical content from the situation. The patient whose sexual repression has not yet been removed, but merely thrust into the background, will then feel confident enough to display all the conditions she attaches to love, all the fantasies of her sexual longing, all the characteristics of her infatuation, and, via all this, open up her own way back to the infantile basis of her love.

However, for one type of woman this attempt to preserve the love-transference for use in the analytical task, but without satisfying it, is doomed to failure. These are women of elemental passion, who will not put up with any surrogates, children of nature who will not accept the mental in place of the material, who in the words of the poet can only be reached 'by soup-logic with dumpling-reasoning'.[4] With this type you have a choice to make: either return her love or suffer the full hostility of a woman scorned. Neither case furthers the cause of the therapy. All you can do is retire defeated and perhaps contemplate the problem of how the capacity for neurosis can be combined with such an implacable need for love.

The question of how to make other women, less violently in love, evolve an understanding of analytical thinking is one that has no doubt similarly preoccupied many analysts. Above all you have to bring out the unmistakable part played by resistance in this 'love'. Really falling in love would make the patient cooperative and increase her willingness to solve the problems of her case, just because the man she loves demands it. Real love would make her want to get to the end of the cure, in order to prove herself worthy in the eyes of the doctor and prepare for a reality in which there was room for the inclination to love. Instead of this the patient, you would say, behaves obstinately and rebelliously, has thrown off all interest in the treatment, and clearly has no respect for the extremely well-founded convictions of the doctor. She thus produces a resistance in the guise of infatuation, and, furthermore, she has no scruples about placing him on the proverbial horns of a dilemma. For if he were to decline, as his duty and his understanding oblige him to do, she would be able to play the part of the woman scorned, and by way of revenge deny herself recovery at his hands, just as she is doing at this moment through her supposed infatuation.

The second argument against the authenticity of this love is the assertion that it bears not a single new trait arising out of the present situation, but is composed entirely of repetitions and pale imitations of earlier reactions, including infantile ones. You will undertake to demonstrate this to the patient through a detailed analysis of her stance in love.

Add to these arguments the requisite measure of patience, and you will usually succeed in overcoming this difficult situation and proceed to work – the infatuation having been either modified or 'knocked on the head' – towards exposing the infantile choice of love-objects and the fantasy that was woven around it. However, I would like to cast a critical light on the arguments in question, and ask whether we are telling the patient the truth when we use them, or in our serious difficulties taking refuge in concealment and misrepresentations. In other words: can the love that manifests itself in therapy really not be seen as genuine?

I believe we have told the patient the truth, but not the whole truth we would tell if we had no regard for the outcome. Of our two arguments, the first is the stronger. The role of resistance in love-transference is beyond dispute and very considerable. But the resistance did not create this love; it finds it ready-made, makes use of it and exaggerates its self-expression. And the resistance does not invalidate the authenticity of the phenomenon. Our second argument is much weaker; it is true that this infatuation consists of reissuing old components and repeating infantile reactions. But that is always the essence of falling in love. Everybody repeats childhood patterns. It is precisely what stems from its conditioning in childhood that lends infatuation its compulsive character, with its overtones of the pathological. Perhaps love in transference has slightly less freedom than the love that occurs ordinarily in life and is called normal; it shows more clearly its dependence on its infantile predecessor, and it proves to be less adaptable and flexible, but that is all – the differences are not essential.

What other ways are there to tell if love is genuine? By its productivity, its usefulness in achieving love's goals? In this respect love in transference does not seem inferior to any other; you have the impression you could achieve anything by its means.

To sum up: you have no right to deny the title of 'genuine' love to an infatuation that makes its appearance during analytical treatment. If it appears so far from normal, this is easily explained by the circumstance that falling in love even outside analytical therapy is more reminiscent of abnormal than normal mental phenomena. All the same, it has a few outstanding characteristics that assure it of a special place. It is 1. provoked by the situation; 2. it is highly intensified by the resistance that dominates this situation; and 3. it manages to pay little regard to reality. It is less astute, less concerned about the consequences, more blind in its estimate of the loved one, than we are willing to concede to a normal state of love. But we must not forget that it is precisely these departures from the norm that constitute the essence of falling in love.

It is the first of these three qualities of transference-love that decisively affects the doctor's course of action. He has coaxed this infatuation into life by initiating an analytical treatment to cure the neurosis; for him it is the inevitable result of a medical situation, similar to physically laying bare a sick person, or having some life-and-death secret confided to him. For him, the medical situation dictates that he must not gain any personal advantage from the infatuation. The willingness of the patient makes no difference to this; it simply throws all the responsibility back upon himself. As he must know, this was precisely the healing mechanism anticipated by the patient. After successfully surmounting all the difficulties, she will often confess what she imagined when she embarked on the course of therapy: if she behaved well, in the end she would be rewarded with the doctor's affection.

For the doctor, ethical motives now combine with technical ones to restrain him from offering the patient any loving relationship. He must keep his objective in mind; the woman must have her capacity for love, which is invaluable to her but has been impeded by child-hood fixations, placed freely at her disposal. But instead of depleting it during therapy she should save it for the real-life demands it will make on her when her treatment is over. He must not repeat with her the scene at the dog-racing stadium where a string of sausages is held up as a prize, and some joker ruins the race by throwing a single sausage on to the track. The dogs all fall upon it and forget the race and the enticing string of sausages in the distance awaiting the winner. I do not want to claim that it is always easy for the doctor to stay within the bounds that ethics and technique prescribe for him. Particularly for a younger and still unattached man it may be a difficult assignment. Sexual love undoubtedly has a prime place among life's experiences, and the uniting of mental and physical satisfaction in the act of love is one of its high points. Everybody knows this, apart from a few weird fanatics, and arranges his life accordingly; only in scientific circles does anyone make a fuss about admitting it. On the other hand, it is difficult for the man to play the part of the one who rejects and refuses the woman when she makes advances to him, and a fine woman who confesses her passion radiates a magic beyond compare, for all her neurosis and resistances. It is not the crudely sensual desire of a patient that presents the temptation. On the contrary, that will tend to have an off-putting effect, and all your reserves of tolerance will be required for you to accept it as a natural phenomenon. The more refined stirrings of desire in the female, inhibited in its aims, are perhaps the ones that pose the danger of making you forget your clinical methodology and responsibility, for the sake of a wonderful experience.

And yet it is out of the question for the analyst to give way. However highly he prizes love, he must value more highly still his opportunity to lift the patient over a decisive stage in her life. She has to learn from him how to subdue the pleasure-principle, to renounce immediate but socially unsuitable satisfaction in favour of the kind that is more distant, perhaps altogether less certain, but psychologically and socially irreproachable. To achieve this self-conquest she has to be taken through the primordial age of her mental development and by this means acquire that enhanced mental freedom that distinguishes conscious mental activity – in the systematic sense – from unconscious.

The analytical psychotherapist thus has to conduct a threefold struggle: the one in his own mind against the forces that would like to pull him down below the analytical level; the external one against the opponents who question the importance he ascribes to the sexual drives and refuse to let him make use of them in his scientific technique; and in analysis, the struggle against his patients, who initially behave like his opponents, but then make clear that an overestimation of sexual life has them in its grip, and would like to make the doctor captive to their socially ungovernable passions.

The lay people whose attitude to psychoanalysis I mentioned at the beginning will no doubt seize upon this discussion as a further opportunity to draw the world's attention to the dangers of this therapeutic method. Psychoanalysts know that they are working with the most explosive forces, and that they need to deploy the same care and conscientiousness as the chemist. But when has a chemist ever been banned on account of danger from dealing with the explosive materials whose reactive properties make them indispensable to him? It is strange that psychoanalysis is obliged to fight afresh for all the privileges long since granted to other medical procedures. I am not in favour of giving up harmless methods of treatment. They are adequate for treating many cases, and after all human society has no more need of the *furor sanandi* [mania for healing] than of any other kind of fanaticism. But to believe that these disorders ought to be conquerable by operating innocuous little mechanisms would be to underestimate very badly the origins and practical significance of the psycho-neuroses. No, in medical practice there will always be room for the *ferrum* and the *ignis* alongside the *medicina* [iron, fire, medicine], and so the professional, unabated practice of psychoanalysis, not afraid to handle the most dangerous mental impulses and harness them for the patient's benefit, will continue to be indispensable.

(1915)

Notes

1. 'Zur Geschichte der psychoanalytischen Bewegung' ['On the History of the Psychoanalytical Movement'] (1914), *Gesammelte Werke*, Vol. X.

2. It is well known that transference can be expressed in other, less tender ways, but this aspect will not be dealt with in this essay.

3. See the essay 'Erinnern, Wiederholen und Durcharbeiten' ['Remembering, Repeating and Working Through'], *Gesammelte Werke*, Vol. X, pp. 126–36.

4. [This is a quotation from Heinrich Heine's poem 'Die Wanderratten' (The Wandering Rats): townspeople plagued by an influx of rats attempt to repel them with weapons and with reasoning. Both fail, the latter because:

> *Im hungrigen Magen Eingang finden*
> *Nur Suppenlogik mit Knödelgründen,*
> *Nur Argumente von Rinderbraten,*
> *Begleitet mit Göttinger Wurstzitaten*

(A hungry stomach is open to access only by soup logic with dumpling reasons, only roast-beef arguments, accompanied by quotes from Göttingen sausages.)]

Resistance to Psychoanalysis

When an infant in its nurse's arms turns away howling from the sight of a stranger's face; when a pious man says a prayer for the beginning of a new portion of time,[1] or greets the year's first fruits with a special blessing; or when a farmer refuses to buy a scythe that does not bear a trademark familiar to his parents: the diversity of all these situations is obvious, and they would surely all appear to derive from different kinds of motivation.

Yet it would be a mistake to overlook their shared features. In every case there is the same display of reluctance, expressed by the child in a primal way, ceremonially appeased by the pious man, and motivating a decision by the farmer. The source of this reluctance, however, lies in the demands made by change on our emotional life, the mental effort it costs us, and the accompanying insecurity, rising to an anxious anticipation. It would be interesting to investigate emotional reactions to novelty as such; for under certain circumstances, beyond the primary ones, you may also observe the opposite: a hunger for stimulation that throws itself eagerly upon anything new, precisely because it *is* new.

In scientific work there should be no fear of the new. In its condition of permanent incompleteness and inadequacy, science is bound to seek redemption in new discoveries and new conceptions. To avoid being all too easily deceived, science is well advised to arm itself with scepticism and accept nothing new until it has passed rigorous examination. However, from time to time this scepticism displays two unexpected characteristics. It fiercely resists innovation, while showing a respectful restraint towards what is already well known and accepted; and it is content to employ the latter to condemn what it has not yet investigated. Thus it shows itself to be a continuation of the primitive reaction to novelty, a cover behind which this reaction is preserved. Everyone knows how often it has happened in the history of scientific research that innovations have met with intense and obstinate resistance, although it later became clear that resistance had been wrong and that the novelty was valuable and significant. As a rule, it was certain specific factors in the new that triggered off the resistance, and on the other hand numerous factors needed to work together to create a breakthrough against the primitive reaction.

The present author developed *psychoanalysis* almost thirty years ago on the basis of Joseph Breuer's findings in Vienna concerning the origins of neurotic symptoms. It had a particularly bad reception. It was undeniably an innovation, even though, aside from these discoveries, it engaged with a mass of material already known from other sources, the results of the theories of the great neuropathologist Charcot, and perceptions derived from the sphere of hypnotic phenomena. Its original significance was entirely therapeutic in nature; its intention was to produce a new and effective treatment for neurotic disorders. But a chain of circumstances undreamt of at the beginning took psychoanalysis far beyond its original aims. Eventually it could claim to have put our understanding of mental processes on an entirely new footing, and therefore to be important for all areas of knowledge founded on psychology. After a decade of neglect it suddenly became the object of the most widespread interest – and unleashed a storm of outraged disapproval.

The form this resistance has taken need not detain us here. Suffice it to note that the conflict around this innovation is by no means at an end. But it is clear already how it will develop. The opposition has not succeeded in suppressing the movement. Psychoanalysis, of which I was the sole representative twenty years ago, has since acquired many important and active adherents. Medics and non-medics alike, they have used analysis as a treatment for neurosis, and have applied it as a method in psychological research and as an aid to scientific work in a whole range of areas of intellectual life. Our attention here will be focused entirely on the reasons for resistance to psychoanalysis, especially noting what it is composed of, and the differing valence of its components.

Clinical [as against analytical] observation is obliged to relate the neuroses to the toxicants, or to such conditions as Badow's Disease [Graves' disease, exophthalmic goitre]. These are conditions arising either out of an excess or a relative lack of certain very powerful substances, either created in the body itself or introduced from outside; that is to say, disturbances of the chemical balance, toxic states. If anyone could isolate or demonstrate the existence of such a substance or substances involved in neuroses, his discovery would not need to fear any objections from doctors. However, we are nowhere near it at the moment. We can only start from the picture presented by the neurotic symptoms, which in the case of hysteria, for example, is composed both of physical and mental disturbances.

Charcot's experiments and Breuer's clinical observations taught us that even the physical symptoms of hysteria are psychogenetic, that is, the effects of mental processes that are out of control. Through hypnosis it was possible artificially to induce at will the physical symptoms of hysteria.

This new knowledge was taken up by psychoanalysis, which began to pose questions for itself about the nature of the mental processes that had such unusual consequences. But this line of research was not to the liking of that generation of doctors. Medics had been taught to value nothing but anatomical, physical and chemical factors. They had not been trained to respect ideas of psychological causation, so they greeted them with indifference or aversion. It was apparent also that they doubted whether matters psychological could be treated with scientific precision. Overreacting as they did to a now obsolete kind of medicine that was dominated by the outlook of the so-called nature-philosophy,[2] abstractions such as those with which psychology is obliged to work seemed to them hazy, fanciful and mystical. They refused to believe in remarkable phenomena that might have been a starting-point for research. Patients with the symptoms of hysterical neurosis were thought to be shamming, and the phenomena of hypnosis were a trick. Even the psychiatrists, unavoidably confronted as they were by the strangest, most bizarre of psychological phenomena, showed no inclination to notice their details or to follow up their connections. They were satisfied to classify the colourful variety of these pathological effects, as far as possible tracing them back to some physical, anatomical or chemical disturbance. In this materialist, or rather mechanistic phase, medicine made great strides; but it also short-sightedly failed to recognize some of the most prominent and most difficult problems in life.

It is understandable that medical men with such an attitude to the mind did not like psychoanalysis and were loath to accept its demand that they should re-educate themselves and view many things in a new light. By the same token, however, one would have expected that the new theory would have appealed all the more to philosophers. After all, they were used to deploying abstract concepts – malicious tongues might even say 'vague phrases' – at the highest level in their explanations of the cosmos, and could not possibly object to the expansion of the sphere of psychology initiated by psychoanalysis. But here there was another stumbling block. 'The mind' meant different things to philosophers than to psychoanalysts. The great majority of philosophers only refer to the mind in connection with the phenomenon of consciousness. The world of the conscious is for them coextensive with the area of the mind. They consign whatever else might be going on in the somewhat intangible sphere of 'inner life' to the physical preconditions for mental activity or processes parallel to it. More precisely, mental life has no other content than that of the phenomena of consciousness, and therefore the science of the mind, psychology, has no other object of study. The layman thinks the same.

What can a philosopher say, therefore, to a theory like psychoanalysis, which holds that inner life is, on the contrary, essentially *unconscious*, and that consciousness is a quality that might or might not put in an appearance during a given mental act, and that changes nothing about this act if it does *not* appear? He will naturally say that an unconscious mental life is preposterous, a *contradictio in adjecto* [contradiction in terms]; he fails to notice that with this verdict he is simply repeating his own – perhaps too narrow – definition of mental life. His certainty is made easy for him, because the philosopher does not know the material studied by the analyst that has forced him to believe in unconscious mental acts. He has not taken account of hypnosis, has not striven to interpret dreams: like the doctors, he thinks that dreams are meaningless products of reduced mental activity during sleep. He is practically unaware that there are such things as obsessions and delusions, and would be hard-pressed if challenged to explain them in terms of his psychological theories. The analyst likewise declines to say what the unconscious is, but he can refer to the area of phenomena the observation of which has thrust acceptance of the unconscious upon him. The philosopher, who knows no kind of observation other than self-observation, cannot follow him there. Thus the position of psycho-analysis midway between medicine and philosophy has brought it nothing but disadvantages. The medics consider it a speculative system and do not want to believe that, like every other science, it rests on the patient and painstaking processing of the facts of the perceived world. The philosophers, measuring it by the yardstick of their own elaborately constructed system-formations, find that it proceeds from impossible premises, and criticize its chief concepts – still being developed – for lack of clarity and precision.

The above circumstances are enough to explain the unwilling and hesitant reception of analysis in scientific circles. But they do not account for the outbursts of indignation, scorn and mockery, nor the disregard for the rules of logic and good taste in polemical argument. Such a response suggests that the reaction aroused is more than a purely intellectual one, that strong emotional forces have been invoked; and indeed there is plenty in the content of psychoanalytic theory to provoke an impassioned reaction in [lay] people, and not just in scientists.

Let us take first and foremost the great significance for inner life that psychoanalysis allocates to the so-called sex drives. According to psychoanalytic theory, the symptoms of neuroses are a distorted, substitute means to satisfy the forces of sexual drives denied direct satisfaction by inner resistances. When analysis subsequently reached out beyond its original area of operations and was applied to normal mental life, it tried to show that those same sexual components, diverted away from their immediate goals and channelled into other things, are the most important contributions to the cultural achievements of individuals and of the community. These assertions were not entirely new. The philosopher Schopenhauer, in unforgettably vigorous language, emphasized the unique significance of sexual life. And sexuality as understood by psychoanalysis was far from coterminous with the urge to intercourse of the sexes or the production of pleasurable sensations in the genitals. To a large extent it coincided with the comprehensive and all-inclusive Eros of Plato's *Symposium*.

But our opponents forgot these illustrious predecessors. They fell upon psychoanalysis as though it were guilty of assassinating the dignity of the human race. They accused it of 'pan-sexualism', although the psychoanalytic theory of the drives had always been strictly dualistic, and alongside the sex drives had never failed to acknowledge others, to which, indeed, it ascribed the power to repress the sex drives. The duality was at first identified as sexual versus ego-drives, and in later versions of the theory it is expressed as Eros versus the death- or destruction-drive. The partial derivation of art, religion or social order from the effect of sexual forces, among others, was held to debase the highest cultural achievements, and it was emphatically proclaimed that mankind had other interests, not just a constant preoccupation with sex. What was forgotten in all this zeal was that even animals have other interests (after all, they are only fitfully and periodically subject to sexuality, not permanently, as human beings are), and that nobody had ever doubted these other interests of mankind; and that the proof of derivation from sources in the primal animal drives does nothing to alter the value of a cultural achievement.

Illogicality and injustice on this scale call for some explanation. Their source is not hard to find. Human culture rests on two pillars: one is control of natural forces, the other is holding our drives in check. Slaves in chains carry the throne of their mistress. Among the inventory of drives that have been harnessed for useful ends, the sex drives – in the narrowest sense – stand out for their power and wildness. Woe betide if they should break loose; the throne would be overturned, the mistress trampled underfoot. Society knows this – and does not want to talk about it.

But why not? What harm could it do to discuss it? Psychoanalysis has never advocated the unchaining of our anti-social drives; on the contrary, it has warned against them and advised better control. But society is not interested in any disclosure of this state of affairs, because in more ways than one it suffers from a bad conscience. First, it has set up a high ideal of morality (morality is limitation of the drives), which it requires all its members to fulfil, and it does not care how difficult it may be for some individuals to comply. But it is not so wealthy or so well organized that it can afford to compensate individuals appropriately for the high cost of renouncing their drives. It is therefore left to individuals to try to obtain adequate compensation for the sacrifice imposed on them, in order to maintain their mental equilibrium. In general, though, they are forced, psychologically speaking, to live beyond their means, while the unsatisfied claims of their drives make the demands of culture seem like a constant pressure.

In this way society maintains a state of *cultural hypocrisy*, which is inevitably accompanied by a feeling of insecurity and a need to fence off this undeniable instability by prohibiting criticism and discussion. This observation applies to all the drive-impulses, including therefore all the egoistic ones; to what extent it can be applied to any conceivable culture, and not just to the ones that have emerged so far, will not be investigated here. We can add that, as regards the sex drives in the narrower sense, in most people they are inadequately and, psychologically speaking, incorrectly controlled, and are therefore the most likely to break loose.

Psychoanalysis reveals the weakness of this system and counsels changes to it. It proposes a relaxation of rigorous drive-repression, creating instead more space for truthfulness. Certain drive-impulses, which society has gone too far in repressing, should be allowed a greater measure of gratification. In other cases, the unsuitable method of restraint by means of repression should be replaced by a better and more reliable procedure. As a result of this critique, psychoanalysis has been thought to be 'hostile to culture', and outlawed as a 'social danger'. This resistance cannot last for ever; in the long run no human institution can escape the impact of justified critical insight, but so far people's attitudes to psychoanalysis have been dominated by this fear, which unleashes passions and disparages the claims of logical argumentation.

With its theory of the drives, psychoanalysis had offended the individual in so far as he thought of himself as a member of the social community. Another part of its theory offered an insult to every single person in the most sensitive point of his own psychological development. Psychoanalysis put an end to the fairy tale of a-sexual childhood. It proved that sexual interests and activities are present from the beginning of children's lives; it showed the transformation they undergo; how around children's fifth year these interests and activities are subject to inhibitions, and then how, from puberty onwards, they enter the service of procreation. Psychoanalysis recognized that infantile sexual life reaches its peak in the so-called Oedipus complex, in an emotional attachment of the child to its other-sex parent, combined with an attitude of rivalry towards the same-sex one; a tendency that, in this phase of development, still extends without inhibition directly into sexual desire. This is so easy to confirm that it would really take a great deal of effort to overlook it. The fact is that every individual has experienced this phase, and then invested much energy in repressing its content and forgetting it. The horror of incest and a powerful guilt-complex are the residue of this primordial phase of individual life. Perhaps the course of events was very similar in the prehistoric phase of man in general, so that the beginnings of morality, religion and social order were extremely closely connected with the transcending of man's primordial origins. This prehistory, which later seemed to him so inglorious, was something of which the adult refused to be reminded. He began to rage when psychoanalysis proposed to lift the veil of amnesia from his childhood years. There was only one way out, therefore: the claims of psychoanalysis must be false and this alleged new science a tissue of fantasies and distortions.

The powerful resistances against psychoanalysis were not of an intellectual nature, then, but stemmed from emotional sources. This explained both their vehemence and their threadbare logic. The situation ran according to a simple formula: *en masse*, people reacted towards psychoanalysis in exactly the same way as the individual neurotic, who had been accepted into therapy because he had problems, but to whom you had the task of demonstrating by patient work that everything had indeed come about precisely as you claimed. Neither had you invented it all yourself, but learned about it from the study of other neurotic patients through several decades of solid application.

This situation was at one and the same time rather startling and rather comforting. Startling because it was no small matter to have the whole human race as your patient; and comforting because everything followed the course that psychoanalytic theory said it must.

If we review the resistances to psychoanalysis described above, it must be said that only a few of them are of the type usually aroused by most scientific innovations of any note. The greater part of them came about because the theory offended powerful human feelings. There was the same reaction to Darwin's theory of evolution, which tore down the dividing wall between man and animal that arrogance had created. I previously referred to this analogy in a short essay ('Eine Schwierigkeit der Psychoanalyse' [A Problem of Psychoanalysis], *Imago*, 1917). There I stressed that the psychoanalytical conception of the relationship between the conscious I [ego] and the over-powerful unconscious signified a serious affront to human self-regard. This I called the *psychological* affront, and I ranged it alongside the *biological* affront caused by the theory of evolution and the earlier *cosmological* affront brought about by Copernicus's discovery.

Purely external circumstances have also contributed to bolstering the resistance to psychoanalysis. It is not easy to arrive at an independent judgement about matters of analysis if you have not undergone it yourself or practised it on someone else. You cannot practise analysis without training in a particular, very delicate technique and, until recently, there was no easily accessible opportunity to learn psychoanalysis and its technique. This situation has now been improved by the founding (in 1920) of the Berlin Psychoanalytical Polyclinic and School. Soon afterwards (in 1922) a very similar institution was created in Vienna.

Finally, may the present author raise with all due restraint the question of whether his own personality as a Jew who never cared to hide his Jewishness has had some part to play in the antipathy of those around him to psychoanalysis. This kind of argument has rarely been voiced publicly; but we have unfortunately become so suspicious that we cannot help surmising that this factor has not entirely failed to have an influence. It may not be purely accidental, either, that the first advocate of psychoanalysis was a Jew. Declaring your faith in it needed a certain willingness to take upon yourself the fate of being in solitary opposition, a fate more familiar to Jews than to anyone else.

(1925)

Notes

1. [There seems to be a reference here to the place of special prayers to mark the passage of time in Jewish worship.]

2. [The term used by Freud, *Naturphilosophie*, has had two incarnations in the history of German science. The first was the sense in which it was used by Idealist philosophy, particularly Schelling, Kant and Hegel, for their accommodation of scientific research *a priori* to certain philosophical preconceptions. The other incarnation, which Freud is probably referring to, is that of Eduard von Hartmann (1842–1906), who wrote about the theory of perception and the philosophical basis of science in books such as *The World-View of Modern Physics* (1902).]

The Question of Lay Analysis

Conversations with an impartial listener

Introduction

The title of this short publication is not comprehensible at first sight. I shall therefore explain it: laymen = non-medics, and the question is, should non-doctors be allowed to practise analysis? This question is subject to both chronological and geographical determinants. Chronological, in that until now no one has cared about who practises analysis. Indeed, there has been far too little concern. The only consensus was that *no one* should practise it; the various reasons for this were all grounded in the same aversion. Thus the demand that only doctors undertake analysis corresponds to a new and apparently more sympathetic attitude to analysis – as long as this attitude can escape the suspicion of being merely a somewhat modified version of the previous one. It concedes that, under certain circumstances, analytical treatment may take place, but only at the hands of a doctor. The aim here is to examine the reason for this limitation.

The question is geographically determined, because it is not of equal moment in every country. In Germany and America, it amounts to an academic discussion, for in those countries a sick person can elect to be treated in any way and by anybody he likes. Any quack can treat anybody, as long as he takes responsibility for his actions. The law does not intervene until called upon to provide redress for some actual harm done to the sick person. But in Austria, the country in which and for which I am writing, the law operates preventively; it prohibits a non-doctor from treating the sick, irrespective of what the outcome might be.[1] Thus in this country there is a practical point to the question of whether a layman, that is, a non-doctor, can treat the sick through psychoanalysis. No sooner is the question raised, however, than it seems to be decided by the wording of the legal statutes. People with nervous disorders are sick, laymen are non-doctors, psychoanalysis is a procedure for curing or improving nervous conditions, and all such treatment is the preserve of doctors. Consequently it is illegal for laymen to treat nervous disorders, and if nevertheless it does occur, it is a punishable offence. In view of such a simple state of affairs, one hardly dares involve oneself in the question of lay analysis. However, there are a few complications with which the law does not concern itself, and which therefore require consideration. It may transpire that the sick people in this case are not like other sick people, that the laymen are not actually laymen, and that the doctors do not quite live up to expectations or to what we permit them to base their claims on. If this can be established, then we can fairly demand that the law should not be applied unmodified to the present case.

I

Whether that happens will depend upon people who are not obliged to inform themselves about the particulars of analytic treatment. Our task is to educate these impartial persons about it, assuming them to be uninformed at the moment. We regret that we cannot invite them to eavesdrop upon such a treatment. The 'analytical situation' tolerates no third party. Furthermore, individual sessions are very uneven. For the most part, such (unauthorized) listeners, coming along to a session chosen at random, would form no useful impression. There is the danger that they would not understand the business taking place between analyst and patient, or they would be bored. For good or ill, they will have to be content with our information, which we will try to present in as reliable a manner as possible.

Let us assume that the patient is suffering from uncontrollable mood-swings, or a dispirited state of dejection that he feels is sapping his energy through loss of confidence in his own judgement. Or he may suffer from painful self-consciousness in the company of strangers. He may perceive, uncomprehendingly, that it has become hard not only to carry on with his work, but also to cope with any serious decision or undertaking. One day, he unaccountably finds himself suffering from an embarrassing attack of anxiety, and since then has hardly been able to bring himself to cross the road alone or to travel by train; he may have had to give up doing both these things altogether. Or else – and this is very strange – his thoughts go their own way and cannot be brought back under his control by an effort of will. They pursue problems that do not matter to him, but from which he cannot tear himself away. He is forced to carry out the most ridiculous tasks, such as counting the windows in house-fronts, and when it comes to simple actions like posting a letter or turning off a gas-jet, he finds himself doubting a moment afterwards whether he has really done it. All this is perhaps no more than irritating and irksome. But the condition becomes unbearable when he suddenly cannot shake off the idea that he has pushed a child under the wheels of a car, or thrown a stranger off a bridge into the water, or when he wonders whether he is not the murderer sought by the police as the perpetrator of a crime that has come to light today. It is obvious nonsense, he knows that himself, he has never harmed anybody, but the sensation, the guilt feelings, could not be stronger if he himself really were the man wanted for murder.

Or again, our patient – a female one this time, let us say – is suffering in a different way and in a different area. She is a pianist, but her fingers are cramped and will not obey her. When she thinks about going out to a social gathering, she starts to feel the call of nature coming on, the relieving of which is incompatible with sociability. Hence she has given up attending social occasions, balls, theatre performances and concerts. She is beset at the most inconvenient times by violent headaches or other painful sensations. She may perhaps be sick every time she eats, and in the long run this might become a dangerous condition. Finally, she regrettably cannot bear any excitement, something that is after all an inevitable part of life. The effect is that she suffers fainting fits, often combined with muscle cramps, reminiscent of the frightening conditions of some disease.

Other sufferers feel troubled in that particular area where emotional life coincides with demands made on the body. Men find themselves incapable of giving expression to their most tender impulses towards the opposite sex, while in relation to objects which barely command their affection, the whole range of responses remains at their disposal. Or their sensuality ties them to people they despise, and from whom they would like to be freed. Or perhaps the same sensuality sets them conditions whose fulfilment is repulsive even to themselves. Women who are affected feel themselves prevented by anxiety and disgust, or by nameless impediments, from complying with the demands of sexual life; or, if they have given way to love, they find that they are cheated of the pleasure that is the reward nature offers for such compliance.

All these people recognize that they are ill, and seek out doctors who are supposed to cure such nervous disorders. And the doctors do indeed have a list of categories to fit these complaints. According to their standpoint, they diagnose them under various names: neurasthenia, psychasthenia, phobias, obsessive neuroses, hysteria. They examine the organs that produce the symptoms, be they heart, stomach, intestines or genitals, and pronounce them healthy. They advise taking a break from one's usual life-style, rest and recuperation, fortifying procedures and medical tonics, and they achieve temporary relief – or even nothing at all. Eventually the sufferer hears that there are people who specialize exclusively in these disorders, and they enter into analysis with them.

Our impartial listener, whom I imagine as being present throughout, has been showing signs of impatience at this discussion of nervous symptoms. Now he becomes sharp and alert, and expresses himself accordingly: 'So, now we are going to see what treatment the analyst provides for the patient the doctor could not help.'

All that goes on between analyst and patient is that they talk to each other. The analyst neither uses instruments, even for the purpose of examination, nor prescribes medicines. If at all possible, he lets the patient stay in his own surroundings and his own familiar circumstances while treating him. Of course, this is not a condition of treatment, and cannot always be carried out. The analyst gives the patient an appointment, lets him talk, listens to him, then talks to him while he listens.

Our impartial interlocutor's expression now shows unmistakable signs of relief and relaxation, but also clearly betrays a certain disdain. It is as though he is thinking: is that all? Words, words, words, as Prince Hamlet says. He surely also recalls Mephisto's mocking speech about what an easy business it is to handle words, lines that no German will ever forget.[2]

He then says: 'So it's a kind of magic; you talk and just blow away his complaint.'

Quite right, it *would* be magic, if it worked more rapidly. Speed is the essence of magic; instant success, you might say. But analytic treatment takes months and even years; such slow magic can no longer be called miraculous. Incidentally, we should not despise the *word*. It is after all a powerful instrument, the means to let each other know about our feelings, the way to achieve influence over others. Words can have an unutterably positive effect, or inflict terrible injury. To be sure, in the very beginning was the deed, the word came later; in many circumstances it was a cultural step forward when the deed was reduced to the word. But the word was originally a form of magic, a magic act, and it has preserved much of its old force.

The impartial listener continues: 'If we assume that the patient is no better primed to understand the analytic treatment than I am, how do you propose to make him believe in the magic of the word or of talking, which is supposed to free him from his sufferings?'

Naturally, the ground must be prepared for the patient, and there is a simple way of doing this. He must be asked to be completely open with his analyst, not to deliberately hold back anything that comes into his head and, as matters progress, to overcome any reservations he has that might prevent him from talking about many of his thoughts or memories. Every individual knows that there are things he would be very loath to tell anybody else, or that he would not dream of telling at all. These are his most 'personal' matters. He also has a sense – and this represents a great advance in psychological self-knowledge – that there are other things that you do not want to

99

admit even to yourself, that you would prefer to hide from yourself, and that you abruptly shut down and drive out of your mind if they do crop up. Perhaps the patient himself notices the germ of a very remarkable psychological problem in this situation, where your own thoughts are supposed to be kept secret from yourself. It is as though the self is no longer the unity he has always taken it to be, as though there were something else in him, which can set itself up in opposition to this self. He may have a shadowy intimation of something like an opposition between one's self and one's mental life in a broader sense. Now, if he accepts the demands of analysis that he should hold nothing back, it will be easy for him to anticipate that novel effects might result from communicating and exchanging thoughts under these unusual conditions.

'I see', says our impartial listener, 'you assume that every neurotic is oppressed by something, some secret, and by inducing him to talk about it, you relieve him of pressure and do him good. That's the principle of the confessional, which has always been used by the Catholic Church to maintain its power over men's minds.'

Yes and no, we are obliged to reply. Confession does indeed come into analysis, and forms an introduction to it, as it were. But it is very far from coinciding with the core of analysis or explaining its effect. In the confessional the sinner says what he knows, whereas in analysis the neurotic is supposed to say more than that. And it has never been claimed that confession has developed the power to eliminate the direct symptoms of illness.

'In that case, I don't understand it after all', comes the reply. 'What is that supposed to mean, "say more than he knows"? Although, certainly, I can imagine that as an analyst you could gain more influence over your patients than the father confessor does over his penitents, because you spend more time and effort on them and deal with them more individually; and that you use this increased influence to wean them off their unhealthy thoughts, talk them out of their anxieties, etc. It would certainly be strange if this method led to control over purely physical symptoms such as vomiting, diarrhoea or cramp, but I am aware that such influence is possible under hypnosis, where you use suggestion to bond people to you personally, even if you don't intend to, and your therapeutic miracles are in fact the result of hypnotic suggestion. But, as far as I'm aware, hypnotherapy works much faster than your analysis, which as you say takes months and years.'

Our impartial listener is neither as ignorant nor at such a loss as we first thought. It is evident that he is trying to get a grip on psychoanalysis by referring to previous knowledge, and to link it to something he already knows. We are now faced with the difficult task of explaining to him that this will not work, that analysis is a unique process, something new and different in kind, which can only be grasped with the help of new insights – or assumptions, if you like. But we still owe him a response to his last remarks.

What you say about the personal influence of the analyst is certainly very striking. Such an influence does indeed exist and plays a significant part in analysis. But not the same one as in hypnotism. It ought to be possible to demonstrate to you that the two situations are completely different. Perhaps it is enough to say that we don't use this personal influence – the 'suggestive' factor – in order to suppress the symptoms of suffering, as happens with hypnotic suggestion. Moreover, it would be wrong to believe that this factor is the sole vehicle and promoter of treatment. Initially it certainly is; but later it controverts our analytical purposes and obliges us to take extensive counter-measures. Let me give you an example to show how far removed distraction and dissuasion are from the technique of analysis. If our patient suffers from guilt feelings, as though he had committed some serious crime, we don't advise him to get over his agonies of conscience by asserting his indisputable innocence. He has already tried to do that himself, and failed. Instead, we point out to him that such a strong and long-lasting feeling must be grounded in something real, something we might be able to identify.

'I would be surprised', opines the impartial listener, 'if agreeing with the patient about his guilt-feelings could lay them to rest. But what are your analytical intentions, and what steps do you take with the patient?'

II

If I want you to understand what I am saying, I had better tell you
something about a psychological theory that is not known, or not
honoured, outside analytical circles. From this theory it will not be
difficult to deduce what we require from the patient and how we
achieve it. I shall present it dogmatically, as though it were a fully
perfected theoretical construct. But do not imagine it came about
in its present form all at once like a philosophical system. We
developed it very slowly, fighting for every little gain, continuously
modifying it through constant contact with observation, until it
eventually took on a shape that seemed adequate for our purposes.
Just a few years ago I would have had to dress this theory up in
different language. But I cannot promise you that the current form
of expression will remain the definitive one. As you know, science is
no revelation. Even well past its infancy, it lacks the characteristics
of certainty, stability, infallibility that the human mind so longs for.
But such as it is, it is all we can get. If you remember as well that
our science is very young, hardly as old as the century itself, and that
it deals with pretty much the most difficult material that human
research can be faced with, then you will be in the right frame of
mind to listen to my account of the topic. But don't hesitate to
interrupt me when you can't follow me or when you need further
explanations.

'I'm interrupting you even before you start. You say you want to
present me with a new psychology, but I wouldn't have said that
psychology is a new science. There have been plenty of psychologies
and psychologists, and even as a schoolboy I heard about great
achievements in this field.'

I don't propose to dispute them. But if you take a closer look, I
think you'll want to assign these great achievements more to the
field of sensory physiology. The study of mental life was hampered
in its development by a single essential scientific misconception.
What does it consist of, as now taught in the academies? Apart from
those valuable insights into sensory physiology, it offers a number

of divisions and definitions of our mental processes which language usage has made the common property of all educated people. This is obviously not sufficient for a grasp of our mental life. Haven't you noticed that every philosopher, writer, historian and biographer constructs his own psychology and puts forward his own assumptions about the relations and purposes of mental acts, all more or less appealing and each as unreliable as the other? There is clearly no common basis. And that is also why, on psychological terrain, there is no respect and no authority. Everybody can poach on it as much as they like. If you raise a problem in physics or chemistry, people who do not have specialist knowledge will keep quiet. But if you risk making a psychological statement, you have to expect everybody to contradict and argue with you. There probably is no 'specialist knowledge' on this territory. Everybody has a mental life, and therefore everyone thinks he is a psychologist. But this hardly seems to me a sufficient qualification. There is a story about a woman who applied for a job as a nanny and was asked whether she was good with young children. Certainly, she replied, I was once a young child myself.

'And this "common basis" of mental life that all the psychologists have so far missed is something you think you have discovered by observing sick people?'

I don't believe the value of our findings is diminished by their origins. Embryology, for example, would inspire no confidence if it could not straightforwardly explain the cause of congenital deformities. But I've already told you about people whose thoughts have a life of their own, so that they are forced to brood about problems they don't have the slightest interest in. Do you think academic psychology has ever managed to contribute in the very least to explaining such an anomaly? And yet we have all experienced the way our thoughts take off on their own at night and produce things we don't understand, that we find weird and disturbing, reminding us of unhealthy symptoms. I'm talking about our dreams. Popular opinion has always maintained that dreams have a meaning, a value, that they are significant. Academic psychology has never been able to explain the meaning of dreams. It has never known what to do with dreaming; any explanations it put forward have been unpsychological ones, such as attributing them to sense stimuli, or to varying depths of the sleeping state in different parts of the brain, etc. But it has to be said that a psychology that cannot explain dreaming is not useful for interpreting ordinary mental life either, and does not deserve the name of science.

'You're becoming aggressive, so you must have touched on a sensitive spot. I have heard that analysis sets great store by dreams, interpreting them, tracing memories of real events that lie behind them, etc. But I've also heard that the interpretation of dreams is subject to the whim of the analysts, and they themselves have not reached agreement about how to interpret dreams and what justifies drawing conclusions from them. If that is the case, you're not entitled to lay so much stress on the advantages of analysis over academic psychology.'

There is a great deal in what you say. It is true that the interpretation of dreams has assumed unique importance both for the theory and the practice of analysis. If I seem aggressive, that is only a form of defence for me. But when I think of all the mayhem created by analysts interpreting dreams, I'm tempted to give in and agree with the pessimistic statement of our great satirist Nestroy: all progress is only half as good as it first looks! But you've got to admit it's always been the same; people confuse and distort everything they get their hands on. With a little care and self-discipline you can surely avoid most of the hazards of dream-interpretation. But aren't you concerned that we'll never get to my explanation if we keep getting distracted in this way?

'Yes, if I've understood you rightly you wanted to tell me about the thinking behind the new psychology.'

I did not want to start there. My intention is to let you know what conception of the structure of the mental apparatus we have formed during our analytical studies.

'May I ask what you mean by "the mental apparatus", and what it is constructed from?'

It will soon become clear what the mental apparatus is. I would prefer you not to ask what material it is constructed from. That is not a psychological question, and is as unimportant to psychology as the question of whether a telescope is made of metal or cardboard is to optics. We won't consider the material perspective at all, unlike the spatial one. For we really do conceive of the unknown apparatus that serves mental functions as an instrument made of various parts – which we call command centres – each in charge of a particular function, and all having a fixed spatial relationship to each other. That is to say, the spatial relationship of 'in front' and 'behind', 'superficial' and 'profound' amounts for us in the first instance to nothing more than a representation of the regular sequence of these functions. Are you still following me?

'Not really, though perhaps I will understand it better later on; but at any rate that's a strange anatomy of the mind, long ago abandoned by natural scientists.'

What do you expect? It's an interim concept, like so many others in the sciences. The early ones have always been fairly rough. *Open to revision* [original in English], you might say in such cases. I think it is superfluous here to make use of the 'as though' formula that has become so popular. The value of such a 'fiction', as the philosopher Vaihinger would call it, depends upon how much you can do with it.

So, to continue: we take our stand upon the ground of popular wisdom and recognize in human beings a mental organization inserted between sensory stimuli and their perception of bodily needs on the one hand, and their motor actions on the other, and for a certain purpose negotiating between them. We call this organization the I [Ego].[3] But this is nothing new; everybody assumes such an organization, as long as they aren't philosophers, and some do even though they are philosophers. But we don't think this exhausts the description of the mental apparatus. Apart from the I, we recognize another area of the mind that is larger, grander and darker than the I, and we call this the It [Id]. We will go on to deal with the relationship between the two.

You will probably object to our using mere pronouns to describe these two mental command centres or provinces, instead of choosing sonorous Greek nouns. But in psychoanalysis we love to stay in touch with popular ways of thinking, and we prefer to press their concepts into the service of science rather than to reject them. We can't take much credit for this, because it's something we have to do: our patients need to understand our theories, and they are often very intelligent but not always highly educated. The impersonal 'It' links up directly with certain expressions used by ordinary people. 'It shot right through me', they will say; 'It was something inside me that was stronger than me.' *'C'était plus fort que moi.'*

In psychology we can only describe things by using analogies. There's nothing unusual about that; it happens everywhere else too. But we have to keep changing these analogies; none of them lasts long enough for our purposes. So, to help you see the relationship between I and It, I want you to imagine the I as a kind of façade of the It, a foreground or if you like an outer layer or shell. The latter analogy is worth holding on to. We know that shells owe their particular qualities to the modifying influence of the external medium to which they are exposed. So let us imagine that the I is the outer layer of the mental apparatus, the It, modified by the influence of the external world (by reality). You can see from this how seriously we in psychoanalysis take spatial concepts. The I for us really is the surface, the It the deeper layer – as seen from outside, naturally. The I is situated between reality and the It, the actual mental realm.

'I'm not going to ask you yet how you can know all this. Just tell me first what you gain from this separation of an I from an It, what makes you do it?'

Your question sets me on the right path to continue. The significant and valuable thing to realize is that the I and the It in many ways diverge a good deal from each other. Different rules apply to the course of mental acts in the I than in the It; the I has different intentions and uses different means. A lot could be said about this, but can I just give you an analogy and an example? Think of the difference between the front and the hinterland that developed during the war. We were not surprised that things happened differently at the front than in the hinterland, and that many things that had to be forbidden at the front were permitted in the hinterland. The decisive influence was of course the proximity of the enemy; for mental life it is the proximity of the outside world. 'Outside', 'foreign' and 'enemy' were once synonymous concepts. And now for the example: in the It there are no conflicts; contradictions and antitheses stand calmly side by side and are often resolved by constructing compromises. The I in such cases does, however, experience a conflict that needs deciding, and the decision consists of one aspiration being relinquished in favour of another. The I is an organization that is distinguished by a very curious striving for unification, for synthesis. The It does not have this characteristic; it lacks concentration, so to speak. Its individual aspirations pursue their goals independently and without reference to each other.

'Given the existence of such an important mental hinterland, how do you account for the fact that it has been overlooked until now, the age of analysis?'

This takes us back to one of your earlier questions. Psychology had blocked off its own access to the territory of the It by maintaining a premise which looks pretty plausible, but which is untenable. It is the premise that we are conscious of all mental acts, that consciousness is the hallmark of mental life, and that if there are unconscious processes taking place in our brains then they are not worthy of the name of mental act and are no concern of psychology.

'I must say that seems self-evident to me.'

Yes, that's what the psychologists say too. But it's easy to demonstrate that it's wrong, i.e. that it's a completely inappropriate division. The most casual self-observation shows us that ideas occur to us that must have gone through some sort of preparatory phase. But you know nothing about the preliminary stages of your thoughts, although they are obviously also a part of your mental life; only the end result enters your consciousness. Occasionally you can become aware of these preparatory thought-formations retrospectively, by a kind of reconstruction.

'It was probably a matter of your attention being distracted, so that you didn't notice these preparations.'

You're evading the point! That won't get around the fact that acts of a mental nature occur in you, and often they are very complicated ones, of which your consciousness is not aware, and which you know nothing about. Or would you want to assert that a certain degree more or less of your 'attention' makes all the difference between a mental and a non-mental act? In any case, why are we arguing? There are experiments in hypnosis that have incontrovertibly demonstrated to everybody willing to learn that such unconscious thoughts exist.

'I don't deny it, but I think I understand you at last. What you call the I is the consciousness, and your It is the so-called subconscious we've been hearing so much about lately. But why all this dressing up in new names?'

It's not a matter of dressing anything up; those other names are unusable. And don't try to give me literature instead of science. If somebody refers to the subconscious, I don't know whether he is talking about location, something lying in the mind somewhere below consciousness; or qualitatively, in terms of a different consciousness, a subterranean one, as it were. Probably it isn't clear to him either. The only acceptable distinction is between conscious and unconscious. But it would be a fatal error to believe that this distinction is coterminous with the split between I and It. Admittedly, it would be wonderful if it were so simple, our theory would have an easy time of it, but it isn't so simple. It's certainly true that everything that goes on in the It is unconscious, and remains so; and that it is only processes in the I that can become conscious. But not all of them are, not always and not necessarily, and large parts of the I can remain permanently unconscious.

How a mental process becomes conscious is a complicated matter. I cannot forbear from telling you – dogmatically, once again – our assumption about this. You will recall that the I is the outer, peripheral layer of the It. Well, we believe that on the extreme outer surface of this I there is a special control mechanism, a system, an organ, which is directed towards the outer world. Only the stimulation of this organ can give rise to what we call consciousness. It can either be aroused from outside, so that with the help of the sense organs it absorbs outside stimuli, or internally, where it can register first the sensations in the It and then the processes of the I.

'This is all getting worse and worse and leaving me behind. You invited me to discuss the issue of whether lay people, that is non-medics, should undertake analytical procedures. So why all this discussion about speculative and obscure theories that you can't make me believe in?'

I know I can't convince you. It's not possible and it isn't my intention. When we teach our students the theory of psychoanalysis, it's noticeable how little impact we make on them at first. They accept the teachings of psychoanalysis as coolly as they did the other abstractions they were brought up on. One or two seem to want to be convinced, but there is no indication that they are. However, we demand that everybody who sets out to analyse others should first submit himself to analysis. It is only in the course of this 'self-analysis' (as it is misleadingly called), when they have really experienced at first hand physically, or rather mentally, the processes psychoanalysis describes, that they acquire the convictions that are going to guide them later as analysts. So how could I expect to convince someone like you, an impartial onlooker, of the rightness of our theories, when I can only give you an incomplete, abbreviated and therefore opaque presentation of them without the benefit of reinforcement through your own personal experience?

My intention is a different one. The question we are considering is not whether analysis makes sense or not, whether what it puts forward is right or grossly mistaken. I am setting our theories before you because that is the best way to explain the thinking behind analysis, what conditions its approach to the individual patient, and the steps it takes with him. That in turn throws a certain light upon the question of lay analysis. Anyway, you can relax now, the worst is over; what comes next will be easier to follow. For now, though, allow me to catch my breath for a moment.

III

'I'm expecting you to tell me how you can derive from psychoanalytical theory an idea of the way that neurotic conditions come about.'

I shall try to do so. For this purpose, though, we must study our I and our It from a different point of view, a dynamic one, that is, with reference to the forces at work in and between them. Up till now we have only attempted to describe the mental apparatus.

'As long as it doesn't turn out to be as incomprehensible as before!'

I hope not. Things will soon become clear to you. Well then, we assume that the forces which provoke activity in the mental apparatus are produced by physical organs as an expression of the body's chief needs. You will recall the words of our great philosopher-poet: hunger and love.[4] Quite a respectable pair of forces, by the way! In so far as these physical needs act as stimuli for mental activity, we call them drives [*Triebe*], a word that many other modern languages envy us.[5] These drives fulfil the It; to put it briefly, all the energy in the It derives from them. But the forces of the I have one and the same source: they originate in those of the It. What do these drives want? Gratification; i.e. to create conditions in which the body's wants can be quenched. The reduction of the tension of wanting is experienced by our organ of consciousness as pleasurable, whereas any increase in it is soon felt to be unpleasant. From these swings arises the cycle of pleasure–dis-pleasure[6] sensations by which the whole activity of the mental apparatus regulates its activity. We talk about the 'dominance of the pleasure principle'.

The situation becomes unbearable if the demands of the drives are not satisfied by the It. Experience shows that such gratification can only be achieved with the help of the external world. This is where the I, the part of the It that faces the outside world, goes into action. If the power that gets the whole vehicle moving comes from the It, it is the I that takes over the steering, as it were, and without that no destination will ever be reached. The drives in the It insist on instant, ruthless gratification, but by doing so they achieve nothing, or even incur palpable harm. The task of the I is to prevent this failure, and mediate between the demands of the It and the objections of the real outside world. Its activity takes two directions. On one hand, with the help of its sensory organ, the system of consciousness, it observes the outside world in order to seize the favourable moment for harmless gratification. On the other hand, it influences the It and reins in its 'passions'; it makes the drives postpone their gratification, and even, if it recognizes the necessity of doing so, makes them modify their aims or give them up in return for compensation. Taming the urges of the It in this way replaces the previously decisive pleasure principle with the so-called reality principle, which pursues the same ends but respects the conditions imposed by the real world outside. Later the I learns that there is another way to ensure gratification apart from this kind of conformity to the outside world. You can intervene in the outside world to achieve change, and thereby deliberately create the conditions that make gratification possible. This activity then becomes the highest achievement of the I: knowing when it is better to control your passions and submit to reality, and when to join forces with them and resist the outside world – this is the be-all and end-all of life-mastery.

'And is the It prepared to put up with such domination by the I, even though, from what you say, it is the stronger party of the two?'

Yes, things go well if the I is in full control of its organization and its powers, has access to all parts of the It and is able to influence them. For there is no natural opposition between the I and the It; they belong together and in a healthy state they are practically indistinguishable.

'That all sounds fine, but with this ideal relationship I can't see the tiniest gap for an unhealthy disorder to enter in.'

You are right; as long as the I and its relationship to the It fulfil these ideal requirements, there is no neurotic disorder. The point where the illness breaks in is situated in an unexpected place, although anyone familiar with general pathology will not be surprised to find confirmation of the fact that it is precisely the most important developments and modifications that bear the seed of illness, of functional breakdown.

'That's too erudite for me, I can't follow you.'

I'll have to start with something more general. You know that a small living being is a really pathetic, helpless thing in the face of an over-powerful outside world full of destructive effects. A primitive being that has not evolved an adequate organization of the I is exposed to all these 'traumas'. It lives for nothing but the 'blind' gratification of its drives and is frequently destroyed by them. The modification of the I is above all a life-saving move. There is nothing to be learned from destruction, but if you successfully survive a trauma you will notice that another, similar situation is imminent, and signal the approach of danger by a brief repetition of the impressions experienced in the trauma, with an attack of anxiety. This response to the perception of danger leads to a flight reaction, which serves to preserve life long enough to gain the strength to confront the dangers of the outer world in a more active way, perhaps even with aggression.

'This is all a long way from what you promised me.'

You have no idea how close I have come to fulfilling my promise. Even for those beings who go on to develop a viable organization of the I, this I is feeble in their childhood years and poorly differentiated from the It. Just imagine what happens when this powerless I is confronted with a drive-demand on the part of the It, which the I would like to resist because it senses that the gratifying of this desire is dangerous. It would summon up a traumatic situation, a clash with the outside world, which the I cannot control because it is not yet strong enough to do so. The I then deals with this danger posed by the drive by treating it as though it were a danger from without; it attempts to escape, withdrawing from its share in the It and leaving the latter to its fate when it rejects all the contributions the I usually makes to controlling these impulses from the drive. We say that the I is repressing these instinctual urges. Momentarily this has the effect of fending off the danger; but there is a price to pay for mixing up the internal and the external. You cannot run away from yourself. By the act of repression the I indulges the pleasure principle, which it usually disciplines, and must suffer the consequences. These consist in the fact that the I has permanently restricted its own sphere of influence. The repressed impulse is now isolated, left to its own devices, inaccessible but also beyond influencing. It goes its own way. Even later, when it has grown stronger, the I can no longer remove this repression. Its synthesis has been disturbed, and a part of the It remains forbidden territory for the I. The isolated impulse, meanwhile, is not inactive either. It knows how to obtain redress for having its normal gratification denied to it. It produces psychic derivatives which stand in for this gratification; linking up with other processes that, by using its influence, it tears away from the I, it breaks through into the I and into the consciousness as a distorted and unrecognizable substitute formation, creating what we call a symptom. Suddenly we are faced with a situation of neurotic disorder: an I whose synthesis is inhibited and that has no influence on some areas of the It; an I that must renounce many of its activities in order to avoid another clash with what has been repressed; an I that exhausts itself in attempts, for the most part futile, to resist the symptoms, the derivatives of the repressed urges; and an It in which individual drives have broken away to pursue their own ends without consideration for the interests of the whole person, from now on obeying only the laws of primitive psychology that rule in the depths of the It.

Surveying the situation as a whole, we have developed a simple formula for the origins of a neurosis: the I has attempted in an inappropriate fashion to suppress certain parts of the It; this attempt has failed and the It has taken its revenge. The neurosis is therefore the outcome of a conflict between the I and the It. Detailed examination reveals that the I enters into this conflict because it is completely intent on maintaining its compliance with the outside world. The opposition runs between the outside world and the It, and because the I, in accordance with its deepest nature, has sided with the outside world, it finds itself in conflict with the It. But note that it is not the fact of this conflict that creates the conditions for illness – after all, such differences between reality and the It are unavoidable, and it is the permanent task of the I to mediate between the two – but that in dealing with the conflict the I has used inadequate means, those of repression. But this in itself is based in the fact that at the time it was faced with the task the I was undeveloped and powerless. Significant repression always happens in early childhood.

'What a strange course of events! But I'm going to follow your advice and not be critical, since all you want to do is show me the ideas psychoanalysis has about the origins of neurosis and then how it sets about combating it. I've got several questions, and I'll return to a few of them later. But at the moment I feel tempted to take your line of thought further and risk putting forward a theory of my own. You have expanded upon the relationship between the outside world, the I and the It, and have put forward as a condition of neurosis that the I in its dependence on the outside world should combat the It. Isn't the opposite case conceivable too? In other words, that in such a conflict the I allows itself to be carried away by the It and abandons its respect for the outside world? What happens in a case like that? With my layman's notion of the nature of mental problems, I would have thought this decision on the part of the I might be the cause of the problems. This kind of turning away from reality seems to be central to mental sickness, after all.'

Yes, I've thought of that myself, and I think it's correct, although to prove it would involve discussing some really complicated matters. Neurosis and psychosis clearly have a close affinity, but there must be a decisive point at which they part company. This point could well be the participation of the I in this kind of conflict. In both cases the It would persist in its characteristic blind intransigence.

'But please continue. What can your theory tell us about the treatment of neurotic illness?'

Our therapeutic aim is easy to outline. We want to restore the I, release it from its limitations, and give it back the dominance over the It that it lost as the result of its earlier repressions. This is the sole point of analysis; our whole technique is directed to this end. We must locate the repressions that have occurred and induce the I to correct them with our help, to find a better way of dealing with conflict than flight. Since these repressions are rooted in early childhood, our analytical work takes us back to that period as well. It is the symptoms, dreams and free ideas of the sufferer that point the way towards the mostly forgotten conflict situations that we want to bring back to life in the patient's memory. Of course we first have to interpret and translate these indicators, for under the influence of the psychology of the It they have taken on what we perceive as strange forms of expression. On the basis of the ideas, thoughts and memories that the patient is able to pass on to us, not without an inner struggle, we can assume that they are connected with what is being repressed or are derivatives of it. By urging the sufferer to overcome his reluctance to communicate, we educate his I to conquer its tendency to flight and to be capable of bearing the approach of the repressed. Ultimately, if we have succeeded in re-creating the circumstances of the repression in his memory, his compliance is splendidly rewarded. The effects of the lapse of time work in his favour, and whatever had made his childhood I take flight now appears to his grown-up and stronger I to be just child's-play.

IV

'Everything you've told me so far has been psychology. It has often sounded unappealing, remote, obscure, but it has all been, if I may put it like this, neat and tidy. Now, I didn't know much about your psychoanalysis before, but a rumour had reached me that it hardly deserved that description. It makes me wonder whether you're holding something back, since you haven't touched on anything of the kind I'm thinking of. And I can't suppress another doubt, either. The neuroses are, as you say yourself, disorders of mental life. Are you saying that such things as our ethics, our conscience, our ideals play no part at all in these acute disturbances?'

So, what you miss in our discussions so far is any consideration of either lower or higher things. However, that's because we have not yet dealt with the contents of mental life at all. But allow me for once to play the part of the one who interrupts and hold up the progress of this discussion. The reason why I have given you so much psychology is that I wanted you to get the impression that analytical work is applied psychology; a psychology, furthermore, that is not known outside analysis. The analyst must first and fore-most have acquired knowledge of this psychology (depth psychology or psychology of the unconscious); at least of as much as we know about it so far. We'll need all this for our later conclusions. But for now – what did you mean by your 'neat and tidy' allusion?

'Well, everybody says that in analysis the most intimate and . . . the nastiest sides of sexual life are brought out, in all their detail. If that's the case – though from your psychological explanations I haven't gathered that it necessarily is – that would be a powerful argument for allowing no one but doctors to offer such treatment. How could you possibly dream of granting such dangerous liberties to other people, whose discretion you can't be sure of and for whose character nobody has vouched?'

It is true, doctors do enjoy certain prerogatives in the sexual field; they are also allowed to inspect the genitalia. Although in the past they were not allowed to in the Orient, and certain idealistic reformers – you know who I mean – have attacked these preroga-tives. But your first question was whether this does apply in psycho-analysis, and why it must be so? Yes, it is the case.

It has to be the case, first because analysis is based on total integrity. Bank balances, for example, are treated there with the same thoroughness and openness, and people say things that you would normally keep back from any fellow citizen, even if he isn't a competitor or a tax-man. I won't deny that this duty of integrity places the analyst under a heavy moral obligation: on the contrary, this is something I myself would emphatically stress. In the second place, these intimate matters must be accessible because among the ultimate and proximate causes of neurotic illnesses, factors arising in sexual life play a part that is extremely important, outstanding, perhaps very specific. What else can the analyst do but get as close as possible to the topic, the material that the sick person brings to him? The analyst never lures him on to sexual territory; he doesn't say in advance 'I'm going to deal with the intimacies of your sexual life'! He lets him start talking about anything he chooses, and calmly bides his time until the patient himself gets on to sexual topics. I always used to remind my students that our opponents told us we would come across cases where the sexual factor played no part; so we should take care never to introduce it, so as not to ruin our chances of finding such a case. Well, so far none of us has been so fortunate.

I know of course that our acknowledgement of sexuality has become – whether explicitly or not – the most powerful motive for others' hostility to analysis. Can that shake our commitment? It only serves to show us how neurotic our entire culture is, since supposedly normal people do not act very differently from neurotic ones. At the time when, in German learned societies, solemn judgement was being delivered on psychoanalysis – nowadays things have gone rather quiet – one speaker claimed particular authority because, after his lecture, he allowed the patients to express themselves as well, clearly for diagnostic purposes and in order to put the analysts' assertions to the test. But, he added, if they start talking about sexual matters, I shut them up. What do you think of this way of offering proof? The learned society cheered him instead of being suitably ashamed on his behalf. Only the triumphant certainty bestowed by sharing a common prejudice can explain the careless logic of this speaker. Years later some students of mine succumbed to the need to liberate human society from the yoke of sexuality placed upon it by psychoanalysis. One of them declared that sexual matters did not mean sexuality, but something else, something abstract and mystical. Another even said that sexual life was only one of the areas in which people wanted to pursue their driving need for power and domination. They were much applauded, at least in the short term.

'Here I'd venture to take sides, for once. It seems to me quite risky to assert that sexuality is not a natural, primordial need of living beings, but the expression of something else. You only have to think of the example of animals.'

That doesn't matter. There is no potion too absurd for society to swallow, as long as it is promoted as an antidote to the terrifying predominance of sexuality.

Furthermore, I have to admit to you that I find your own reluctance to accept that the sexual factor plays such a big part in the origins of neuroses difficult to reconcile with your task of remaining impartial. Aren't you afraid that such an antipathy might interfere with your ability to arrive at a fair judgement?

'I'm sorry you should say that. Your confidence in me seems to be shaken. Why didn't you choose somebody else to be the neutral party, then?'

Because that somebody else would have thought exactly the same as you. But if he had been willing to recognize the importance of sexual life right from the start, then the world would have cried, 'He's not impartial, he's just one of your supporters.' No, I certainly have not given up expecting to influence your opinions. But I admit that this question is different from the one we were dealing with earlier. In our psychological discussions I wasn't concerned whether you believed me or not, as long as you had the impression that it was a matter of purely psychological problems. This time, on the question of sexuality, I want you to become open to the insight that your most powerful motive for resistance is precisely the preconceived animosity you share with so many others.

'But I haven't had the experience that gives you such unshakeable confidence.'

All right, perhaps I can now continue with my account. Sexual life is not only a titillating subject, but a serious scientific problem as well. There was so much that was new to learn, so many strange things to explain. I have already told you that analysis must reach back into the early childhood years of the patient, because it is in that period and during the weak stages of the I that the decisive repressions occur. But surely children have no sexual life; doesn't it only start in puberty? On the contrary, we discovered that sexual impulses are a part of life from the moment of birth onwards, and that it is precisely to ward off these drives that the infantile I uses repressions. A strange coincidence, is it not, that the infant resists the power of sexuality just as the speaker did in the learned society, and later those students of mine who constructed their own theories? What is happening here? The most general answer would be that our whole culture has been built up at the expense of sexuality, but there is much more to be said about it.

The discovery of childhood sexuality is among those revelations of which one has to be ashamed. It seems that some paediatricians have always known about it, and some children's nurses. Intelligent men who call themselves child psychologists then talked in reproachful tones about 'the loss of childhood innocence'. Always emotion instead of argument! This sort of thing is always happening in our political bodies. Somebody from the opposition stands up and denounces some mismanagement in the civil service, army, judiciary, etc. Whereupon somebody else, preferably in the government, declares that such observations are an insult to the honour of the state, the military, the dynasty or even the nation. Therefore they effectively amount to untruths. Such feelings cannot tolerate insults.

The sexual life of a child is naturally different from that of an adult. The sexual function undergoes a complicated development from its beginnings to the final form so familiar to us. Its growth combines numerous partial drives, each with its own object, and passes through different phases of organization, until it finally puts itself at the service of procreation. Not all of the partial drives are usable just as they are in the final outcome; they must be diverted, modified, in part repressed. Such an extensive development does not always run its course unimpaired; there are developmental checks, partial fixations on early stages of development. Where the operation of the sexual function later encounters obstacles, sexual urges – the libido, as we say – are often inclined to revert to such points of fixation. The study of childhood sexuality and the transformations it undergoes up to maturity has also given us the key to understanding the so-called sexual perversions, which people used to describe with all the required signs of repulsion, but whose origins nobody could explain. This whole area is extraordinarily interesting, but for the purposes of our present discussion there is little point in telling you more about it. To find your way around in it, you obviously need anatomical and physiological knowledge, not all of which is obtainable at medical school, unfortunately. But familiarity with cultural history and mythology is also essential.

'Even after all that, I still haven't got any notion of childhood sexuality.'

I shall dwell rather longer on the topic, then. In any case, I don't find it easy to tear myself away from it. You see, the most remarkable thing about the sexual life of children is that its whole, very far-reaching development takes place in the first five years of life. From there until puberty there stretches out the so-called latency period, in which – normally – sexuality makes no progress; on the contrary, sexual urges decline in force and much that the child had already known or put into effect is relinquished and forgotten. In this phase of life, after the early blossom of sexuality has wilted away, all those attitudes of the I are formed that, like shame, disgust or morality, are designed to withstand the stormy assault of puberty and channel newly awakening sexual desire. This so-called dual-phase onset of sexual life has a good deal to do with the origins of neurotic illness. It seems to be unique to human beings; perhaps it is one of the conditions for the human privilege of becoming neurotic. Before psychoanalysis, the early period of sexual life was just as neglected as, in another area, the background of conscious mental life. You will be right to suspect that the two aspects are intimately related.

There is a lot that is surprising to report about the contents, changes and results of this early sexuality. For example: you will surely be astonished to hear that boys so often suffer from a fear of being eaten by their father. (And aren't you surprised to learn that I am placing this fear among the expressions of sexual life?) I might remind you of the mythological story you may remember from your schooldays, about the god Chronos devouring his children. It is a myth that must have seemed very strange to you when you first heard it! But I doubt whether any of us gave it much thought at the time. Nowadays we can recall a number of tales featuring a devouring animal, such as the wolf, and in him we recognize the father in disguise. This gives me a nice opportunity to point out to you that mythology and the world of fairy tales are not intelligible at all without a knowledge of children's sexual life. This is a secondary gain from analytical studies.

You will be no less surprised to learn that the male child suffers from the fear that his father will deprive him of his sexual organ, and that this fear of castration has an enormous influence on shaping his character and in deciding his sexual orientation. Here too mythology will encourage your belief in psychoanalysis. The same Chronos who devours his children had emasculated his father Uranus, and then in revenge is himself emasculated by his son Zeus, who has been rescued through his mother's cunning. If you are inclined to assume that everything that psychoanalysts say about early childhood sexuality derives from the wild imagination of the analysts, you might at least admit that this imagination has produced the same creations as the imaginative efforts of primitive people, laid down in their myths and tales. Another more attractive and probably more accurate interpretation would be that the same archaic factors can be found at work in the mental life of children as once prevailed in the primeval times of human culture. In a condensed form, the child would then be repeating in his mental development the history of the race, in the same way that this has long been recognized in embryology.

A further characteristic of early childhood sexuality is that the actual female genital organ does not feature in it – the child has not yet discovered it. All the emphasis is on the male organ, all interest centres on whether it is present or not. We know less about the sexual life of small girls than we do about boys. We need not be ashamed of this difference; for, after all, the sexual life of adult females is a *dark continent* [original in English] for psychology. But we have recognized that girls feel strongly their lack of a sexual organ equal in status to the male one, and therefore feel inferior, and that this 'penis envy' gives rise to a whole series of typically female reactions.

Also peculiar to children is that the two kinds of excremental function possess sexual interest. Education draws a sharp line here, which is obliterated again by the practice of jokes. It may seem disagreeable to us, but we know that with children it takes quite a long while for disgust to set in. This is not denied even by those who otherwise defend the seraphic purity of the childish mind.

But there is nothing else that commands our attention as much as the fact that the child regularly directs his sexual desires at the people he is most closely related to, primarily at his mother and father, therefore, and in second place at his siblings. For the boy the mother is the first object of his love, for the girl the father, as long as a bisexual predisposition does not simultaneously favour the reverse attitudes. The other parent is viewed as an interfering rival and quite often regarded with deep hostility. Do not misunderstand me; I am not saying that the child wants merely that kind of tenderness from his favoured parent that we grown-ups would like to see as the essence of the parent–child relationship. No, analysis leaves us in no doubt that, beyond this tenderness, the desires of the child strive for what we would see as sensual gratification, as far as the child can imagine it. It is easy to understand that the child has no grasp of the true facts of sexual congress, and he substitutes for them other notions derived from his experiences and feelings. Normally the summit of his desires is the intention of giving birth to a child or – in some vague way – of fathering one. In his ignorance, the boy does not exclude himself from the desire to have a baby. We call this whole mental structure the Oedipus complex, after the familiar Greek legend. By the end of the early stage of sexuality the norm should be that it is left behind, thoroughly broken down and transformed, and the outcome of this transformation is designed to produce great results in later mental life. But, as a rule, the transition is not thorough enough, and puberty provokes a revival of the complex, which can have serious consequences.

I am surprised you have not said anything yet. That can hardly betoken acceptance on your part. By claiming that the first sexual object of choice for the infant is an incestuous one (to use the technical term), analysis has offended against the most sacred feelings of humanity and knows exactly how much incredulity, protest and accusation to expect. It has not been disappointed. Nothing has done more to lose it support among contemporaries than its putting forward of the Oedipus complex as a predestined formation common to all humanity. The Greek myth must surely have implied the same, but the majority of people today, whether scholars or not, prefer to believe that nature has deployed an innate abhorrence as protection against the possibility of incest.

First of all, let us call history to our aid. When Julius Caesar entered Egypt, he found that the youthful Queen Cleopatra, who was soon to assume such significance for him, was married to her still younger brother Ptolemy. That was nothing special for the Egyptian dynasty; the Ptolemaic rulers, Greek in origin, had merely continued the custom practised for several millennia by their predecessors, the ancient Pharaohs. But that is just sibling incest, which is judged relatively leniently even today. So let us turn to our main authority on primordial conditions, mythology. It informs us that the myths of all peoples, not only the Greeks, contain an abundance of sexual relationships between fathers and daughters, and even mothers and sons. Both the cosmology and the genealogy of royal houses are founded upon incest. What do you suppose was the purpose of creating these poetic works? In order to brand gods and kings as criminals, to draw down the disgust of humankind upon them? A more likely reason was that incestuous desires are an age-old human heritage and are never entirely suppressed, so that fulfilment of them continued to be allowed to the gods and their descendants even after the majority of ordinary mortals had had to renounce them. In complete accord with these lessons from history and mythology, we find incestuous desires still alive and active in the childhood of the individual.

'I could take it amiss that you were going to withhold all this from me about childhood sexuality. It seems to me very interesting, precisely for its relationship to early human history.'

I was afraid it would take us too far away from our purposes. But we might benefit from it later, after all.

'But tell me, how can you verify the correctness of your analytical results concerning the sexual life of children? Do your convictions rest entirely upon the parallel with mythology and history?'

Oh, not at all. They rest upon direct observation. It happened like this: at first we inferred the content of sexual childhood from the analysis of adults; that is to say, after a lapse of some twenty or thirty years. Later we carried out analyses of the children themselves, and it was no small triumph when these confirmed everything we had conjectured, despite the superimposed layers and the distortions accumulated in the meantime.

'What, you analysed small children, children under six? Is that allowed, and isn't it rather questionable for the children themselves?'

It works very well. It's hard to believe all that is going on in a child of about four or five. Children are mentally very lively at this age; the early phase of sexuality is also a period of intellectual flowering for them. I have the impression that when they enter the latency period they become intellectually inhibited and less bright. Many children from then on also lose their physical charm. And as far as the harmfulness of analysis is concerned, I can tell you that the first child on whom we dared to try the experiment nearly twenty years ago has since become a healthy and capable young man who went through his puberty unproblematically, despite serious psychic trauma. Hopefully, the other 'victims' of analysis have not fared any worse. There is much of interest linked to these child analyses. It is possible that in future they may become even more significant. Their value for theory is beyond question. They give us unambiguous information on questions that remain unresolved in the analysis of adults, and thereby protect the analyst from mistakes that would have serious consequences for him. You can catch at work the factors that cause neuroses, and you cannot help recognizing them. Certainly, in the interests of the child, the analytical influence on him must be combined with pedagogic measures. This is a technique that still awaits further refinement. Practical interest has been aroused, however, by the observation that a very large number of our children undergo an unmistakably neurotic phase. Now that we have learned to sharpen our vision, we are tempted to say that child neurosis is not the exception but the rule, as though, on the route from infantile predisposition to social culture, it is hardly to be avoided. In most cases this attack of neurosis is spontaneously beaten off; but does it not regularly imprint its traces even on the average healthy person? On the other hand, in later neuroses we never fail to identify a link with the childish illness, which for its part does not need to have been particularly noticeable. There is a close analogy with tuberculosis, where the specialists tell us that everybody has suffered a bout of this infection once in their childhood. For the neuroses, however, it is not a matter of immunization, but of predisposition.

I want to return to your question about what verification we have. In a very general sense we have convinced ourselves through direct analytical observation of children that we have interpreted correctly what adults have told us about their childhood. In a series of cases, though, we have evolved another method of confirmation. From the material of analysis we reconstructed certain external processes, significant events in childhood, of which the conscious memory of the patient had no recall at all. By fortunate chance and from inquiries among parents and carers we acquired indisputable evidence that these reconstructed events really did take place in that way. This did not apply very often, naturally, but when it did it had an overwhelming impact. You have to realize that the correct reconstruction of such forgotten childhood experiences always has a considerable therapeutic effect, whether they can be objectively confirmed or not. They owe their importance to the fact that they occurred at such an early age, at a time when they were still able to have a traumatic effect on the I in its weak state.

'But what kinds of events can it be that analysis needs to discover?'

Various kinds. First and foremost, impressions capable of having a lasting effect on the incipient sexual life of the child; witnessing sexual contacts between grown-ups, for example, or having sexual experiences with a grown-up or with another child – none of these is such a rare occurrence – or overhearing conversations that the child understood either at the time, or only later, from which it drew conclusions about secret or mysterious things; or utterances or actions of the child himself which demonstrate a significant degree of tenderness or hostility to other persons. It is particularly important in analysis to recall the forgotten sexual activities of the child himself and also the intervention of adults who put an end to them.

'That is my cue to ask a question I have had in mind for some time. What are these "sexual activities" of the child in this early phase which, as you say, were overlooked before the introduction of analysis?'

The most regular and essential of these sexual activities, strangely enough, had not been overlooked at all; that is to say, it was not strange at all, given that they could not possibly be overlooked. The child's sexual impulses find their main outlet in self-gratification through stimulation of the genitals, in reality of the male genitals. Adults had always known how extraordinarily widespread this 'bad habit' was; it was regarded as a sin and severely punished. Don't ask me how you could reconcile observation of these immoral tendencies in the child – children do it, they themselves say, because it is pleasurable – with theories about their innate purity and lack of sensuality. It is the opposition who owe you an explanation of this riddle. For us there is a more important problem: what attitude should we take to sexual activities in early childhood? While we know the responsibility we take upon ourselves by repressing them, we do not dare to give them completely free rein. Among uncivilized races and in the lower classes of civilized peoples there seems to be no attempt to control children's sexuality. Although this probably creates a powerful defence against later attack from individual neuroses, does it not also mean an exceptional loss of potential for civilized achievement? It really looks as though we are facing a new Scylla and Charybdis here.

I am happy to leave you to decide whether the interest provoked by the study of sexual life among neurotics results in an atmosphere favourable to arousing prurience.

V

'I think I see what you are aiming at. You want to show me the kinds of knowledge needed for practising analysis, so that I can judge whether only doctors should be allowed to do so. Well, so far not much about medicine has emerged, just a lot of psychology and some biology or sexual science. But perhaps we haven't yet reached the end?'

Certainly not, there are many gaps to be filled in. Can I make a request to you? Would you care to describe to me your present conception of an analytical session? As though you had to conduct one yourself?

'Well, that could be fun. It's really not my intention to resolve our dispute by experimenting like that. But I will do you the favour; on your head be it. So, I assume the patient comes along with a complaint. I promise him a cure or improvement as long as he follows my directions. I demand that he should be absolutely honest and tell me what he knows and anything that occurs to him, and not to deviate from this resolve however uncomfortable it makes him to say certain things. Have I done well to remember that rule?'

Yes, and you should add that it does not matter that what occurs to him seems unimportant or silly.

'That as well. Then he begins to tell me something and I listen. From what he says I work out what impressions, experiences, and desires he has repressed, because they occurred at a time when his I was still weak and was afraid of them, instead of dealing with them. Once he's learnt this from me, he transports himself back to the earlier situation and this time with my help he fares better. Then the limitations forced upon his I disappear, and he's put right. How was that?'

Bravo, bravo! I can see I shall be accused once more of training a non-doctor to be an analyst. You have caught on really well.

'I've only repeated what I heard from you, like reciting something you've learned by heart. I really have no idea how I would do it, and I can't understand why such a job should take an hour a day for months on end. Ordinary people haven't usually experienced all that much, and it's probably always the same things that are repressed in childhood.'

There's a lot to be learned in the actual practice of analysis. For example, you would not find it all that easy to deduce from the patient's words what experiences he has forgotten or what impulses he has repressed. He says something to you that at first makes no more sense to you than to him. You have to decide to interpret in a very particular way the material the analysand has dutifully delivered to you. It's similar to refining precious metal from ore by particular processes. This prepares you for working through many tons of ore to gain perhaps just a little of the valuable material.

'But how do you process the raw material, to stay with your simile?'

By assuming that the statements and ideas of the patient are just distorted versions of what you are looking for; allusions, as it were, from which you have to divine what they are hiding. In a word, you first have to interpret this material, be it memories, notions or dreams. This you will do, of course, in the light of the expectations that your professional knowledge has allowed you to form while you were listening.

'Interpret! That's an awful word. I don't like hearing it, and it takes all my confidence away. If everything depends on my interpretation, who will vouchsafe that I'm interpreting correctly? Then everything is left to my own caprice.'

Calm down, things are not quite that bad. Why are you exempting your own mental processes from the laws that you acknowledge for others? If you have achieved a certain self-discipline and acquired particular knowledge, your interpretations will not be influenced by your personal idiosyncrasies and will be accurate. I don't say that the personality of the analyst is irrelevant at this stage of the task. You need quite a fine ear for what has been unconsciously repressed, and not everybody has this to the same degree. And, above all, this links up with the duty of the analyst to make himself fit to receive analytical material without prejudice, by submitting to a profound self-analysis. Certainly, something always remains that is analogous to the 'personal equation' in astronomical observations; this individual factor will always play a bigger part in psychoanalysis than elsewhere. An abnormal person can still become a respectable physicist, whereas as an analyst he will always be handicapped by his own abnormality when it comes to forming an undistorted picture of mental life. Since no one can prove somebody else is abnormal, general agreement about matters of depth psychology will be especially difficult to reach. Many psychologists even say it's hopeless and that any fool will have the right to proclaim his foolishness as wisdom. I must confess that I'm rather more optimistic in this respect. Our experience tells us that, even in psychology, a fairly satisfactory level of agreement is achievable. Every area of research has its own particular difficulties, which we must try to eliminate. Moreover, in the psychoanalytical art of interpretation much can be learned; it is like studying the material of a different science, which is connected with the strange indirect form of representation through symbols.

'Well, I'm no longer interested in taking on an analytical session, even in my imagination. Who knows what sort of surprises I might be in for.'

You're quite right to give up any such intention. You can see how much training and practice would be needed. If you have established the right interpretation, there's yet another task ahead. You have to wait for the right moment to pass on your interpretation to the patient with some hope of success.

'How do you recognize the right moment every time?'

That is a matter of tact, which can become highly refined through experience. It's a bad mistake to try to shorten the analysis by off-loading your interpretations on to the patient the moment you have arrived at them. You will make him express resistance, rejection, indignation, but won't succeed in making him overcome his repressions. The rule is to wait until he has made so much progress towards them that he has only a few more steps to take, guided by your suggested interpretation.

'I don't think I would ever learn that. And when I have followed these precautions in my interpretation, then what?'

Then a discovery awaits you that you are not prepared for.

'And that is?'

That you have been wrong about your patient, that you cannot depend at all upon his cooperation and willingness, that he is prepared to place all sorts of obstacles in the way of your mutual enterprise; in other words, he does not want to get better at all.

'Hold on, this is the weirdest thing you've told me yet! And I don't believe it, either. The patient who is suffering so much, who complains so movingly about his problems, who has made such sacrifices for the sake of treatment, doesn't want to get better! I'm sure you don't mean it like that.'

Brace yourself for this . . . I do mean it. What I've just said is the truth, not the whole truth, admittedly, but a very considerable part of it. The sufferer does indeed want to get better, but then again he doesn't. His I has lost its unity, and that is why he cannot assert a unified will. He would not be a neurotic otherwise.

'Were I to be cautious, my name would not be Tell.'[7]

The derivatives of what has been repressed have broken through into his I, and are asserting themselves there. The I has as little control over tendencies stemming from that source as it does over what is repressed, and generally knows nothing about them. This is a special kind of ill person, who creates difficulties we have not learned to expect. All our social institutions are geared to people with a unified, normal I, which one can classify as good or evil, which either performs its proper function or has been switched off as a result of some overwhelming influence. Hence the legal alternative: either responsible or not responsible. These distinctions are not at all appropriate for neurotics. It must be admitted that it is difficult to make the normal demands of society fit their psychological condition. We saw this on a large scale in the last war. Were the neurotics who shirked military service malingerers or not? They were both. If they were treated like malingerers and illness was made really uncomfortable for them, they got better; once supposedly cured and returned to the military, they promptly escaped back into illness again. Nothing could be done with them. And the same applies to neurotics in civilian life. They complain about their illness, but exploit it as much as they can; when you try to take it away from them, they defend it like the proverbial lioness defending her young – though it would make no sense to reproach them for this contradiction.

'But wouldn't it be best not to treat these difficult people at all, then, but leave them to their own devices? I can't believe it's worth while taking as much trouble with every one of these patients as you indicate that you do.'

I cannot agree with your suggestion. It is undoubtedly better to accept the complications of life instead of resisting them. It may be that not all the neurotics that we treat are worth the trouble of analysing, but there are also very worthwhile people among them. We must set ourselves the goal of ensuring that the smallest possible number of people enter civilized life with such poor mental equipment. That is why we must gather much experience and learn to understand much. Every analysis can be instructive and help us gain new explanations, quite apart from the personal value of individual patients.

'But if the I of the patient has conceived the will to keep the illness, then it must be able to cite reasons and motives for this too, and justify itself somehow. But it's impossible to see why somebody should want to be ill, what good it does him.'

Not at all, it's not so hard to imagine. Think of the shell-shock cases[8] who don't have to serve any longer, because they are ill. In civilian life neurotic illness can be used defensively, to cover up inadequacy in a profession and in competitive situations; in family life it can be used to force the others to make sacrifices and offer proof of their love or to impose one's will upon them. All of this lies pretty well on the surface; we sum it up as 'illness gain'. The remarkable thing, though, is that the sick person, his I, knows nothing about this whole chain of motivation, with its consistent line of action. We combat the influence of these tendencies by forcing the I to take note of them. But there are other, more profound motives for holding on to a sick condition, and these are not so easy to deal with. Without another excursus into psychological theory, however, you can't understand them.

'Just keep on with your explanation; a bit more theory hardly matters at this stage.'

When I explained to you the relationship of the I and the It, I withheld from you an important part of the theory of the mental apparatus. You see, we were obliged to assume that a separate authority had established itself, which we call the Super-I. This Super-I occupies a special position between the I and the It. It belongs to the I, shares the latter's high degree of psychological organization, but enjoys a particularly close relationship to the It. In reality it is the repository of the earliest objects seized upon by the It, the heir to the Oedipus complex after the closure of the latter. This Super-I can oppose itself to the I, treat it like an object, and sometimes deals with it very harshly. It is as important for the I to stay on good terms with the Super-I as with the It. Any falling-out between the I and the Super-I has great significance for mental life. You have already guessed that the Super-I is the vehicle of the phenomenon we call the conscience. It is very important for mental health that the Super-I is formed normally, that is to say that it has become sufficiently impersonal. This is precisely not the case with the neurotic whose Oedipus complex has not undergone the proper transformation. His Super-I still confronts the I like a stern father confronting a child, and his moral activity remains at the primitive level of the I allowing itself to be punished by the Super-I. The illness is used as the means of 'self-punishment'; the neurotic is obliged to behave as though he is dominated by a guilt-feeling that can only be assuaged by illness as a punishment.

'All this sounds really mysterious. The strangest thing about it is that the sufferer does not become conscious of the power of his conscience.'

Yes, we are only just beginning to appreciate the meaning of all these important conditions. That is why my explanation has inevitably turned out to be rather obscure. But now let's move on. We call all the forces opposed to the work of recovery the patient's 'resistances'. The gain from his illness is the source of one such resistance; his 'unconscious guilt-feeling' represents the resistance of the Super-I. It is the most powerful factor, and the one we fear most.

In our treatment we encounter other resistances, too. If anxiety in early years has induced the I to engage in a repression, this anxiety will persist, and will express itself in the present as a resistance if the I confronts an encounter with the repressed. One can imagine that the attempt to push an instinctual process along the new path opened up for it, when for decades the path it has taken has been different, is not unproblematic. You could call that the resistance of the It. Battling with all these resistances is the main part of our work during analytical treatment; the task of interpretation dwindles into insignificance by comparison. This struggle and the conquering of resistances changes and strengthens the I of the patient so much that we have no worries about his future behaviour after the end of the treatment. On the other hand, you can see why treatment takes so long. It is not the time that development takes, nor the richness of the material, that is decisive. It's more a matter of whether the path is free. Over a stretch of territory which you could cross by train in a few short hours in peace-time, an army can be held up for weeks by enemy resistance. Such struggles take time in mental life, too. I am sorry to say that, so far, all attempts substantially to speed up analytical treatment have failed. The best way to shorten the process seems to be to carry it out correctly.

'If I had ever been tempted to try to do your job for you and attempt to analyse somebody, what you've just told me about resistances would have cured me of it. But what about the personal influence you have admitted exists? Doesn't that help against these resistances?'

I'm glad you brought that up at this point. This personal influence is our most powerful dynamic weapon; it is the new factor we introduce into the situation and the way we can bring some action into it. The intellectual content of our explanations cannot achieve this, because the patient, who shares all the prejudices of his environment, does not necessarily believe us any more than our scientific critics do. The neurotic gets down to the work in hand because he believes the analyst, and he believes him because he develops a special emotional attitude to the person of the analyst. Children likewise only believe people to whom they are attached. I have already told you how we make use of this particularly strong 'suggestive' influence. Not to suppress the symptoms – this distinguishes the analytical method from other psychotherapeutic procedures – but as a driving force to make the I of the patient conquer his resistances.

'Well, supposing that succeeds, doesn't everything go smoothly from then on?'

Yes, it should. But it turns out that there is an unexpected complication. Perhaps the biggest surprise for the analyst was to discover that the emotional relationship the patient develops with him is of a very special kind. The very first doctor who attempted an analysis – it was not me – came across this phenomenon, and was shaken by it. For this emotional relationship – to put it plainly – is a kind of falling in love. Strange, isn't it? Especially when you consider that the analyst does nothing to provoke it, that, on the contrary, in personal terms he keeps a distance between himself and the patient, and wraps himself in a certain reserve. And when, furthermore, you discover that this peculiar romantic attachment is oblivious to the question of what other actual appealing features the love-object might have, and surmounts all the factors involved in personal attraction, those of age, sex and class. This love is nothing short of inevitable. Not that this kind of spontaneous falling in love is otherwise rare. As you know, the opposite is demonstrated often enough, but in the situation of analysis it comes about quite regularly, although there is no obvious rational reason why it should. You might think that in the patient–analyst relationship there would be no need for the former to conceive more than a degree of respect, trust, gratitude and human goodwill towards the analyst. Instead of that, there is this romantic attraction, which itself gives the impression of a pathological phenomenon.

'Well, I would have thought that would favour your analytical project. When you're in love, you're compliant and do all you can to please the other person.'

Yes, initially it is favourable, but eventually, when this love has strengthened its hold, its real nature comes to the fore, and a good deal about it is incompatible with the task of analysis. The patient's love is not content with obeying; it becomes demanding, craving tender and sensual gratification, claiming exclusiveness, developing jealous emotions, and more and more showing its negative side, its willingness to indulge in animosity and desire for revenge when it cannot get its own way. At the same time, like other romantic obsessions, it puts anything significant out of mind, and blots out any interest in treatment and in recovery. In short, there is no doubt that it has replaced the neurosis, and our work has succeeded only in driving out one form of illness with another.

'That sounds bleak. What do you do about it? You ought to give up the analysis, but since, as you say, this is the result in every case, it seems impossible to carry out any analysis at all.'

We first of all use the situation in order to learn from it. What we gain in that way can help us to control it. Isn't it well worth noting that we succeed in transforming a given neurosis, whatever its content, into a state of pathological romantic obsession?

We are unshakeably confirmed by this experience in our conviction that the neurosis is grounded in some aspect of erotic life that has been applied to abnormal purposes. With this insight we have found our feet again, and feel we can go on to make the obsession itself the object of analysis. And we make another observation, too. The attachment to the analyst does not always express itself so clearly and sharply as I have tried to indicate. And why does that not happen? It doesn't take long to work out. To the same extent that the totally sensual and the hostile sides of his attachment try to come to the fore, the resistance of the patient to them is aroused. Before our eyes he struggles with them, attempts to repress them. And now we understand the process. The patient is repeating, in the form of attachment to the analyst, mental experiences that he has lived through once before. He has transferred on to the analyst mental attitudes that lay primed in him, and were intimately related to the origins of his neurosis. Before our eyes he also repeats his defensive actions of that period, and wants to repeat in his relationship with the analyst all the ups and downs of that phase of his life. What he shows us is the core of his intimate life-story; he reproduces it concretely, as though happening now, instead of recalling it. This is the solution to the puzzle of transference, and the analysis can be continued precisely with the help of this new situation, which had appeared so threatening to it.

'That's very subtle. And is it easy to get the patient to believe he's not in love, just re-enacting some old drama?'

Everything depends on your doing so, and achieving it is where the real skill of manipulating 'transference' comes in. You can see that at this point the demands made on analytical technique are intensified to the highest level. Here is where you can make your most crass mistakes or obtain your greatest successes. It would make no sense to escape from these difficulties by suppressing or neglecting the transference. Whatever else you did after that, it would not deserve to be called an analysis. Neither would it make sense, and it would also be cowardly, to send the patient away as soon as his transference-neurosis begins to bother you. That would be roughly like conjuring up spirits and then running away as soon as they appear.

It is true that sometimes you have no choice; there are cases where you cannot get control of the unbridled transference and you have to break off the analysis, but at least you must always wrestle to the best of your ability with the demon spirits. To indulge the demands of the transference, to fulfil the desires of the patient for tender and sensual gratification, is not only quite rightly ruled out by ethical considerations, but also completely ineffectual as a means to the end of analysis. The neurotic cannot be cured by enabling him to repeat, without correction, an unconscious cliché that has been latent in him. If you enter into compromises with him by trading partial gratification in return for his continuing cooperation in the analysis, you have to be careful not to get into the ridiculous situation of the priest who is supposed to be converting the sick insurance agent. The sick man remains unconverted, but the priest goes away insured. The only possible way out of the transference situation is to take the patient back to the past, either as he really experienced it, or as it is given shape by the wish-fulfilment activity of his imagination. And this demands a great deal of skill, patience, calm and self-denial from the analyst.

'And where do you think the neurotic experienced the original model of his transferred attachment?'

In his childhood, usually in a relationship to a parent. You remember the significance we were obliged to ascribe to these earliest emotional relationships. This is where we come full circle.

'Have you really finished? My mind is reeling a bit from being told so much. But just one more thing: where can one learn whatever is needed for practising analysis?'

At the moment there are two institutes where psychoanalytical training goes on. The first, in Berlin, was established by Dr Max Eitingon of the Analytical Society there. The second is maintained by the Vienna Psychoanalytical Society at its own expense and with considerable sacrifice. The authorities take an interest only to the extent of creating a number of difficulties for these newly fledged ventures. A third teaching institute is supposed to be opening in London under the direction of Dr E. Jones of the Society there. At these institutes the candidates are themselves analysed, receive theoretical tuition in lectures about all the subjects they need, and are mentored by older, experienced analysts when they are allowed to take their first steps in analysing some minor cases. Such a training is expected to last two years. Naturally, even after this time you are still a beginner, hardly a master of the art. What you still lack must be acquired by practice and by exchange of ideas in the psychoanalytical societies, where younger members mingle with older ones. But anyone who has been through this course of instruction, has been analysed himself; has grasped as much as can be taught at present about the psychology of the unconscious; knows about the science of sexual life; and has learnt the delicate technique of psychoanalysis, the art of interpretation, combating resistances and manipulating transference – such a person is no longer a layman in the field of psychoanalysis. He is equipped to undertake the treatment of neurotic disturbances, and in time will achieve all that can be demanded of this therapy.

VI

'You have made great efforts to show me what psychoanalysis is, and what knowledge is needed in order to practise it with prospects of success. All right, it hasn't done me any harm to listen to you. But I don't know how you expect my judgement to be influenced by your explanations. What I see before me is a case that is in no way exceptional. The neuroses are a special kind of illness, analysis is a special method for treating them, a medical specialization. It is the usual rule in other cases that a doctor who has chosen a branch of medicine to specialize in will not be satisfied with just the training his diploma has confirmed, especially if he wants to settle in a big city, which is the only place able to sustain specialists. Someone who wants to be a surgeon looks for a surgical clinic where he can spend a few years. The same applies to the ophthalmologist, laryngologist, etc., and especially to the psychiatrist, who may perhaps never have the chance to work outside a state institution or a sanatorium. It will be the same for the psychoanalyst: anyone who opts for this new medical specialization will embark after completing his studies on the two-year training course at a teaching institute such as you mentioned, if it really does take that long. He will then recognize that it is in his interest to cultivate contacts with colleagues in a psychoanalytical society, and everything proceeds in the most orderly fashion. I can't see where there can be any room for lay analysis in all this.'

We will always welcome any doctor who does what you have just promised in his name. Four-fifths of the people that I acknowledge as my students are doctors anyway. But permit me to sketch for you the way that doctors' relationships to analysis have really developed and the direction they are likely to take in future. Doctors do not have any exclusive claim to ownership of analysis: on the contrary, until recently they could not find enough ways to damage it, from the most facetious mockery to the most serious slander. You will reply, rightly, that all that belongs to the past and need not influence the future. I agree, but I'm afraid the future will be different from what you have predicted.

Allow me to give the term 'medical impostor' the meaning it deserves, instead of its legal sense. As far as the law is concerned, somebody who treats sick people without the proper credentials recognized by the state is a charlatan. I would prefer a different definition: a charlatan is somebody who carries out a treatment without the necessary knowledge and abilities. Based on this defi-nition, I would venture the observation that – not only in European countries – in analysis, doctors form the largest contingent of impos-tors. They often carry out analytical treatment, without having studied it and without understanding it.

There is no point in your protesting that this is irresponsible, and you don't believe doctors capable of it. After all, you say, a doctor knows that a medical diploma is not a licence to hunt, and a sick person is not fair game. One must always allow that a doctor is acting in good faith, even if he is perhaps subject to error.

The facts remain: I hope they bear the interpretation you put upon them. But I will try to explain to you that a doctor is capable of behaving in matters psychoanalytical in a way he would take care to avoid in every other area.

The first thing to bear in mind is that, at medical school, the doctor has undergone a training that is more or less the opposite of the one he would need as preparation for psychoanalysis. His attention is directed towards objectively ascertainable anatomical, physical and chemical facts; on his proper understanding of them and his ability to influence them depends his success as a doctor. The problem of life is placed within this field of vision, in so far as it has revealed itself to us until now in the interplay of forces that are also shown to be at work in inorganic nature. He is not inspired to take any interest in the mental aspects of life phenomena. The study of higher mental achievements is no concern of medicine; it is the territory of some other faculty. Psychiatry alone is supposed to preoccupy itself with disturbances of mental functions, but we know in what way and for what purposes it does so. It looks for the physical conditions of mental disturbance and treats them like other causes of illness.

Psychiatry is right to do so, and medical training is obviously excellent. If you say of the former that it is one-sided, you have to establish the standpoint from which this characterization can be seen as an accusation. Strictly speaking, every science is one-sided; it has to be, to limit itself to certain contents, perspectives, methods. It is an absurdity, which I will not take part in, to play off one science against another. Physics does not devalue chemistry; it cannot replace it, but neither can it be represented by chemistry. Psychoanalysis is undoubtedly quite especially one-sided, as the science of the mental unconscious. So we will not contest the right of the medical sciences to be one-sided.

The standpoint we are looking for is only to be found by switching from scientific medicine to the practical art of healing. A sick person is a complicated being; he can remind us that mental phenomena, hard to grasp as they are, cannot be banished from the picture of life. The neurotic especially is an unwelcome complication, an embarrassment to practical medicine as much as to the law and the military. But he exists, and he is the particular concern of medicine. And medical education contributes nothing, absolutely nothing, towards acknowledging or treating him. Given the close connections between things that we divide into physical and mental, it is predictable that the day will come when paths of cognition and also, hopefully, of influence, will open up between the biological study of the organs and chemistry, and the territory of the phenomena of neurosis. That day seems far off; at the moment these pathological conditions are not accessible from the medical side.

It would be tolerable if all that medical education did was to deny doctors any orientation in the area of the neuroses. But it does more than this: it instils in them an erroneous and damaging attitude. Doctors whose interest in the psychic factors of life has not been awakened are all too prepared to disparage them and mock them as unscientific. Consequently they cannot take anything very seriously which is to do with these factors, and do not feel the responsibilities they impose. They fall prey to the layman's disrespect for psychological research and take the easy option. You have to treat neurotics, because they are sick and have presented themselves to the doctor; and you have to keep trying new things. But why give yourself the bother of long preparation? You can manage without it: who knows how useful all that stuff that is taught in the analytical institutes really is? The less they know about the subject, the bolder they are. Humility is found only in those who really know, for they know how inadequate this knowledge is.

The comparison of analytical specialization with the other branches of medicine that you put forward to appease me is therefore not applicable. Medical schools themselves offer the opportunity of further training in surgery, ophthalmology, etc. The analytical institutes are few in number, young in years and lacking in authority. Medical schools have not recognized them and take no notice of them. A young doctor has had to believe so much that his teachers have told him that he has had little opportunity to form any opinions of his own. And in an area where there is as yet no acknowledged authority, he will happily seize the chance to play the critic himself for a change.

There are other circumstances that favour his role as a charlatan. If he were to undertake eye operations without adequate preparation, then the failure of his cataract removals and iridectomies and the absence of patients would soon put an end to his bold venture. The practice of analysis is comparatively harmless for him. The public has been spoilt by what is on average a positive outcome of eye operations and expects a cure at the hands of the surgeon. But when the 'nerve doctor' fails to restore his patients to health, nobody is surprised. The rate of success in therapy for neurotics has not spoilt people, and the nerve doctor at least 'took a lot of trouble over them'. There's just not much you can do, nature will have to do its bit to help, or time. So for women there is first menstruation, then marriage, later the menopause. At the end, death is really helpful. And the measures the doctor has taken with the patient are so inconspicuous that no accusation will stick to them. After all, he hasn't used any instruments or medicines; he has only talked to him and attempted to persuade him to do or not to do something. That can't do any harm, particularly if care has been taken not to touch upon anything painful or upsetting. The medical analyst who has steered clear of rigorous instruction cannot fail to try to improve on analysis, to draw its poison fangs and make it comfortable for the sufferer. And it is a good thing if that is as far as he has gone, for if he has really dared to awaken resistances, and then not known how to deal with them, then he may have made himself really unpopular.

In all fairness, it must be admitted that the activities of an untrained analyst are less harmful for the patient than those of an unskilled surgeon. The potential harm amounts only to a wasted outlay on the part of the patient, and reduced or impaired chances of recovery. In addition, the good name of analytical therapy is diminished. This is all undesirable enough, but it bears no comparison with the threat posed by the scalpel of a fake surgeon. In my opinion there need be no fear of a grave or permanent deterioration of a psychological condition as a result of the unskilled employment of analysis. Disagreeable reactions fade away after a while. Compared to the life traumas that have induced the illness, the doctor's small-scale bungling is not worth discussing. It is just that the inappropriate attempt at therapy has done nothing for the patient.

'I've listened to your description of the medical fraud at work in analysis without interrupting you, but I have the impression that you are dominated by animosity towards the medical profession, and you yourself have indicated a historical explanation for this. But I'll grant you one thing: if analysis is going to take place, it should be undertaken by people who have been thoroughly trained for it. And you don't believe that the doctors who are taking up analysis will eventually do what is needed to acquire this training?'

I'm afraid not. As long as the attitude of medical schools to the analytical teaching institutes remains unaltered, the doctors will find the temptation to make it easy for themselves too great.

'But you seem to be systematically avoiding any direct statement about the question of lay analysis. I would guess that you are actually suggesting that because the doctors who want to do analysis cannot be subjected to any controls, then for reasons of revenge, as it were, and in order to punish them, they should have their monopoly of analysis taken away, and this medical activity should be opened up to lay people.'

I do not know if you are guessing my motives correctly. Later, perhaps, I can give you evidence of a less biased attitude on my part. But my emphasis is on the demand that nobody should be allowed to practise analysis unless he has acquired the right to do so through a specific training. Whether the person concerned is a doctor or not, seems to me a secondary matter.

'So what sort of specific suggestions would you like to make?'

I have not got that far yet, and I don't know if I ever will. I'd like to raise another question with you, and, by way of introduction, also touch on a particular point. It has been said that, at the behest of the doctors' organization, the relevant authorities are proposing to prohibit laymen in general from practising analysis. This prohibition would also include the non-medical members of the Psychoanalytical Society, who have enjoyed an excellent training and then perfected their expertise through practice. If the prohibition is adopted, we should have a state of affairs where a number of people are prevented from carrying out an activity, although we can be certain that they are very good at it, while the same activity is opened up to others to whom there is no question of applying a similar guarantee. That is hardly what you might call successful law-making. At the same time, this special problem is neither very important, nor hard to resolve. It concerns only a handful of people, who won't come to much harm. They will probably emigrate to Germany, where, without any legal prescription to hinder them, their competence will soon win recognition. If you want to spare them that and soften the harshness of the law for them, it is easy to do so by following certain legal precedents. In monarchical Austria it repeatedly happened that notorious quacks were licensed *ad personam* [with a special personal licence] to practise certain branches of medicine, because people were convinced they had genuine skills. These cases mainly concerned peasant healers, and as a rule they were vouched for by one of those archduchesses who used to be so numerous. But the same ought to be possible for city-dwellers, purely on the basis of specialist guarantees. More significant would be the effect of such a prohibition on the Vienna analytical teaching institute, which from then on would not be able to accept non-medical candidates for training. This would mean that, once again, a strand of intellectual activity that is able to develop freely elsewhere would be suppressed in our fatherland. I am the last to claim any competence in evaluating laws and decrees. But what I do see is that stressing our law on charlatans does not serve the purpose of aligning us with German conditions, which is obviously the aim at present, and that there is something anachronistic about applying this law to the case of psychoanalysis, since at the time of its introduction psychoanalysis did not yet exist, and the particular nature of neurotic illnesses had not yet been recognized.

I now come to a discussion of a question that seems to me more important. Is the practice of psychoanalysis a matter that should be subject to bureaucratic intervention at all, or is it more advisable to let it follow its own natural course? I am certainly not going to make a decision on this, but I am taking the liberty of putting it to you for consideration. In our fatherland there has existed from time immemorial a veritable *furor prohibendi* [mania for prohibition], a tendency to impose tutelage on others, to intervene and to prohibit, with results that we know have not been exactly good. It seems that in the new, republican Austria not much has changed as yet. I assume that you have an important voice in any decision about the case of psychoanalysis, which is our present concern; I don't know whether you will have any wish or enough influence to oppose these bureaucratic tendencies. At any rate, I will not spare you my humble thoughts on this question. I feel that a superfluity of decrees and prohibitions damages the authority of the law. It's a matter of observation: where there are only a few laws, they are carefully observed; where your every move is dogged by prohibitions, you are positively tempted to disregard them. Moreover, you don't have to be an anarchist to be open to the insight that, given their origins, laws and decrees cannot claim sanctity and inviolability. They are often inadequate in content and offend our sense of justice either now or after some time; and in view of the slowness of those who lead our society there is no other way to correct such unsuitable laws than to violate them whole-heartedly. It is also advisable, if you want to maintain respect for laws and decrees, not to pass any whose observation or infringement you cannot monitor.

A lot that we have said about the practice of analysis by doctors could be repeated here with reference to lay analysis, which the law would like to suppress. Analysis is a very inconspicuous process; it uses neither medicines nor instruments, and consists only of conversations and exchange of information. It will not be easy to prove that a lay person has been practising 'analysis' if he claims that he has only offered comfort and explanations, and that he is only trying to assert a beneficial human influence upon somebody in need of help with mental problems: you can't forbid him from doing so simply because doctors sometimes do it as well.

In the English-speaking countries the practices of 'Christian Science' are widespread, a kind of dialectical denial of the evils of life by appealing to the teachings of the Christian religion. I do not hesitate to say that this represents a regrettable aberration of the human mind, but who in America or England would dream of prohibiting it or imposing punishments for it? Do the higher authorities here feel so sure of the right path to redemption that they dare to hinder everybody else from 'seeking salvation after their own fashion'?[9] Even admitting that many people left to themselves incur risk and harm, would it not be better for the authorities carefully to demarcate the areas that are supposed to be out of bounds, and otherwise as far as possible leave ordinary souls to be educated by experience and their influence upon each other? Psychoanalysis is something so new in the world; the public at large are so poorly informed about it; and the attitude of official science towards it is still so much in flux, that it seems to me premature to be intervening in its development through legal prescriptions. Let us leave sick persons themselves to discover that it is harmful to them to look for psychological help from people who have not learnt how to give it. Let us enlighten them about it and warn them against it, and then we will have saved ourselves the trouble of forbidding it to them. On Italian country roads the power-lines carry the simple and effective inscription: *Chi tocca, muore* ['Touch and you die']. That is perfectly sufficient to regulate the treatment of low-slung wires by passers-by. The equivalent German warnings are superfluously and insultingly verbose: *Das Berühren der Leitungsdrähte ist, weil lebensgefährlich, strengstens verboten* [Touching the power-lines is strictly forbidden because of mortal danger]. Why the prohibition? Anyone who values their life will impose it on themselves, while those determined to kill themselves in this way will not ask for permission.

'But there are cases that you could cite as precedents in the question of lay analysis. I am thinking of laymen practising hypnosis, and the recent legal prohibition from holding occult sessions and founding societies of that kind.'

I cannot say that I am an admirer of these measures. The latter is an utterly blatant arrogation of authority by the police at the expense of intellectual freedom. I'm beyond suspicion of believing very much in so-called occult phenomena, let alone longing for them to be recognized. But such prohibitions won't stifle people's interest in this supposed secret world. On the contrary, great harm may have been done by shutting the door on the opportunity for disinterested curiosity to arrive at a liberating verdict on these oppressive possibilities. But again, this applies only to Austria. In other countries even research into the 'paranormal' encounters no legal obstacles.

The case of hypnosis is rather different from that of analysis. Hypnosis is the invocation of an abnormal mental state and nowadays serves lay people only for putting on a show. If hypnotherapy, initially so promising, had not declined, its circumstances would be similar to those of analysis. Incidentally, the history of hypnosis provides a precedent for the fate of analysis, but from a different direction. When I was a young student of neuropathology, the doctors campaigned passionately against hypnosis, declared it to be a swindle, a trap set by the devil and a highly dangerous intervention. Today they monopolize this same hypnosis, use it boldly as a method of medical examination, and for many neurologists it is still the mainstay of their therapy.

But I have already told you that I do not propose to make suggestions which rest on a decision about whether it is right for the law to regulate in analytical matters, or to let them go their own way. I know that to be a question of principle, where the inclinations of the key people will have more influence than any arguments. I have already put together all the points that seem to me to speak in favour of *laissez-faire*. If the decision goes the other way, in favour of a policy of active intervention, then the single feeble and unjust measure of banning non-medics from analysis seems to me an inadequate achievement. You would need to take more concerns into account: establishing, for everybody who wants to engage in it, the terms under which analytical practice is permitted; setting up some authority that can provide information about what analysis is and what preparation is needed for it; and promoting the opportunity for training in analysis. So, either leave it alone, or create order and clarity, but don't intervene through a single prohibition, mechanically derived from a regulation that has now become inadequate.

VII

'Yes, but the doctors! What about the doctors? I can't make you enter into the real topic of our discussions. You're still evading me. It's a question of whether or not doctors should be given the exclusive right to practise analysis – after they have fulfilled certain conditions, if you like. The majority of doctors in analysis are not the charlatans that you make them out to be. You say yourself that the overwhelming majority of your students and supporters are doctors. It has come to my ears that they don't share your views about lay analysis at all. I can obviously assume that most of your students support your demands for proper training etc., and yet these students find it possible to reconcile all that with excluding lay people from practising analysis. Is that so, and if it is, how do you explain it?'

I can see that you are well informed: yes, it's true. Not all, but a fair number of my medical collaborators are not on my side in this, and support the exclusive claim of doctors to treat neurotics analytically. You can see from this that differences of opinion are permitted even in our camp. My bias is well known, and this disagreement over the question of lay analysis does not cancel out our good rapport. How can I explain my students' position? I don't know for sure, but I think it is a matter of status-consciousness. Their development has been different from mine, and they still feel uncomfortable about their isolation from their colleagues. They would like to be accepted as full members of the *profession* [original in English], and for the sake of this tolerance they are ready to sacrifice a position whose vital importance is not apparent to them. Perhaps it is something different: to attribute competitive motives to them would be not only to accuse them of a debased outlook, but also to credit them with short-sightedness. After all, they are always ready to introduce new doctors into analysis, and in terms of their material situation it can only be a matter of indifference to them whether they share the available patients with colleagues or laymen. But there is probably something else to consider. These students of mine may well be influenced by certain factors which give doctors an indisputable advantage in analysis over lay people.

'Give them an advantage? That's it. So you do finally admit this advantage? That settles the question.'

It's not an admission I find difficult to make. This might show you that I am not so blinded with passion as you assume. I put off mentioning these circumstances because raising them requires further theoretical discussion.

'How do you mean?'

First of all, there's the question of diagnosis. If you accept for treatment a patient who suffers from so-called nervous disturbances, you want to be sure in advance – as far as you can – that he is suitable for therapy, that this really is a way of helping him. And that is only the case if he really has a neurosis.

'I should have thought you would see that from the phenomena, from the symptoms he complains about.'

This is where another complication arises. It isn't always accurately identified. The patient may show all the outer signs of a neurosis, and yet be suffering from something else entirely, the beginnings of an incurable mental illness, or the initial stages of degenerative brain disease. The distinction – differential diagnosis – cannot always easily be made, nor instantaneously at all stages. Naturally, only a doctor can take responsibility for such a decision. As I have said, it is not always easy for him. The case can look harmless for a long time, before it reveals its malignant nature. Neurotics are indeed constantly worried that they may be becoming mentally ill. But if a doctor fails for a while to recognize such a condition or remains unclear about it, it does not matter very much; no harm has been done and no superfluous steps have been taken. Admittedly, treating the patient analytically would not have done him any harm, either, but it would have stood revealed as an unnecessary expense. In addition, there would certainly be plenty of people ready to blame the bad outcome on the analysis. Unjustly, of course, but you have to avoid offering such grounds.

'That's very discouraging. It undermines everything you have been telling me about the nature and origin of neuroses.'

Not at all. It once again reinforces the point that neurotics are a nuisance and an embarrassment for everybody concerned; including the analyst, therefore. But perhaps I can clear up your confusion again by presenting my information in more correct language. It is probably more accurate to say about the cases we are discussing that they have evolved a neurosis, but that the latter is not psychogenetic, but somagenetic; it has physical, not mental origins. Do you follow me?'

'Yes, I do; but I can't reconcile this with the other aspects, the psychological ones.'

Well, it can be done, as long as you bear in mind the complications of the living substance. What did we identify as the essence of a neurosis? The fact that the I, having been raised to the level of the higher organization of the mental apparatus by the influence of the outside world, is not capable of fulfilling its function as a mediator between the It and reality; that in its weakness it withdraws from instinctual elements of the It and reaps the consequences of this denial by having to endure limitations, symptoms and unsuccessful reaction formations.

In all of us, such weakness of the I regularly occurs in childhood, and that is why the experiences of the earliest childhood years have so much importance for later life. Under the extraordinary pressure of this childhood phase – in a few years we have to cover the enormous evolutionary distance between the stone-age primitive and the participant in modern-day culture, and in particular we have to ward off the drive-impulses of the early sexual stage – our I seeks refuge in repressions, and exposes itself to a childhood neurosis whose residue it takes forward as a predisposition to neurotic illness in later life. Now, everything depends on how fate treats this grown-up being. If life becomes too hard, and the distance between the demands of the drives and the claims of reality too wide, then the efforts of the I to reconcile the two may fail. They are all the more likely to do so, the more the I is inhibited by the predisposition it has carried forward from infancy. The process of repression then repeats itself; the drives break free from the control of the I, creating substitute gratification for themselves by taking the route of regression, and the poor I ends up becoming helplessly neurotic.

Let us keep this firmly in mind: the centre and pivotal point of the whole situation is the relative strength of the organization of the I. By doing so, we will find it easier to complete our overview of causation. We already recognize as, so to speak, normal causes of neurosis the weakness of the childhood I, the task of overcoming the early sexual urges and the effects of more or less random childhood experiences. But is it not possible that other factors play a part, stemming from the time before the infant's life began? For example, an innate strength and uncontrollability in the instinctual life of the It, which from the beginning made excessive demands on the I? Or a particular developmental weakness of the I, whose causes are unknown? Self-evidently these factors acquire causal significance; in many cases they are paramount. We always have to reckon with the power of the drives in the It. Where it is excessively developed, the prospects for our therapy are not good. We still do not know enough about developmental inhibitions of the I. But there you have the cases of neurosis with an essentially constitutional basis. Hardly any neurosis comes about without the help of some such constitutional, congenital factor.

But if the relative weakness of the I is the decisive agent in the coming about of the neurosis, then it must also be possible for a later physical illness, if it results in a weakening of the I, to cause a neurosis. And that again is very often the case. Such a physical disorder can affect the life of the drives in the It, increasing the power of the drives beyond the limit that the I can cope with. The normal model for such processes would be, for example, the changes that take place in females because of the disturbances caused by menstruation and the menopause. Or a general physical illness, even maybe an organic disease of the central nervous system, attacks the system by which the mental apparatus gains its sustenance, forcing it to slacken off in its functioning and to cease its more subtle operations, which include the maintenance of the organization of the I. All these cases produce roughly the same picture of a neurosis. The neurosis always has the same psychological mechanisms, but, as we recognize, the most manifold, often complex causation.

'I'm liking you more now; at last you're talking like a doctor. All

I'm waiting for now is for you to admit that such a complicated medical affair as a neurosis can only be dealt with by a doctor.'

I'm afraid you're overshooting the mark there. What we have been talking about was a matter of pathology; in analysis we are concerned with a therapeutic process. I concede, in fact I demand, that in every case considered for analytical treatment the doctor should first make the diagnosis. Fortunately, the great majority of cases we are called upon to deal with are psychogenetic in nature and not suspected of being pathological. Once the doctor has confirmed that, he can safely leave the treatment to a lay analyst. That is the way it has always been in our analytical societies. Thanks to the close contact between medical and non-medical members the danger of confusion has been avoided almost entirely. There is a second kind of case where the analyst has to call upon the doctor for help. In the course of analytical treatment symptoms – most likely physical – may appear that cause doubt about whether they belong to the context of the neurosis, or are related to a separate organic illness presenting itself as a disorder. This decision must once again be left to the doctor.

'So the lay analyst can't do without the doctor even during analysis. Yet another argument against his usefulness.'

No, you can't concoct an argument against the lay analyst out of this possibility, for in the same circumstances the doctor would have acted no differently.

'I don't understand that.'

There is a technical instruction that when such ambiguous symptoms appear during treatment the analyst shall not rely on his own judgement, but call in the opinion of somebody not involved in the case, a specialist perhaps, even if the analyst is a doctor himself and has not lost confidence in his medical expertise.

'And why prescribe something that seems to me so superfluous?'

It is not superfluous; there are in fact several reasons for it. First of all, it is difficult for one person to combine organic and mental treatment. Second, the relationship of transference can make it inadvisable for the analyst to carry out a physical examination of the patient. And third, the analyst has every reason to doubt his objectivity, since his interest is so intensely focused on mental factors.

'Your attitude to lay analysis is becoming clear to me now. You insist there should be lay analysts. But since you can't deny their inadequacy for their task, you are putting forward everything that can excuse and ease their existence. But I don't see why there should be lay analysts, since they can only ever be second-class therapists. I'm willing to disregard the few laymen who have already been trained as analysts, but no new ones should be created, and the teaching institutes should undertake not to accept any more lay people for training.'

I would agree with you, if it could be shown that this restriction would serve all possible interests. You must accept that there are three kinds of interest involved: that of the patients, that of the doctors, and – *last not least* [original in English] – that of science, which of course includes the interests of all future patients. Shall we take these three points together?

All right; for the patient it does not matter whether the analyst is a doctor or not, as long as the possibility of misjudging his condition has been ruled out by the required medical assessment at the beginning and in the event of incidents occurring during the treatment. It is far more important to him that the analyst has the necessary personal qualities to make him trustworthy, and that he has gained the knowledge and the insights, as well as the experience, that alone can enable him to fulfil his task. You might think that the analyst's authority must suffer if the patient knows that he is not a doctor, and in many situations cannot help being dependent upon a doctor. We have of course never failed to inform patients about the analyst's qualifications, and have been able to satisfy ourselves that any prejudices about status were not reflected in the patients, who were prepared to accept a cure from whatever quarter it was offered to them – something that doctors found out a long time ago, incidentally, to their profound annoyance. Moreover, the lay people who are practising analysis today are not just anybody, but educated people, PhDs, teachers, and individual women with a great deal of experience of life and outstanding personalities. The analysis to which all candidates for an analytical teaching institute must submit is, at the same time, the best way of gauging their personal suitability for practising this demanding activity.

Now for the doctors' interests. I do not believe that they can gain from incorporating psychoanalysis into medicine. Medical studies already last five years, and the final examination is not completed until well into the sixth year. Every few years new demands are made on the student, and if he did not meet them he would have to be declared under-equipped for the future. Access to a medical career is very difficult, and pursuing it neither very satisfying nor very advantageous. If one adopts the clearly justifiable demand that doctors should also be acquainted with the mental aspect of illness, and extends medical education to include some preparation for analysis, that means a further lengthening of the curriculum and therefore of the time spent studying. I don't know if the doctors would be happy to draw such a conclusion from their claim upon psychoanalysis. But it can hardly be denied. And this at a time when the material conditions of existence for the classes from whom doctors are recruited have deteriorated so much that the younger generation are forced to become self-sufficient as soon as possible.

Perhaps you would prefer not to burden medical studies with preparation for analytical practice, and regard it as more advisable for future analysts to concern themselves with the required training only after they have qualified as doctors. You might say that the loss of time involved hardly matters, since a young man under thirty will never enjoy that trust from the patient that is a prerequisite of mental health care. One could reply by saying that a newly qualified doctor in the physical health field hardly enjoys great respect among patients either, and that a young analyst would do better to fill his time by working at a psychoanalytic clinic under the control of experienced practitioners.

But it seems to me more important that with this suggestion you are advocating a squandering of time that, in these difficult days, really cannot be justified economically. It is true that analytical training overlaps with medical education, but it does not include it and is not included by it. If we were founding a university institution for the study of psychoanalysis (which at the moment sounds like pure fantasy), then it would have to teach a great deal that is taught in medical faculties: aside from depth psychology, which would always be the centrepiece, an introduction to biology; as much study of sexual life as possible; some acquaintance with psychiatric syndromes. On the other hand, the analytical syllabus would include subjects that are far removed from medicine, and with which doctors would never come into contact: cultural history, mythology, the psychology of religion and literary studies. Without a good knowledge of these areas the analyst would face most of his material with incomprehension. At the same time, the better part of what is taught at medical schools is not needed for his purposes. Whether it be knowledge of the tarsal bone, the composition of the hydrocarbons, the paths of the cerebral neurones, everything medicine has discovered about bacillus infections and treatment for them, about serum reactions and tissue regeneration; all of it is without doubt extremely valuable, but it is completely irrelevant to him, it has nothing to do with him. It neither helps him to understand a neurosis, nor does this knowledge contribute to the honing of that intellectual capacity on which his activity makes the greatest demands. It will not do to object that the case is similar when the doctor takes up another medical specialization, for example dentistry. The two cases cannot be equated: the grand perspective of pathology remains important for dentistry; the body of knowledge about inflammation, suppuration, necrosis, or the interaction of physical organs. But the experience of the analyst takes him into a different world, with different phenomena and different laws. However well philosophy succeeds in transcending the gulf between mind and body, our experience is that for the time being they are separate, especially where our practical efforts are concerned.

It is unfair and impractical to force a person who wishes to relieve others of the pain of a phobia or an obsession to take a detour via medical studies. It will not succeed, either, if it does not manage entirely to suppress analysis. Imagine a landscape in which there are two paths leading to a particular vantage-point, one of them short and straight, the other long, winding and circuitous. You put up a notice warning that the short path is closed; perhaps it passes some flowerbeds that you want to protect. The only chance that your notice will be respected is if the short path is steep and difficult, while the longer one follows a gentle incline. If the situation is different, and by contrast the detour is the more difficult path, then I leave you to guess how useful your notice will be and the fate in store for your flowerbeds. I am afraid you will succeed no better in forcing lay people to study medicine than I will in persuading doctors to pursue analytical studies. You know human nature as well as I do.

'If you are right that analysis can't be practised without special training, but also that it would overburden medical study if you added preparation for analysis to it, and that medical knowledge is largely superfluous for the analyst, what happens to the aim of producing the ideal medical personality competent to meet all the demands of his profession?'

I cannot predict what will be the way out of these difficulties, and it is not my job to pronounce on it. I can only see two things: first, that for you analysis is an embarrassment, and you'd prefer it not to exist – of course, neurotics are an embarrassment, too – and, second, that for the time being you want all interests to be taken into account if the doctors decide to tolerate a class of therapist who will relieve them of the labour of treating the extremely frequent psychogenetic neuroses, and who will serve these patients well by staying in constant touch with them.

'Is that your last word on the subject, or would you like to add something?'

Certainly, I wanted to consider yet another interest, the third that I mentioned, namely science. What I wanted to say about it does not affect you very deeply, but it's all the more important to me for that.

You see, we do not consider it desirable at all that psychoanalysis should be swallowed up by medicine and then be stored away in the psychiatry textbooks, under the heading of therapy, alongside procedures like hypnotic suggestion, auto-suggestion, persuasion, that draw upon our ignorance and owe their short-lived effects to the sluggishness and cowardice of the mass of people. It deserves a better fate and I hope that is what it will have. As 'depth psychology', the theory of the unconscious mind, it could become indispensable to all the branches of knowledge which are to do with the history of the rise of human culture and its great institutions such as art, religion and the social order. It seems to me that it has already helped these disciplines to solve their problems, but these are only small contributions compared to what could be achieved if cultural historians, psychologists of religion, language researchers, etc. would themselves agree to operate with the new research methods put at their disposal. The use of analysis in the therapy of neuroses is only one application; the future may perhaps reveal that it is not the most important. In any case it would be unreasonable to sacrifice all other applications for the sake of just one, simply because this area of application happens to coincide with the sphere of medical interests.

For here another nexus is revealed, one in which it would be harmful to interfere. If the representatives of the various arts disciplines are to learn psychoanalysis in order to apply its methods and approach to their own subject, it is not good enough for them just to depend on the results published in the analytical literature. They will have to learn about analysis in the only possible way, by submitting themselves to analysis. Thus, in addition to the neurotics who need psychoanalysis, there would be a second group of persons, who accept analysis out of intellectual motives, but would surely welcome the heightening of their powers that would be a by-product. To carry out these analyses a number of analysts would be required, for whom a knowledge of medicine would be particularly unimportant. But these people – let us call them teaching analysts – would need to have undergone an especially careful training. And if this training is to be brought to life for them, they must be given the opportunity to acquire experience from particularly instructive and conclusive cases. But since healthy people not motivated by the desire for knowledge do not submit themselves to analysis, it can only be neurotics by whom the teaching analysts – under carefully controlled conditions – can be educated for their later, non-medical role. The whole thing requires a certain amount of freedom of movement and is incompatible with petty restrictions.

Perhaps you do not believe in these purely theoretical interests of psychoanalysis, or you deny them any influence on the practical question of lay analysis. In that case I must remind you that there is yet another area of application for psychoanalysis that is taken from the sphere of the law on fraudulent medics, and to which the doctors are hardly likely to lay claim. I mean its pedagogical use. When a child begins to display the signs of an unwelcome development, becoming bad-tempered and obstinate and losing concentration, there is little the paediatrician or even the school doctor can do for him, even when the child produces clearly neurotic symptoms such as anxieties, loss of appetite, vomiting or disturbed sleep. A treatment combining analytical guidance with educational measures, carried out by people not above concerning themselves with the conditions of the child's milieu, and who understand how to achieve access to the child's state of mind, can produce two results: to put an end to the neurotic symptoms, and to reverse the incipient character-change. Our insight into the meaning of the often inconspicuous childhood neuroses as a predisposition for serious disorders in later life points to these analyses of children as an excellent route to prevention. Psychoanalysis undeniably still has enemies: I do not know what means they have at their disposal to spike the guns of these pedagogical analysts or analytical pedagogues, but I do not think it will be easy to do. However, one can never be too sure.

Incidentally, coming back to the question of treating adult neurotics, we have not exhausted all aspects of this either. Our culture imposes an almost unbearable pressure on us; it needs reforming. Is it too much of a fantasy to expect that psychoanalysis, despite its difficulties, might be destined to prepare humanity for such a reform? Perhaps it will occur to an American – once again – to invest some money into training in analysis the *social workers* [original in English] of his country and making them into an auxiliary force to combat cultural neuroses.

'Aha, a new kind of Salvation Army.'

Why not? Our imagination always works with some pattern in mind. The flood of eager learners who will then stream into Europe will have to bypass Vienna, because here the development

of analysis may have succumbed to the premature trauma of prohibition. You are smiling? I am not saying this in order to try to soften
your judgement, certainly not. I know you do not believe me, and I
cannot guarantee that these things will happen. But one thing I do
know. It is not so very important what decision you make about the
question of lay analysis. It might have an effect locally. But what
matters, the inner potential for the development of psychoanalysis,
cannot be affected by decrees and prohibitions.

(1926)

Notes

1. The same applies in France.
2. [The reference is to Scene IV of Goethe's *Faust*, where Mephistopheles
apes an academic advising a student on his choice of faculty: 'For if your
meaning's threatened with stagnation, the words come in, to save the
situation: or furnish you a universal system. Thus words will serve us grandly
for a creed, where every syllable is guaranteed' (*Faust: Part One*, translated
by Philip Wayne, Harmondsworth: Penguin, 1949, p. 97.)]
3. [Because Freud deliberately draws attention here to the colloquial nature
of his terminology, in translating this essay I have been obliged to use the
terms 'the I' and 'the It', instead of the 'Ego' and the 'Id' which have become
familiar to English readers of Freud since he was first translated. It can be
argued that Freud here gives the best possible reason why this Latinate
translation was a bad idea in the first place.]
4. [The reference here is to Schiller's poem of 1795, 'Die Weltweisen' (The
Worldly-Wise), whose last lines run:

> *Einstweilen bis den Bau der Welt*
> *Philosophie zusammenhält*
> *Erhält sie [die Natur] das Getriebe*
> *Durch Hunger und durch Liebe.*

(Meanwhile, until philosophy can hold the world-structure together,
(Nature) will maintain the whole busy affair by hunger and by love.)]
5. [Although the *Shorter Oxford Dictionary* shows that the term 'drive' in
a psychological sense, as the equivalent of *Trieb*, did occur as early as 1918,

it does not seem to have gained any kind of currency until the 1930s, and a spot-check reveals it does not appear in this sense in some standard English dictionaries of the 1920s and even the 1950s.]

6. [For an explanation of the use of the form 'dis-pleasure', see note 4 in 'Analysis Terminable and Interminable', p. 207.]

7. [A line from Schiller's drama *William Tell*.]

8. ['Shell shock' is more accurately and more helpfully referred to in German as *Kriegsneurose*, and its victims are therefore 'war neurotics', *Kriegsneurotiker*, which is the term that Freud uses here.]

9. [A famous saying of Frederick the Great of Prussia.]

Postscript to 'The Question of Lay Analysis'

The immediate occasion for writing the short publication to which the present discussions[1] relate, was a charge of fraudulent medical practice that was levelled against our non-medical colleague Dr Th.[eodor] Reik by the Viennese authorities. It is probably now common knowledge that, after preliminary investigations had taken place and various expert reports had been called in, this charge was dropped. I don't think this success was due to my book; rather, the prosecution's case was too weak, and the alleged victim was not entirely trustworthy.

Halting proceedings against Dr Reik probably does not imply a decision in principle on the question of lay analysis by the Viennese court. When I invented the figure of the 'impartial' interlocutor in my polemical piece, I had in mind the person of one of our more senior officials, a well-disposed man of uncommon integrity, with whom I myself had a conversation about the Reik case and to whom I subsequently sent a private paper about it at his request. I knew I had not succeeded in winning him over to my point of view, and that is why I did not end my dialogue with the impartial person in agreement.

Neither did I expect to succeed in bringing about a united position among analysts themselves on the question of lay analysis. Anyone in this gathering who compares the views of the Hungarian Society with those of the New York group will probably assume that my publication achieved nothing at all, with everybody maintaining the position he held before. But I do not believe this either. I think that many colleagues will have moderated their extreme partiality: most have accepted my opinion that the problem of lay analysis cannot be solved by traditional ideas, because it arises out of a novel situation and therefore needs a new kind of judgement.

The overall direction of my approach also seems to have been well received. I foregrounded the proposition that it was not important whether the analyst had a medical diploma, only whether he had acquired the special training needed for practising analysis. This tied up with the question, eagerly discussed by colleagues, about what training is most suitable for the analyst.

I believed, and I still maintain, that it is not the kind prescribed by the university for future doctors. So-called medical training strikes me as a laboriously long way round to get to the analytical profession. It gives the analyst much that is indispensable, but also weighs him down with too much that he can never utilize, and it entails the risk that his interests as well as his style of thought will be diverted from coming to terms with psychological phenomena. A curriculum for the analyst has yet to be created: it will have to embrace the subject matter of the humanities, of psychology, cultural history and sociology, as well as that of anatomy, biology and evolutionary history. There is so much to learn that one would be justified in leaving out of the syllabus everything that has no direct bearing on the activity of analysis, but only contributes indirectly, like any other kind of study, to the training of the intellect and of sensory observation.

Against this proposal it is easy to raise the objection that there are no such university institutions; that this is just an ideal requirement. Yes, it is an ideal, but it is one that can be realized and must be realized. For all their youthful inadequacies, our teaching institutes are the beginning of such a realization.

It will not have escaped my readers' notice that I have taken for granted above something that is still fiercely contested in our debates. Namely, that psychoanalysis is not a medical specialization. I cannot understand how anyone can resist recognizing this. Psychoanalysis is part of psychology, not medical psychology, in the old sense, or psychology of the processes of illness, but psychology pure and simple; by no means the whole of psychology, but its basis, perhaps even its foundations.

Do not be misled by the possibility of applying it for medical purposes: electricity and radiology have also been used in medicine, but the science of both is physics. Even historical arguments cannot alter this derivation. The whole of the theory of electricity began with the observation of nervous reflexes, but nobody would want to claim that it is part of physiology. It is said of psychoanalysis that it was invented by a doctor in his efforts to help the sick. But that is obviously irrelevant to an assessment of it. And this historical argument is really dangerous.

Continuing along these lines, you might remember how unfriendly, indeed how spitefully dismissive the medical profession was towards analysis; it would follow from this that they still have no claim on analysis. And actually – although I reject such a conclusion – I am still mistrustful enough to be unsure whether the doctors' courting of psychoanalysis, seen from the standpoint of libido theory, stems from the first or the second of Karl Abraham's 'lower levels': whether it is a matter of taking possession in order to destroy or in order to preserve the object.

To stay with the historical argument for a moment: since it concerns me as a person, I can give those who are interested some insight into my own motivation. After forty-one years of activity as a doctor, my self-knowledge told me I had not actually been a proper doctor. I became a doctor through being deflected against my will from my original intention, and the great triumph of my life is that after a long detour I found my initial direction again.

From my early years I do not recall any desire to help suffering people, and my sadistic tendency was not great, so that this derivative of it did not need to develop. Neither did I ever play 'doctors'; my infantile curiosity clearly took a different direction. In my youth I developed an overwhelming desire to understand some of the mysteries of this world and perhaps to contribute something towards solving them. Enrolling in the medical faculty seemed the best route to this, but then I tried – unsuccessfully – zoology and chemistry, until under the influence of von Brückes, the greatest authority ever to influence me, I stuck with physiology, which at that time was admittedly over-restricted to histology.

So I had completed all the medical examinations without the least interest in becoming a doctor, until a word of warning from my revered teacher told me that in my miserable material circumstances I must avoid a career in theory. So I moved from the histology of the nervous system to neuropathology, and then, thanks to some new ideas in the field, I began to work on neuroses. However, I do not think my lack of a proper vocation as a doctor did my patients much harm. For the sufferer does not gain very much if the doctor's therapeutic interest is emotionally over-emphasized. For him it is best if he works coolly and as correctly as possible.

The preceding report has certainly not contributed very much to clarifying the problems of lay analysis. It was only meant to reinforce my personal legitimation, whenever I happen to be the one who is defending the intrinsic value of psychoanalysis and its independence from medical application. Here the objection will be raised that it is an academic question, of no practical interest at all, whether psychoanalysis as a science is a branch of medicine or of psychology. The real question is a different one, it is said – precisely the question of the application of analysis to treating patients. To the extent that it claims to be applicable, it will have to tolerate being absorbed into medicine as a specialism, like radiology for example, and submit to the rules governing all therapeutic methods. I acknowledge that, I admit it, but what I want to see is that the therapy should be prevented from killing off the science.

Unfortunately, all comparisons only take us so far. There comes a point where the two things being compared part company. The case of analysis is different from that of radiology; physicists do not need sick people in order to study the laws governing x-rays. But analysis has no raw material other than the processes of the human mind, and can only be learnt from people. Because of the particular circumstances involved, which are fairly obvious, a neurotic human being presents more instructive and accessible material than a normal person, and if somebody who wishes to learn and apply analysis is deprived of this material, his educational opportunities will have been reduced by a good half. Far be it from me to demand, of course, that the interests of the neurosis-sufferer should be sacrificed to those of teaching and of scientific research. My brief essay on the question of lay analysis is precisely concerned to show that if certain provisos are observed, the two interests can be reconciled, and not least that such a solution also serves medical interests, if the latter are properly appreciated.

I mentioned all these provisos myself in my essay, and I may say that in this area the recent discussion has added nothing new. Furthermore, I should like to point out that it often places the emphasis in a way that does not do justice to reality. The point often made about the difficulties of differential diagnosis and the uncertainties of diagnosing physical symptoms, which make medical knowledge or medical intervention necessary, is perfectly accurate. But the number of cases in which such doubts never arise and in which no doctor is needed, is incomparably larger. These cases may be scientifically utterly uninteresting, but in life itself they play an important enough role to justify the occupation of the lay analyst, who is completely competent to deal with them. Some while ago I analysed a colleague who developed a particularly fierce resistance to anyone who is not a doctor engaging in a medical activity. I was able to say to him: we have been working now for more than three months. At what point in our analysis did I have any occasion to call upon my knowledge as a doctor? He admitted that there had been no such reason.

Neither do I have much respect for the argument that the lay analyst, because he must be prepared to consult the doctor, can enjoy no authority with the patient and has a status no higher than that of an auxiliary, a masseur or the like. The analogy is once again inappropriate, apart from the fact that the patient tends to bestow authority according to his emotional transference, and that the possession of a medical diploma impresses him far less than the doctor thinks. The professional lay analyst will have no trouble gaining the respect due to him as a secular pastor. The phrase 'secular pastoral care' could well be used to describe in general the function the analyst has to fulfil towards the public, be he doctor or layman. Our friends among the Protestant, and latterly also the Catholic, clergy often liberate their charges from the mental impediments in their life by restoring their faith, after offering them a piece of analytical enlightenment about their conflicts.

Our opponents, the Adlerian individual psychologists, aim to bring about the same change, among those who have lost confidence and competence, by arousing their interest in social community, after they have illuminated a single corner of their mental life and shown them the part played in their illness by their self-centred and suspicious impulses. Both methods, which owe their force to their dependence on analysis, have a place in psychotherapy. We analysts set ourselves the goal of the most complete and far-reaching analysis of the patient that is possible; we do not aim to ease his burden by enrolling him in a Catholic, Protestant or socialist community, but to enrich him from his own inner resources by directing towards his I the energies that through repression are pent up and inaccessible in his unconscious, as well as those other energies that the I has had to waste in maintaining the repressions. What we are thus doing is pastoral care in the best sense.

Have we aimed too high? Are the majority of our patients even worth all the effort we put into this work? Is it not more economical to prop up a defective structure from outside rather than to reform it from within? I cannot say, but there is one thing I do know. From the beginning there was a mutual dependence in psychoanalysis between healing and researching: insight brought success; you could not carry out treatment without learning something new; you gained no enlightenment without experiencing its benign effect. Our analytical procedure is the only one in which this precious correspondence is maintained. Only by carrying out analytical pastoral care do we deepen our dawning insight into human mental life. The prospect of scientific gain has been the noblest, most gratifying aspect of analytical work. Can we sacrifice it to just any practical considerations?

Some contributions to this discussion give me cause to suspect that, in one respect, my essay on the question of lay analysts has been misunderstood. Doctors are being defended against me, as though I had declared them universally unfit to practise analysis, and had spread the word to keep doctors out. Well, that is not my intention at all. This impression was no doubt created because, in my polemically motivated presentation, I had to declare the untrained medical analysts more dangerous than the laymen. I could make my real views on this question clearer by echoing a cynicism that [the satirical magazine] *Simplicissimus* once employed about women. One man complained about the weaknesses and difficulties of the fair sex, upon which the other observed: but a woman is the best thing of its kind that we have. I must admit that as long as we do not have the teaching institutes we would like for training analysts, then medically educated people are the best material for future analysts. But allow us to ask that they do not substitute their education for training; that they overcome the partiality that is encouraged by teaching at medical schools; and that they resist the temptation to flirt with endocrinology and the autonomous nervous system, where it is a matter of understanding psychological facts by means of secondary psychological concepts.

Equally, I share the expectation that all problems related to the connections between psychic phenomena and their organic, anatomical and chemical basis should only be tackled by people who have studied both areas, that is to say by medical analysts. But we should not forget that this is not all there is to psychoanalysis, and that for its other aspect we cannot do without the collaboration of people trained in the humanities. For practical reasons we have adopted the habit, in our published work as much as elsewhere, of distinguishing medical analysis from the applications of analysis. That is not correct. The real dividing line runs between scientific psychoanalysis and its application in medical and non-medical areas.

The most vehement rejection of lay analysis in these discussions is represented by our American colleagues. A few remarks in reply to them do not seem out of place. It is hardly a misuse of analysis for polemical ends if I express the view that their resistance is entirely due to practical factors. They can see that, in their country, lay analysts are responsible for a good deal of mischief and abuse of analysis, and are thereby harming patients as well as the reputation of analysis. So it is understandable that in their outrage they want to distance themselves from these pests and to exclude lay people from participating in analysis at all. But this state of affairs is sufficient in itself to reduce the significance of their statements. For the question of lay analysis must not be decided by practical considerations alone, and local conditions in America cannot by themselves be decisive for all of us.

The resolution of our American colleagues, essentially governed by practical motives, seems to me impractical, for it cannot change a single one of the factors that dominate the current situation. It amounts to a temptation to indulge in repression. If you cannot impede the activities of the lay analysts, and you are not supported by the public in campaigning against them, would it not be more effective to take their existence into account by offering them opportunities for training, gaining influence over them, and giving them the incentive of a chance to be approved and have their help enlisted by the medical profession, so that they have an interest in raising their ethical and intellectual level?

(1927)

Note

1. This postscript appeared at the end of the published proceedings of a discussion organized by the *Internationale Zeitschrift für Psychoanalyse* [*International Journal of Psychoanalysis*] in the summer of 1927 (numbers 2 and 3 of Volume XIII).

Analysis Terminable and Interminable

I

Experience has taught us that psychoanalytic therapy, setting a person free from his neurotic symptoms, inhibitions and abnormal characteristics, is a lengthy task. That is why from the very beginning attempts have been made to reduce the duration of analyses. Such efforts needed no justification; the most sensible and practical motives could be cited in their support. But there was probably still a vestige at work in them of that impatient disparagement with which an earlier period of medicine regarded the neuroses, as superfluous results of invisible damage. If you really did now have to deal with them, then you wanted to be done with them as soon as possible. Otto Rank, in connection with his book *The Birth Trauma* (1924), made a particularly energetic move in this direction. He assumed that the act of birth was the actual source of neurosis, in that it carried with it the possibility that the 'primal fixation' on the mother might not be overcome and that it might persist as a 'primal repression'. Through subsequent analytical resolution of this primal trauma Rank hoped to eliminate the whole neurosis, so that this single small piece of analysis would obviate the need for any further analytical work. A few short months were to suffice for this achievement. It cannot be disputed that Rank's train of thought was bold and clever; but it could not stand up to critical scrutiny. Incidentally, Rank's attempt was a child of its time, conceived under the impression of the contrast between European post-war misery and American *'prosperity'* [original in English] and designed to adapt the pace of analytical therapy to the frantic tempo of American life. Not much has been heard about anything that Rank's project achieved for sick people. Probably about the same as the fire service would achieve when called out to a house on fire if it did no more than remove an overturned oil lamp from the room where it had caused the fire. It is true that a significant speeding up of the fire-fighting operation could be achieved in this way. The theory and practice of Rank's attempt now belong to the past – just like American *'prosperity'* itself.

Even before the war I myself took another route towards accelerating the pace of analytical treatment. At the time I undertook to treat a young Russian who, spoilt by his wealth and completely helpless, came to Vienna with his personal physician and nurse.[1] In the course of a few years he recovered a good deal of his independence, regained his interest in life, and restored to order his relationship to the people most important to him. But then this progress stalled; the clearing up of the childhood neurosis that clearly underlay his later illness was not getting any further forward. It was clear that the patient found his condition at the time really comfortable, and preferred not to take a single step that might bring the end of the treatment nearer. It was a case of a self-imposed block to recovery, a recovery that was in danger of being wrecked precisely by its own – partial – success. In this situation I resorted to the heroic measure of setting a deadline. At the beginning of a new working season I revealed to the patient that this coming year would be the last for his treatment, regardless of the progress he made in the time left to him. At first he did not believe me, but once he became convinced that I was in deadly earnest he underwent the necessary transformation. His resistances vanished, and in those last months he managed to reproduce all the memories and locate all the connections that the understanding of his early neurosis and the overcoming of his present one seemed to require. When he left me in the high summer of 1914, unaware as we all were of the events that were so soon to unfold, I regarded him as thoroughly and permanently cured.

In a supplement to the case history (1923) I have already reported that this assumption was not justified. When he returned to Vienna towards the end of the war as a penniless refugee I had to help him overcome a part of the transference he had not yet put behind him. This we succeeded in doing within a few months, and I was able to close my postscript with the information that 'the patient, who had been deprived by the war of his home, fortune, and all family connections, has subsequently felt normal and has behaved impeccably'. This verdict has stood the test of the one-and-a-half decades that have since elapsed, but a few reservations need to be added to it. The patient has remained in Vienna, and has established a social position for himself, albeit a modest one. But during this period his sense of well-being has frequently been disrupted by bouts of illness that can only be seen as offshoots of his life-long neurosis. Every time, after a short treatment, these conditions have been relieved by the skill of my ex-student, Dr Ruth Mack Brunswick; I am hoping she will soon be reporting on these experiences herself. In some of these attacks it was a matter of remaining vestiges of the transference, and, for all their short-lived nature, the conditions then displayed distinctly paranoid characteristics. In other bouts, however, the pathogenic material consisted of fragments of his childhood history that had not come to light in my analysis and then subsequently – the simile is inescapable – were shed like stitches after an operation or necrotic pieces of bone. I found the history of this patient's cure nearly as interesting as his case history.

I have since used deadlines again in other cases, as well as noting the experiences of other analysts in this respect. The verdict on the value of applying such 'blackmailing' pressures is unequivocal. They are effective, providing you choose the right moment to use them. But they do not offer any guarantee of a complete end to the task. On the contrary, you can be sure that, while under the pressure of your threat part of the material becomes accessible, another part is held back and as it were buried and lost to the therapeutic project. You must not extend the deadline once it has been firmly laid down; that would endanger the credibility of any sequel. Continuing the cure with another analyst is the most obvious solution, except that we know that a change like this means both a further loss of time and giving up the gains achieved by work done so far. Nor is it easy to agree when the right moment has come to deploy this powerful technical measure; it is a matter of tact. It is impossible to recover from any error of judgement. The saying about the lion only leaping once is not wrong.

II

This discussion about the technical problem of whether it is possible to speed up the slow process of analysis leads us on to another profoundly interesting question: whether there is a natural end to an analysis, and whether it is at all possible to bring an analysis to such a conclusion. The language used among analysts seems to favour such an assumption, for you often hear them saying regretfully or apologetically about a notoriously imperfectible customer: 'His analysis is not yet complete', or 'His analysis isn't finished yet.'

The first thing we need to agree on is what is meant by the ambiguous phrase 'end of an analysis'. In practical terms it is not difficult. The analysis is over when the analyst and the patient stop meeting for analytical sessions. They will do so if two conditions are more or less fulfilled. The first is that the patient is no longer suffering from his symptoms, and has overcome both his inhibitions and his anxieties; the second, that there is no longer any need to fear the return of these pathological states, because the analyst judges that the patient has been made aware of so much that was repressed; much that was incomprehensible has been cleared up; and many inner resistances have been conquered. If external difficulties have prevented you from reaching this goal, then it is better to talk of an incomplete than of an imperfect analysis.

The other meaning of 'the end of an analysis' is much more ambitious. It prompts the query whether the patient has been influenced to the point that no further change can be expected from continuing analysis. It is as though through analysis you could reach a level of absolute psychological normality, which can, furthermore, be trusted to remain stable; when, for example, all occurrences of repression have been resolved and all gaps in memory filled in. You have to consult first of all your own experience, to see if anything like this ever actually occurs, and then the theory, to see if it is at all possible in the first place.

Every analyst will have dealt with a few cases that had this happy ending. You have succeeded in getting rid of the prevailing neurotic disorder, it has not recurred and has not been replaced by a different one. We have quite a good idea of the conditions necessary for these successes to be achieved. The I of the patient must not have been noticeably altered, and the causation of the disorder must essentially be a traumatic one. For the causation of all neurotic disturbances is mixed; they involve either excessively powerful drives, that is, drives that resist taming by the I, or the effect of early, that is to say premature, traumas that an immature I cannot master. As a rule, both factors are involved, working in tandem, the constitutional and the fortuitous. The stronger the first factor is, the more likely it is that the trauma will lead to a fixation and result in a developmental disorder; the more powerful the trauma, the more certain it is to show harmful effects even where the drives operate under normal conditions. There is no doubt that the traumatic causation offers analysis a far more favourable prospect. Only in a predominantly traumatic case can analysis do what it does best, making up for an inadequate decision in the early years through correct adjustment by means of strengthening the I. Only in such cases can you talk about a permanently completed analysis. This is where the analysis has done its job and does not need to go on. But it has to be said that if a patient who has been restored to health in this way never again presents a disorder that puts him in need of analysis, you never know how much of this immunity may be due to his good luck in not having to face any tests that are too hard for him.

The factors that are unfavourable to analysis, and likely to prolong it to the point of inconclusiveness, are the inborn strength of the drives and the unfavourable change brought about in the I – through dislocation and restriction – by its struggle to contain that strength. It is tempting to blame the former, the strength of the drives, for the formation of the latter, the change in the I, but it seems that this change also has its own causation, and in fact we have to admit that as yet we do not know enough about these circumstances. It is only now that they are becoming the object of analytical study. In any case, it seems to me that analysts are not properly focusing their interest in this area. Instead of investigating how analysis brings about a recovery, which I believe has already been adequately explained, they should ask what obstacles stand in the way of an analytical cure.

In this connection I should like to deal with two problems that arise directly out of analytical practice, as the following examples will show. A man who has himself practised analysis with great success, judges that his attitude to both man and woman – to the men who are his competitors, and to the woman whom he loves – is not free of neurotic obstructions. So he puts himself under analysis with another person, whom he regards as superior to himself. This critical illumination of his own inner self is a complete success for him. He marries the woman he loves and makes himself the friend and teacher of his supposed rivals. Many years pass, and his relationship with his former analyst remains unclouded. But then, for no apparent reason, a disorder appears. The analytical subject begins to oppose the analyst, accusing him of failing to give him a complete analysis. He should have known and borne in mind that a transference relationship can never be merely positive; he should have concerned himself with the possibility of a negative transference. The analyst's defence is that at the time of the analysis there was no sign of a negative transference. But even if he had overlooked the merest indications of such a thing, which was not ruled out considering the narrow horizon of analysis in those early days, it would still be doubtful whether he would have had the power to activate a theme or 'complex' (as they say) by a mere hint, if it was not active in the patient himself at the time. To do so would have meant treating the patient in a really unfriendly manner. Moreover, not every good relationship between analyst and analysand during and after the analysis need be regarded as transference. There have been other friendly relationships that have had a real basis and proved to be durable.

I shall go directly on to the second example, which raises the same problem. A girl in her late teens has been excluded from life since puberty due to immobility because of pains in the legs. The condition is obviously hysterical in origin, and has resisted many medical treatments. An analytical cure lasting nine months removes the problem and gives back to this capable and valuable person her right to a share in life. The years after her recovery are not good; disasters in the family, financial losses and, with increasing age, the dwindling of all prospects of happiness in love and marriage. But the former patient courageously withstands all this and is a pillar of strength for her family in difficult times. I cannot remember whether it was twelve or fourteen years after the end of her cure that a gynaecological examination became necessary because of heavy bleeding. A myoma was discovered, which led to a total hysterectomy. From the time of the operation onwards the young woman was ill again. She fell in love with the surgeon, and indulged in masochistic imaginings about the terrible changes inside her, behind which she hid her romantic fantasies. She proved to be inaccessible for any further analysis, and for the rest of her life she never returned to normality.

The successful treatment had taken place so long before that not many claims can be made for it; it falls within my early years of practising. It is at least possible that the second illness had the same roots as the first, which had been successfully overcome, and that it was a transformed expression of the same repressed impulses that had only been partially dealt with in the analysis. But I am inclined to believe that, without the new trauma, there would have been no second outbreak of the neurosis.

These two cases, chosen for a particular purpose from among a large number of this kind, will be enough to launch our discussion about these topics. Sceptics, optimists and ambitious people will make different uses of them. The first group will say that this proves that even a successful analytical treatment does not protect its former beneficiary from falling ill with another neurosis, perhaps even a recurrence of the old ailment. The others will not regard the case as proven. They will object that the two experiences dated from the early days of analysis, twenty and thirty years ago respectively. Since then our insights have become broader and more profound, and our technique has adapted itself to this new knowledge. Today you could demand and expect that an analytical cure should turn out to be lasting, or at least that a second illness should not prove to be a revival, differently expressed, of the earlier disorder. This one experience, they would say, need not make us react so oversensitively that we move to limit the demands we make on our therapy.

I have naturally chosen these two case histories because they date from so long ago. Obviously, the more recent the success of a treatment, the less relevant it is to our present considerations, since we have no means of predicting how a cure will work out in later years. The expectations of the optimists clearly presuppose quite a lot that is not exactly self-evident: first, that it is possible at all to settle a drive-conflict (or rather, a conflict between the I and a drive) finally and for all time; second, that while you are treating somebody for one drive-conflict you can inoculate him, so to speak, against all the other potential conflicts; third, that you have the power to arouse such a pathogenic conflict, which currently betrays no sign of its existence, for the purpose of preventive treatment, and that this would be a wise thing to do. I am throwing up these questions without any wish to answer them at present. Perhaps reliable answers to them are beyond us as yet.

Theoretical reflection will probably enable us to contribute something towards appreciating their significance. But one thing has already become clear to us: the path to fulfilment of our heightened expectations of analytical therapy does not lead to or via any reduction of its length.

III

Analytical experience stretching over many decades, and a change in the style and manner of my activities, encourage me to try to answer the questions raised. In earlier years I had a large number of patients who were understandably keen on quick completion of their treatment. In recent years I have concentrated on analysis for teaching purposes, and a relatively small number of seriously afflicted people have stayed on with me to continue their treatment, though with shorter or longer interruptions from time to time. With these people the therapeutic aim had changed. There was no longer any question of keeping the cure short; the object was exhaustively to investigate the scope of the illness and bring about a profound change in the person.

Of the three factors that we have recognized as decisive for the prospects of analytical theory – the influence of traumas, the constitutional strength of the drives, and transformation of the I – it is only the middle one that will concern us here, the strength of the drives. My first reflection will lead us to doubt whether we have to accept the limitation implied by the adjective constitutional (or congenital). Decisive from the very beginning as the constitutional factor may be, it remains conceivable that a strengthening of the drives occurring in later life could produce the same effect. The formulation would then have to be changed; we would be talking about the current strength of the drives rather than the constitutional strength. The first of our questions ran: 'Is it possible, by means of analytic therapy, permanently and finally to eliminate a conflict between the drive and the I, or a pathogenic demand of the drive on the I?' To avoid misunderstandings, it is probably worth explaining in more detail what is meant by the phrase 'permanently eliminate the demands of a drive'. Certainly not that it is induced to vanish so that it never reappears. In general that is impossible, and would not be desirable. No, what is meant is something else, what might roughly be referred to as the 'taming' of the drive. That is to say, the drive is completely subsumed into the harmony of the I, is open to influence from other tendencies in the I, and no longer follows its own path to gratification. There is no easy answer to the question of the route and the means by which this happens. You have to tell yourself to 'call in the witch' – the witch of metapsychology, that is. Without metapsychological speculation and theorizing – I almost said 'fantasizing' – you cannot move forward an inch. Unfortunately the witch's information is once more neither very clear nor very detailed. Our only clue – an invaluable one, though – is the contrast between primary and secondary processes, and that is what I want to refer to here.

If we now go back to our first question, we find that our new point of view forces us to make a certain decision. The question was whether it is possible to eliminate a drive-conflict permanently and finally, that is, to 'tame' an instinctual demand in this way. The question of the strength of the drive is not mentioned at all in this formulation, but it is precisely upon this that the outcome depends. Let us assume that the analysis achieves for the neurotic what the healthy person does for himself without this help. With the healthy person, however, everyday experience teaches us that every settlement of a drive-conflict is only valid for a certain strength of the drive, or, more accurately, only within a certain relation between the strength of the drive and the strength of the I.[2] If the I is weakened, through illness, exhaustion, etc., then all the instincts that have previously been successfully tamed are able to announce their demands once more and take abnormal routes in their striving for substitute gratification.[3] The irrefutable proof of this assertion is supplied by night-time dreaming, which reacts to the sleeping state of the I by awakening the instinctual demands.

Equally unquestionable is the material from the other side [that of the contingent, as against congenital, influence of the drives]. Twice in the course of individual development significant strengthening of certain drives occurs: at puberty, and around the time of the menopause in women. We are not in the least surprised when previously un-neurotic people become neurotic at these times. The taming of their drives, successfully conducted while the latter were less powerful, fails when they become stronger. The repressions act like dikes holding back a mass of flood-water. The kind of impact we see from these two moments of physiological strengthening of the drives can also happen less predictably as a result of fortuitous influences at any point in life. Strengthening of the drives results from new traumas, enforced privations or the collateral influences of the drives on each other. The result is in every case the same, and reinforces the irresistible might of the quantitative factor in the causation of illness.

Here I have the feeling that I ought to be embarrassed about making all these ponderous observations, since what I am saying has been known for a long time and is self-evident. We have really always behaved as though we knew all this; it is just that our theoretical account has neglected to give the same weight to the aspect of the 'economy' of the psyche as we have to its dynamic and its local aspects. So my excuse is that I am drawing attention to this neglect.

Before we opt for an answer to our question, however, we must listen to an objection whose strong point is that we are probably already prejudiced in its favour. It holds that our arguments all derive from the spontaneous processes taking place between the I and the drive, and assume that analytical therapy can achieve nothing that does not already happen by itself under favourable, normal conditions. But is that really so? Does our therapy not precisely stake a claim to producing a state of affairs that is never spontaneously present in the I, the forging of which constitutes the essential difference between those who have or have not been analysed? Let us examine what this claim is based upon. All the repressions occur in early childhood; they are primitive defence measures on the part of the immature, weak I. In later years, no further repressions come about, but the old ones continue to exist and they are pressed into service by the I to control the drives. New conflicts are dealt with by what we call 'secondary repression'. What we have commonly said about these infantile repressions is no doubt true, that they are fully and completely dependent on the proportional relation of the forces at work, and cannot withstand the increased strength of a drive. But analysis allows the mature and stronger I the opportunity to revise these old repressions; a few are dismantled, others are acknowledged but rebuilt out of more solid material. These new dikes have a very different kind of durability from the earlier ones; they can be trusted not to give way so easily to the flood-waters of intensified drives. The later correction of the original process of repression, which puts an end to the superior strength of the quantitative factor, is thus the real achievement of analytical therapy.

So much for our theory, which we cannot renounce short of an irrefutable obligation to do so. And what does experience make of it? It may not yet be comprehensive enough for us to come to a safe conclusion. Quite often it confirms our expectations, but not always. One has the impression that we should not be surprised if it ultimately turns out that the difference between non-analysed people and the later behaviour of those who have been analysed is not so radical as we expect and maintain, and as we aspire to make it. According to this observation, although analysis might sometimes succeed in eliminating the effect of the strengthened drive, it would not do so regularly. Or perhaps its influence would lie in heightening the power of resistance of the inhibitions, so that after analysis they would be able to confront much stronger demands than they could before analysis, or without it. I am not confident about trying to decide the issue here, and I do not know if it is yet possible to do so.

But you can get closer to understanding this instability in the impact of analysis by approaching it from another direction. We know that the first step towards dealing intellectually with the environment we inhabit is to discover generalizations, rules, and laws that bring order to chaos. While, through this effort, we simplify the world of phenomena, we cannot avoid falsifying it as well, particularly where processes of development and transformation are involved. We are concerned with grasping a qualitative change, and in the process we generally neglect a quantitative factor, at least initially. In reality, transitional states and intermediate stages are much more common than are sharply demarcated, polarized conditions. With developments and transformations our attention is concentrated on the result; we are prone to overlook the fact that such processes are usually more or less imperfectly completed, and therefore, when all is said and done, they are actually only partial changes. That acute satirist of the old Austria, Johann Nestroy, once said: 'All progress is only half as great as it first appears.' One is tempted to ascribe a truly universal validity to this wicked sentence. There are practically always vestigial phenomena, a partial lagging-behind. When a generous sponsor surprises us with an isolated sign of miserliness, or someone who is usually kind to a fault suddenly indulges in a hostile action, these 'vestigial phenomena' are invaluable for research into origins. They show us that these praiseworthy and valuable qualities are based on compensation and over-compensation, which, as was only to be expected, were not completely achieved, not in full measure. Whereas our first description of the development of the libido stated that the original oral stage gives way to a sado-anal one, which in turn is followed by a phallic-genital phase, later research, while not exactly contradicting this, added the correction that these serial substitutions do not happen suddenly but gradually, so that parts of the earlier organization continue alongside the new one. Furthermore, even in normal development the transformation is never totally complete, so that in the final formation remnants of the earlier libido fixations may still survive. We see the same thing in quite different areas. There is not one of the supposedly vanquished misconceptions and superstitions of mankind that does not live on vestigially among us, at the lower levels of civilized nations or even among the highest classes of civilized society. Anything that has once lived clings tenaciously to life. Sometimes you could doubt whether the dragons of old really are extinct.

To turn to the relevance to our case, I mean the answer to our question about the instability of our analytical therapy: it may well be that we do not always fully achieve, and so do not achieve thoroughly enough, our aim of replacing the more permeable repressions with reliable defences suited to the needs of the I. The transformation does take place, but only partially; parts of the old mechanisms remain untouched by analytical efforts. It is hard to prove that this is really so; we have no other way of judging it than in terms of the success achieved, which certainly has to be accounted for in some way. The impression one has during analytical work seems to confirm rather than contradict our assumption. But you cannot make the clarity of our own insight the measure of the degree of conviction we inspire in the patient. It may well lack 'depth', we might say; there is always the matter of the quantitative factor, which it is tempting to overlook. Perhaps the solution is to say that the claim of analysis to cure neuroses through ensuring control of the drives is justified in theory, but not always borne out in practice – because analysis does not always succeed in securing in sufficient measure the basis for managing the drives. The reason for this partial failure is not hard to find. The quantitative factor of the strength of the drive originally set itself up in opposition to the defences of the I; so analysis was called in to help, and the same factor now sets a limit to this new effort. If the drive is over-powerful, the mature I, though reinforced by analysis, fails in its task just as the earlier, helpless I did. Control of the drive is improved, but remains imperfect, because the transformation of the defence mechanism is incomplete. There is nothing surprising about this, because analysis works not with unlimited but with restricted power at its disposal, and the end result always depends on the relative strengths of the elements that are in conflict.

It is doubtless always a good thing to reduce the length of an analytical cure, but the path to accomplishing our therapeutic aim can only go via the strengthening of the auxiliary power we would like to lend to the I. Hypnotism seemed an excellent means to our end; the reason why we had to give it up is well known. No replacement for hypnosis has yet been found, but it is easy from this perspective to understand the – sadly unsuccessful – therapeutic efforts to which a master of analysis like Ferenczi devoted the last years of his life.

IV

The two questions that follow, whether during treatment for a drive-conflict the patient can be protected from such conflicts in the future, and whether it is possible and effective, for the purpose of prevention, to arouse a drive-conflict that has not yet manifested itself – these two questions have to be taken together, for it is obvious that the first task can only be accomplished if the second is as well. In other words, the potential future conflict must be turned into an actual one that is subject to your influence. This new problem is basically only a continuation of the earlier one. If previously it was a matter of preventing the recurrence of the *same* conflict, now it concerns a possible replacement of that conflict by another. The aim here sounds very ambitious, but all we want to do is make clear to ourselves the limits there are to the potential of an analytic therapy.

Much as therapeutic ambition may be tempted to accept such an undertaking, experience has only a straight snub in store for it. If a drive-conflict remains only potential and has not yet expressed itself, then analysis cannot influence it either. The warning about letting sleeping dogs lie, so often cited against our efforts to explore the psychological underworld, is totally inappropriate for the circumstances of mental life. For if the drives cause disorders it is proof that the dogs are not sleeping, and if they really do appear to be asleep, it is not in our power to wake them.

However, this last remark seems to be not quite accurate, and demands more detailed discussion. Let us consider what means we have for activating a drive-conflict that is currently latent. Clearly, there are only two things we can do: either bring about a situation in which it becomes activated, or settle for talking about it in analysis, and drawing attention to its potential occurrence. The first intention can be realized in two ways; first, in reality, and, second, by means of the transference, and in both cases we expose the patient to a certain amount of real suffering through deprivation and damming up of the libido. Now, it is right for us to use such a technique in the ordinary course of analysis. Otherwise, what would be the point of the injunction to carry out the analysis 'by renunciation'? But this is a technique for dealing with a conflict that is already taking place. We try to exacerbate that conflict, and bring it to its most acute form in order to heighten the energy available for a solution. Analytical experience has shown us that every 'better' is an enemy of the good, that at every stage on the way to recovery we have to fight the inertia of the patient, who is always ready to settle for an incomplete resolution.

But when we aim at preventive treatment of an unrealized, merely potential drive-conflict, it is not enough to regulate actual and unavoidable suffering; you would have to decide to create new suffering, and so far this has quite rightly been left to Fate. From every side you would be warned about your arrogance in vying with Fate to carry out such cruel experiments upon poor human creatures. And what would these experiments be like? Can you take responsibility in the name of prophylaxis for ruining a satisfactory marriage or causing a position to be relinquished, with which the security of the analytical subject's existence is bound up?

Fortunately, you are never faced with pondering the justification for such interventions in real life; you simply do not have the authority they would require, and the subject of this therapeutic experiment would surely not want to take part.

If such a thing is effectively ruled out in practice, theory has further objections to it, too. The fact is that analysis works best when the pathogenic experiences lie in the past, so that the I can gain some distance from them. In acute states of crisis analysis is next to useless. The whole attention of the I is taken up with this painful reality and withholds itself from analysis, whose aim is to penetrate beneath this surface and expose past influences. Creating a new conflict will therefore only make analysis harder and prolong it.

It will be objected that this is a completely superfluous discussion. Nobody, it will be said, would dream of trying to make the latent drive-conflict treatable by deliberately provoking a situation of suffering. Neither would this be a laudable prophylactic accomplishment. For example, it is known that a past attack of scarlet fever produces immunity against a recurrence of the same disease. But it does not occur to the specialists to protect a healthy person by infecting him with scarlet fever because he might catch scarlet fever. Protective measures are not allowed to produce the same dangerous situation as the illness itself, only a far milder one, such as that induced by smallpox immunization and many similar processes. So in the analytical prevention of drive-conflicts only the two other methods can be considered: generating new conflicts artificially in the transference, which will lack the quality of reality; and arousing such conflicts in the imagination of the analytical subject by talking to him about them and making him aware of their potential.

I do not know whether you could maintain that the first of these two less drastic processes is absolutely inapplicable in analysis. There is a dearth of investigations specifically focused upon it. But there are obvious problems that make the enterprise look somewhat unpromising. First, your scope for selecting such situations for the transference is extremely limited. The subject himself cannot accommodate all his conflicts within the transference, no more than the analyst is able to summon up all of the patient's possible drive-conflicts out of the transference situation. You can make him jealous or experience unrequited love, but no technical purpose need be involved in this. This kind of thing happens spontaneously in most analyses. Second, you must not forget that all such happenings involve behaving unpleasantly towards the subject, and this damages his affectionate attitude to the analyst, the positive transference which is the strongest motive for the analysand's participation in your joint analytical enterprise. So not very much at all can be expected from these procedures.

There remains only the one method that we probably had in mind at the outset. You tell the patient about the possibility of other drive-conflicts, and also arouse his expectation that something like this might happen to him. You hope that telling and warning him about this will result in activating one of the conflicts in question, but to a modest degree that none the less suffices for treatment. But this time experience gives us an unambiguous answer. The expected result fails to materialize. The patient hears the message all right, but it finds no echo. He may think to himself: 'That's all very interesting, but I don't feel anything like that.' You have increased his knowledge, but changed nothing else about him. The case is roughly the same as with reading psychoanalytical writings. The reader is only 'excited' by those passages that he feels affect him, in other words that affect the conflicts going on in him at the time. Everything else leaves him cold. You can see something similar if you explain sex to children. I am far from saying that this is a harmful or superfluous thing to do, but the preventive effect of this liberal measure has obviously been overestimated. The children now know something they did not know before, but they do not know what to do with their newly acquired knowledge. You become aware that they are not even very keen to sacrifice what you might call those organic sexual theories they have formed, in keeping with and dependent upon their incomplete libido-organization, about the role of the stork, the nature of sexual intercourse and where babies come from. For a long time after they have been enlightened about sex, they go on behaving like primitive tribes who have had Christianity thrust upon them but continue in secret to worship the old idols.

V

We began with the question of how you can shorten the long-winded process of analytical treatment, and then, still led by an interest in matters to do with time, went on to investigate whether permanent healing is possible or even whether future illness can be staved off by preventive treatment. As we went on we recognized certain factors as decisive for the success of our therapeutic efforts: the influence of traumatic causation; the relative strength of the drives that need to be controlled; and something we called the transformation of the I. We only dwelt at length on the second of these factors, and in doing so had reason to acknowledge the outstanding importance of the quantitative factor and to stress that the metapsychological way of looking at things merits consideration whenever you attempt an explanation.

We have said nothing as yet about the third factor, the transformation of the I. If we turn our attention to it, the first impression we get is that there are many questions to be asked and answered here, and that what we have to say about it will prove to be very inadequate. This first impression survives even a longer preoccupation with the problem. It is well known that the analytical situation consists in allying ourselves with the I of the subject in order to subjugate certain uncontrolled parts of his It, and thus incorporate them into the synthesis of the I. The fact that such a collaboration regularly fails to work with psychotics gives our judgement its first firm reference point. The I must be a normal one for us to make such a pact with it. But such a normal I, like normality in general, is an idealized fiction. Unfortunately, the abnormal I, which is no use for our purposes, is no fiction. Every normal person is simply averagely normal; his I approaches that of the psychotic in one respect or another, to a greater or lesser extent, and the extent of his distance from one end and proximity to the other end of the range serves us provisionally as a measure for what is so vaguely called 'the transformation of the I'.

If we ask where all the various kinds and degrees of I-transformation originate, the obvious and unavoidable alternatives are either that they are inborn or acquired. The second case will be easier to handle. If acquired, then certainly in the course of development from the time that life first begins. From the very beginning the I must try to carry out its task of mediating, in the service of the pleasure principle, between the It and the outside world, protecting the It against the dangers of the external world. If it learns in the course of these exertions to take up a defensive position in regard to its own It and to treat its drive-demands like external threats, it does so at least in part because it understands that gratifying the drive would lead to conflicts with the outside world. Under the influence of education, the I then gets used to relocating the scene of the struggle from outside to inside, overcoming internal danger before it becomes an external one, and it is probably just as well that it does so. During this struggle on two fronts – later a third front is added – the I makes use of various procedures to cope with its task, which in general terms is to avoid danger, anxiety and dis-pleasure.[4] We call these procedures 'defence mechanisms'. We do not yet have an exhaustive knowledge of them. Anna Freud's book has given us our first insight into their variety and their complex significance.[5]

It is to one of these mechanisms, that of repression, that we owe the very origins of the study of neurotic processes. There was never any doubt that repression is not the only procedure the I has at its disposal for achieving its objects. But certainly it is something very particular, more distinct from the other mechanisms than they are from each other. I would like to make its relationship to these others clear by using a comparison, though I know that in these areas comparisons do not take you very far.

Suppose, therefore, that we think about the possible fate of a book at a time when books were not yet appearing in multiple copies, but were individually transcribed. Suppose that such a book contains statements that in later times are regarded as undesirable. For example, according to Robert Eisler[6] the writings of Flavius Josephus must have contained passages that offended later Christianity. Official censorship today would simply employ a single defence mechanism, that of confiscating and destroying every copy of the whole edition. At that time various means were used to neutralize the book. Passages were heavily crossed out so that they became unreadable; these could then not be copied out again, and the next scribe provided an unimpeachable text, but with gaps in places, and perhaps unintelligible where that had happened. Or perhaps this was not enough for the authorities, and they wanted to avoid any sign of the book's having been mutilated. So they resorted to distorting the text; they left out single words, or replaced them with others, and they put in whole new sentences. But best of all was to cut out the whole passage and insert a new one that said the exact opposite. The next scribe could then produce a text free from suspicion, but falsified. It no longer contained what the author wanted to convey, and very probably the corrections did not tend towards the truth.

If you do not take the comparison too literally, you could say that repression stands in relation to the other defence mechanisms as omissions relate to textual distortions. In the various forms of that falsification you can find analogies to the variety of I-transformations. You might want to object that this comparison falls down in one essential respect, for the distortion of the text is the work of a tendentious censorship that has no equivalent in the development of the I. But that is not the case, because this tendentiousness is to a large extent represented by the compulsion of the pleasure principle. The psychological apparatus cannot tolerate dis-pleasure, and must fend it off at any cost. If perceptions of reality bring dis-pleasure with them, then it, i.e. the truth, must be sacrificed. You can defend yourself for quite a while against external danger by flight and avoidance of a dangerous situation, until eventually you become strong enough to counteract the threat by actively changing reality. But you cannot take flight from yourself; flight is no help against internal danger, and that is why the defence mechanisms of the I are condemned to falsify internal perceptions and permit us only an inadequate and distorted acquaintance with our It. In its dealings with the It, the I is then crippled by its limitations or blinded by its errors, and what happens in the psyche as a result is inevitably the same as if you go rambling in an area you don't know and are not very sprightly on your legs.

The defence mechanisms serve the purpose of holding dangers at bay. It is undeniable that they succeed in this; it is doubtful whether, during its development, the I can entirely do without them, but what is certain is that they can themselves become dangerous. Often it turns out that the I has paid too high a price for the services they render. The dynamic energy required in order to maintain them, as well as the limitations of the I they nearly always bring with them, prove to be heavy burdens upon the mental economy. Nor are these mechanisms closed down once they have helped the I in its difficult years of development. Naturally, not everybody uses all possible defence mechanisms, only a certain selection of them, but these become fixed in the I. They become ways in which the character responds repeatedly, throughout his whole life, every time a situation similar to the original one recurs. Thus they become infantile traits, and share the fate of the many institutions that try to survive beyond their useful lifespan. 'Reason becomes nonsense, a good deed a trial', as the poet laments. The stronger I of the adult continues to defend itself against dangers which in reality no longer exist; it even feels a compulsion to seek out in reality those situations that can more or less replicate the original danger, in order to justify persisting in its habitual ways of reacting. So it is not difficult to understand how the defence mechanisms prepare and facilitate the onset of a neurosis, by means of an ever-increasing alienation from the external world and permanent weakening of the I.

But we are not currently focusing our interest on the pathogenic role of the defence mechanisms; we want to look at the way that the I-transformation that corresponds to them influences our therapeutic efforts. The material on which to base an answer to this question is supplied in the book by Anna Freud already cited. The essential thing about it is that the subject should repeat these ways of reacting during analysis, in front of our eyes, as it were; in fact, that is the only way we get to know them at all. This is not to say that they make the analysis impossible for us to carry out. It is more that they determine one-half of our analytical task. The other half, first tackled during the early years of analysis, is to reveal what lies hidden in the It. Our therapeutic treatment oscillates constantly during the treatment between a little It-analysis and a little I-analysis. In the first case we want to make conscious a part of the It, and in the other to correct something in the I. The decisive point is that the mechanisms used defensively against erstwhile dangers should recur during the course of treatment as *resistances* to a cure. What it comes down to is that the I should treat the therapy itself as a new danger.

The therapeutic effect is connected in the broadest sense to making conscious what lies repressed in the It; we prepare the way for this by means of interpretations and constructions. But while the I still clings to its earlier defences and does not relinquish its resistances, the interpretation is useful only to us, not to the patient. Now, these resistances, although belonging to the I, are unconscious and in a certain sense self-contained within the I. The analyst finds them easier to identify than the hidden content of the It. It should be enough to treat them as parts of the It and, by making them conscious, to relate them to the rest of the I. In this way one-half of the analytical task would be accomplished; you would not expect to find a resistance to the disclosure of resistances. But what happens is as follows: during work on the resistances, the I – more or less seriously – renounces the contract on which the analytical situation is based. The I no longer supports our attempts at revealing the It; it resists them, reneging on the basic rule of analysis, and allowing no further derivatives of the repressed matter to surface. You cannot expect the patient to be powerfully convinced of the healing power of the analysis. It may well be that he retains a degree of trust in the analyst, which becomes effective when reinforced by the factors of the positive transference when this has been kindled in him by the analyst. But under the influence of the impulses to dis-pleasure that this renewed playing-out of the old defensive conflicts makes him feel, negative transferences are now able to gain the upper hand and completely vitiate the analytical situation.

For the patient the analyst is now just a stranger who makes uncomfortable demands on him, and he behaves towards him exactly like a child who dislikes a stranger and does not believe him. If the analyst tries to demonstrate to the patient one of the distortions that have resulted from his defensiveness, he finds that he does not understand and is not open to good arguments. So there really is resistance to the revealing of resistances, and the defence mechanisms fully deserve the name given to them initially before we had researched them in depth. They are resistances not only against raising the contents of the It to a conscious level, but also against analysis in general and thus against therapy.

We may well call the effect of the defences in the I an 'I-transformation', if we understand this in terms of a distance from the fictive 'normal I' that assures the analyst of unswerving loyalty to its alliance with him. It is thus easy to believe what daily experience tells us, that essentially the outcome of therapy depends upon how strong and deep-rooted these resistances of the I-transformation are. Once more we encounter the importance of the quantitative factor, and once again we are reminded that an analysis only has certain limited amounts of energy at its command to measure up to hostile forces. Indeed, doesn't the victory usually go to the bigger battalions?

VI

The next question is whether all I-transformation – in our sense – takes place during the defensive conflicts of the early period. The answer cannot be in doubt. There is no reason to dispute the existence and significance of original, innate variations in the I. It is even decisive in itself that each individual makes choices – only a few, but invariably employed from then on – from among all the possible defence-mechanisms. This indicates that the individual I is equipped from the beginning with dispositions and tendencies, the types and modalities of which we are not, however, in a position to specify. Moreover, we know that we should not over-emphasize the difference between acquired and inherited characteristics and turn them into opposites. An important part of what is inherited is what our ancestors acquired. When we talk about an 'archaic legacy' we are usually only thinking of the It and seem to assume that no I is present as yet at the beginning of an individual life. But we should remember that It and I are originally one entity, and you do not have to over-elaborate heredity into a mystery in order to entertain the belief that before the I even exists, the lines of development, tendencies and reactions it will later demonstrate have been pre-determined. There is no other possible explanation, for example, for the psychological peculiarities of families, races and nations in their attitude towards analysis. To go even further, analytical experience has forced us to conclude that even certain specific mental features such as symbolism owe their origins entirely to inherited trans-mission. And a number of investigations into the psychology of various peoples lead us to presuppose that other, equally specialized elements of early human development have been laid down in the archaic legacy.

The perception that the characteristics of the I, which we encoun-ter as resistances, are as much conditioned by heredity as acquired through defensive struggles, has meant that the question of their location – in the I or in the It? – has lost much of its point. A further step in our analytical knowledge leads us to different kinds of resistances that we can no longer locate, and that seem to be dependent on fundamental conditions in the mental apparatus. I can only give a few samples of this genre; the whole area is confusing and strange, and not yet sufficiently researched. For example, you come across people whom you want to describe as having an especi-ally 'viscous libido'. The processes that the therapy initiates in them proceed much more slowly with them than with others because, apparently, they cannot make up their minds to detach the content of their libido from one object and transfer it to another, although it is hard to find any particular reasons for their loyalty to the *status quo*. You also meet the opposite type, whose libido seems to be particularly labile, and who rapidly agrees to the relocation of content suggested by the analysis and gives up the earlier location in its favour. It is the sort of difference an artist might be conscious of when working either in hard stone or in soft clay. Unfortunately, the analytical results from this second type often turn out to be quite invalid; the new content-locations are quickly abandoned again, and you have the impression not so much of having worked in clay, but written on water. The warning 'easy come, easy go' is appropriate here.

In another group of cases, you are surprised by a kind of behaviour that you can only relate to the fact that the flexibility you normally expect, the ability to change and develop further, are exhausted. Admittedly, in analysis we are always prepared for a certain amount of psychic inertia. When the analytical undertaking has opened up new paths for the instinctual impulses, we observe almost as a regular thing that it is only after a noticeable hesitation that these options are taken up. We have called this behaviour, perhaps not quite correctly, 'resistance from the It'. But in the cases in question, all movements, relations and distributions of forces prove to be unalterable, fixed and rigid. It is what you find with very old people, resulting from force of habit, the exhaustion of their ability to take anything in, and a kind of psychological entropy. But here we are dealing with individuals who are still young. Our theoretical preparation seems inadequate to give us a proper grasp of the types described; no doubt we need to consider chronological elements, changes within a developmental rhythm in mental life which has not yet been registered.

In yet another group of cases, those variations in the I that can be blamed for being sources of resistance to analytical therapy and obstacles to its success, are different again, and probably even more deeply rooted. Here we are dealing with the very last topic of which psychological research is able to take cognizance: the behaviour of the two basic drives and their distribution, diffusion and disaggregation, which it is difficult to imagine being limited to a single domain of the mental apparatus, whether It, I or Super-I. No stronger impression can be gained of the resistances at work during analysis than that given by a force which defends itself in every possible way against recovery, and wishes at all costs to hang on to illness and suffering. We have surely quite rightly recognized that a part of this force is consciousness of guilt and the need to be punished, and located it in the relationship of the I to the Super-I. But that is only the part that is, so to speak, psychically bound in by the Super-I, and for that reason discernible; various quantities of the same force may be at work who knows where, in bound or free form. If you look at the picture as a whole, adding the phenomena of so many people's inherent masochism to their negative reactions to therapy and the guilt-consciousness of the neurotic, it is impossible to go on thinking that mental events are dominated exclusively by the pursuit of pleasure. These phenomena are unmistakable indications of the existence of a power in mental life that we call – on account of its aims – the aggressive or destructive drive, and which we trace back to the original death-drive of matter imbued with life. It is not a question of contrasting optimistic and pessimistic theories of life; it is only the cooperation and conflict of the two basic drives, Eros and the death-drive, and never just one of them by itself, that accounts for the colourful variety of the phenomena of life.

It would be the most rewarding project for psychological research to clarify how parts of the two kinds of drive integrate with each other, under what conditions these mergers become loosened or fall apart, what disorders correspond to these changes, and with what emotions the scale of perception of the pleasure principle responds to them. Meanwhile we must submit to the superiority of the powers that defeat our efforts. Even trying to influence simple masochism puts our abilities severely to the test.

In studying the phenomena demonstrated by the destructive drive in action, we are not limited to the observation of pathological material. Numerous facts of everyday mental life cry out for such an explanation, and the sharper our vision becomes the more frequently they will attract our notice. This is too new and important a subject to mention simply in passing in this discussion; but I will make do with selecting just a few samples. This one, for example:

It is well known that there have always been, and there still are, people who can take others of the same or the opposite sex as objects of erotic attraction, without either of these leanings detracting from the other. We call these people bisexuals, and accept their existence without being particularly astonished by it. But we have learnt that in this sense everybody is bisexual, and distributes his libido either in a manifest or a latent manner between objects of both sexes. However, there is one thing that strikes us about this. While in the first case the two proclivities have come to an amicable arrangement, in the other case, which is much more frequent, they are in a state of irreconcilable conflict. A man's heterosexuality will not tolerate any homosexuality, and vice versa. If the former is more powerful, it manages to keep the latter in a latent condition and forces it away from actual physical gratification; on the other hand, nothing is more dangerous for a man's heterosexual functioning than disturbance by a latent homosexuality. You might attempt to explain this by saying that there is simply only a certain amount of libido available, for which the two rival tendencies must compete. But it is hard to see why the rivals do not regularly share the available quantity of libido between them, since they can do so in many cases, after all, according to their relative strengths. One has the overwhelming impression that the tendency to conflict is something special, newly added to the situation, irrespective of the quantity of libido. It is hard to see to what we can attribute this kind of tendency to conflict, occurring independently, other than to the intervention of an element of free aggression.

If we accept the above case as an expression of the drive to destruction or aggression, then the question arises whether we should not extend the same conception to other examples of conflict – indeed, whether we should not revise all our knowledge of psychic conflict from this new point of view. For we assume that, on the road of development from primitive to civilized man, a very considerable internalization or turning inward of aggression occurs. Inner conflicts are surely the proper equivalents for the external battles that no longer take place. I am well aware that the dualistic theory, placing a death-drive, or a destructive or aggressive drive, as an equal partner alongside the Eros that makes its presence felt in the libido, has in general not found much favour and has not actually been accepted even among psychoanalysts. My pleasure was thus all the greater when I recently found this theory of ours in the work of one of the greatest thinkers of ancient Greece. For the sake of this confirmation, I am willing to forgo the prestige of being an innovator, especially as, considering the scope of my reading in earlier years, I can never be sure that my supposed innovation was not an effect of unconscious recall.

Empedocles of Akragas (Girgenti),[7] born about 495 BC, comes down to us as one of the most splendid and remarkable figures in the cultural history of ancient Greece. His many-sided personality made its mark in a great variety of activities; he was a researcher and thinker, prophet and magus, politician, philanthropist and herbalist-physician; he is said to have freed the city of Selinunt from malaria, and he was revered like a god by his contemporaries. His mind seems to have united the starkest contrasts: while he is precise and sober in his physical and physiological researches, he is not afraid of obscure mysticism, and constructs the most astonishing and bold speculations about the cosmos. Capelle compares him to Dr Faust, 'to whom many a secret was revealed'. Arising at a time when the realm of science was not yet divided into so many provinces, many of his theories are bound to seem primitive to us now. According to him, the variety of things came about through the mixing of the four elements, earth, water, fire and air. He believed in an animistic nature and in transmigration of souls, but his theoretical construct also incorporates such modern ideas as the development of life in stages and the recognition of the role of chance (*Tyche*) in this development.

What interests us, though, is a doctrine of Empedocles that comes so close to the psychoanalytical theory of the drives that you would be tempted to claim that they are identical, if it were not that the Greek's theory is a cosmic fantasy, while ours is content to base itself on a claim to biological validity. Admittedly, the fact that Empedocles attributes the same animation to the universe as to individual forms of life does a good deal to diminish the significance of this difference.

Thus the philosopher teaches that there are two principles at work in shaping events, both in the secular and the spiritual world, and that they are in perpetual conflict with each other. He calls them φιλία – love – and νεῖκος – strife. One of these forces, which for him are fundamentally 'instinctual natural energies, not at all intelligences directed towards a goal', strives to concentrate the primal particles of the four elements into a unity; the other, by contrast, wants to undo all these mixtures and segregate the elemental particles from each other. He imagines the world-process as a continuous, never-ending succession of periods in which one or other of the fundamental forces is victorious, so that first love and then strife gain their objectives completely and dominate the world, whereupon the other, defeated force asserts itself and overcomes its partner.

Empedocles' two fundamental principles – φιλία and νεῖκος – are in name and function the same as our two primal drives, Eros and destruction; one of them concerned to combine all existing matter into ever greater unities, the other to dissolve these unions and destroy the structures they had created. Of course, we should not be surprised that when it crops up again two-and-a-half millennia later, a number of features of this theory have changed. Aside from our obligation to limit ourselves to bio-psychological matters, Empedocles' four elements are no longer our fundamental materials. Organic life has become sharply distinguished from the inorganic, and we no longer think of the mixing and separating of particles of matter, but of a welding together and disaggregation of the components of the drives. We have, to an extent, given the principle of 'strife' biological foundations by attributing our destructive drive to the death-drive, to the urge of the living to return to a lifeless state. This is not to deny that an analogous drive existed previously, nor to assert that such a drive arose only when life appeared. And nobody can foretell in what form the core of truth in Empedocles' theory will reveal itself to later insights.

VII

A richly informative lecture given by S. Ferenczi in 1927, 'The Problem of Terminating Analysis',[8] ends with the comforting assurance 'that analysis is not an endless process, but can be brought to a natural conclusion with the proper expertise and patience of the analyst'. But it seems to me that his essay, on the whole, reads like a warning not to try to shorten, but to deepen the analysis. Ferenczi added a valuable observation about how decisive it is for success that the analyst should have learnt enough from his own 'aberrations and mistakes' and that he should have 'the weaker points of his own personality' under control. This contributes an important addition to our topic. It is not only the nature of the patient's I, but also the character of the analyst that demands to be numbered among the factors that influence the prospects of analytical therapy and, like resistances, serve to impede them.

It is undeniable that the analysts have not achieved in their own personalities the degree of psychological normality towards which they would like to educate their patients.

Opponents of analysis tend to point with scorn to this fact and use it as an argument for the uselessness of the analytical project. You may dismiss this criticism as unjustifiably demanding. Analysts are people who have learnt to practise a certain skill, but beyond that they are allowed to be human beings like any other. You don't declare that anybody whose internal organs are not healthy is unfit to be a specialist in internal disorders; on the contrary, there are certain advantages to be derived from somebody who is himself threatened with TB specializing in tuberculosis cases. Of course, the two situations are not identical. A doctor suffering from lung or heart disease, if he is able to stay in practice at all, will not be obstructed by his illness either in the diagnosis or the treatment of internal complaints; whereas the analyst's own defects, because of the particular conditions of analytical work, really do interfere with his ability properly to comprehend the patient's circumstances and react to them in a relevant way. So it does make some sense to demand that one of the analyst's qualifications should be a higher level of normality and correctness. In addition, he needs a degree of superiority in order to serve as a model for the patient in certain analytical situations, and as a teacher in others. And finally, we must not forget that the analytical relationship is founded upon the love of truth, that is, upon the acknowledgement of reality, and has no room for false appearances and deception.

Let us pause here a moment to assure the analyst of our whole-hearted sympathy, in view of the heavy demands that his occupation makes upon him. It almost appears that the analyst's work might be the third of those 'impossible' professions in which, even before you begin, you can be sure you will fall short of complete success. The two others, known about for much longer, are education and government. You obviously cannot demand that the future analyst should be perfect before he takes up analysis, or that only people of such high and rare perfection should enter the profession. But where and how is the poor man to acquire the ideal aptitude he will need in his job? The answer is: by undergoing analysis himself, which is the way that preparation for his future vocation begins. For practical reasons this can only be short and incomplete. Its main purpose is to allow the instructor to judge whether the candidate is suitable for further training. It has done its job once it has securely convinced the apprentice that the unconscious exists, conveyed to him the otherwise almost incredible degree of self-perception to be gained from the recurrence of the repressed, and allowed him to sample the technique which has proved uniquely useful in analysis. By itself this would not be sufficient instruction, but we count on the stimulation received in analysis continuing after the end of his sessions, the process of working upon his I being carried forward spontaneously when he himself undertakes analysis, and the process making use, in this new sense, of all his subsequent experiences. This actually does happen, and, in so far as it does, it makes the analytical subject suitable to be an analyst.

Unfortunately, other things happen as well, and in trying to describe what they are, one is thrown back upon impressions. Hostility on one hand, and partiality on the other, create an atmosphere not conducive to objective research. However, it seems that numerous analysts learn to use defence mechanisms that permit them to divert conclusions and demands away from their own person, probably so as to direct them towards other people, so that they themselves avoid change, and evade the critical and corrective influence of analysis. It may be that this confirms what the writer said about the difficulty people have in not misusing power once it is granted to them.[9] In trying to understand this, you cannot help thinking occasionally of an unpleasant analogy with the effects of x-rays handled without special care. It would not be surprising if, in view of his constant deal-ings with the repressions struggling for release within the human mind, all those instinctual demands within the analyst himself, which he can usually manage to keep repressed, were jolted into activity. These are further 'dangers of analysis', which in this case threaten not the passive but the active partner in the analytical situation, and we should not hesitate to confront them. There is no doubt about how it should be done. Every analyst should periodically, about every five years, submit himself to analysis again, and not be ashamed to do so. This would mean that his own analysis, and not only the patients' therapy, would become interminable rather than terminable.

However, this is the moment to avert a misunderstanding. I do not intend to claim that analysis is in general a never-ending task. Whatever your theoretical position on this question, ending an analysis is in my view a practical matter. Every experienced analyst will remember a series of cases in which, *rebus bene gestis* [matters having been satisfactorily concluded], he and the patient were finally parted for good. The distance between practice and theory is much smaller in cases of so-called character analysis. Here it is not easy to envisage a natural conclusion, even if you avoid exaggerated expectations and make no excessive demands on analysis. Nobody is going to set themselves the aim of ironing out all human idiosyn-crasies in favour of a schematic normality, much less demand that someone who has been 'thoroughly analysed' should feel no passions and be subject to no inner conflicts. The analysis should create the optimum psychological conditions for the functioning of the I; its task will then be completed.

VIII

Both in character and in therapeutic analyses you become aware of the fact that two topics emerge prominently and cause the analyst an unusual amount of trouble. You cannot ignore for long the natural law that is expressed in them. The two topics are connected with sexual difference; one of them is as characteristic of males as the other is of females. Despite the dissimilarity of content, there are obvious parallels. Something that is common to both sexes is forced into a different form of expression by the sexual difference.

The two corresponding topics are, in the case of females, *penis envy* – a positive aspiration to possess male genitals – and for males, resistance to a passive or feminine attitude to another man. The common feature was brought out in early psychoanalytic nomenclature: 'response to the castration complex'. Later, Alfred Adler launched a phrase that is highly appropriate for males, 'masculine protest'. I think that 'rejection of femininity' would have been the right description from the beginning for this very remarkable feature of human mental life.

When attempting to build this factor into our theoretical structure we must not forget that by its nature it cannot be accommodated in the same way for both sexes. For the man, the striving for masculinity is from the start appropriate to his I; since a passive attitude presupposes acceptance of castration, it is vigorously suppressed, and often it is only over-compensations that indicate its existence. For the female too the striving for masculinity is appropriate to her I at a certain point, that is to say in the phallic phase, before the development of femininity. But then it succumbs to that significant process of repression upon whose outcome, as so often described, the fate of femininity depends. A great deal will hinge upon whether enough of the masculinity-complex escapes repression and permanently influences character. Large parts of the complex are normally converted in order to contribute to the construction of femininity; the unfulfilled desire for a penis should become the desire for a child and for a man, who possesses the penis. Extraordinarily often, though, we find that the desire for masculinity is preserved in the unconscious, and it emerges out of repression to play a disruptive role.

As can be seen from the foregoing, in both cases it is the aspect of opposing sexuality that falls victim to repression. I have already mentioned elsewhere[10] that this perspective was something that Wilhelm Fliess once made me aware of; he was inclined to declare that the immediate cause and ultimate motive of repression was sexual polarity. If I decline to 'sexualize' repression in that way, that is, to ground it in biology rather than just in psychology, then I am merely repeating the opposition I expressed at the time.

The outstanding importance of these two topics – desire for a penis in females, resistance to a passive attitude on the part of males – did not escape Ferenczi's attention. In a lecture given in 1927 he makes the claim that to be successful, every analyst must have mastered these two complexes.[11] From my own experience I would like to add that I find Ferenczi particularly demanding here. At no other time do you suffer from such a sense of repeated wasted effort, or the feeling that you are preaching 'to thin air', as when you are trying to persuade women to renounce as unrealizable their wish for a penis, or when you would like to convince men that a passive attitude to males does not always mean castration, and that in many situations in life it is indispensable. The stubborn over-compensation of men leads to one of the most powerful resistances to transference. The man does not want to subordinate himself to a father-substitute, does not want to owe him a debt of gratitude, and therefore will not accept a cure at the doctor's hands. No such transference can arise from the woman's desire for a penis; however, what it does give rise to is bouts of severe depression, and an inner conviction that the analytical therapy will be no use and that there is no help for the patient. You will agree with her when you realize that the persistent hope of acquiring the sorely missed male organ is the strongest motive driving her into therapy in the first place.

You also learn from this that it is not important in what form the resistance appears, whether as transference or not. What is decisive is that the resistance does not allow any change to occur, and that everything remains as it is. You often have the impression that with the penis-desire of the female and the male's protest you have penetrated to the 'living rock', and so have come to the end of your active involvement. This must be so, because biology really does serve as the living rock which lies beneath the psychological stratum. The rejection of femininity cannot be anything but a biological fact, a part of that great puzzle of sexuality.[12] It is hard to say whether and when we will succeed in overcoming this factor in an analytical treatment. Our consolation is that we are confident we have offered the analytical subject every possible encouragement to examine and to change his attitude to it.

(1937)

Notes

1. See the paper 'From the History of an Infantile Neurosis', 1918, published with the consent of the patient. The young man's later illness is not dealt with in detail there, but only touched upon where its connection with the childhood neurosis absolutely requires it.

2. A conscientious correction: 'for a certain segment of this relation'.

3. This is by way of justification of the claims to causation of such unspecific factors as overwork, the effects of shock, etc., which always enjoyed general acknowledgement but which psychoanalysis was obliged to push into the background. Health can simply only be described metapsychologically, with reference to the relative strengths of the steering elements of the mental apparatus known to us, or if you like deduced or presumed by us.

4. [The standard translation of the German term *Unlust*, which Freud uses here as an antonym of 'pleasure', in psychological literature is the awkward term 'unpleasure'. Even in Freud's day this was already an antiquated sense of the word *Unlust*, which in modern German has the restrained meaning of 'reluctance', 'lack of enthusiasm'. An older sense of 'displeasure' in English, which now means 'irritation' or 'annoyance', was closer to Freud's implication of 'pain', 'the opposite of pleasure'. I have chosen to use the translation 'dis-pleasure', the hyphen being intended to convey the special usage of the term here, parallel to Freud's special usage of *Unlust*.]

5. Anna Freud, *The Ego and the Defence Mechanisms*, Imago Publishing Co., London, 1946: first edition Vienna, 1936.

6. Robert Eisler, *Jesus Basileus*, Religionswissenschaftliche Bibliothek, first General Editor W. Streitberg, Vol. IX, Heidelberg, Carl Winter, 1929.

7. The following information is taken from Wilhem Capelle, *Die Vorsokratiker* [*The Pre-Socratics*], Alfred Kröner, Leipzig, 1935.

8. *Internationale Zeitschrift für Psychoanalyse*, Vol. XIV, 1928.

9. Anatole France, *La Revolte des anges*.

10. 'Ein Kind wird geschlagen' ['A Child is Beaten'], *Gesammelte Werke*, Vol. XII, p. 222.

11. '. . . every male patient should indicate his overcoming of castration-

anxiety by achieving a sense of equality with the doctor, while all female ones, in order to show that their neurosis is completely vanquished, must come to terms with their masculinity-complex and devote themselves without rancour to the imaginative possibilities of the female role' (loc. cit. [see note 8], p. 8).

12. We must not be misled by the phrase 'masculine protest' to assume that the male's rejection concerns the passive attitude, the social aspect of femininity, so to speak. That is contradicted by the observation, which is easy to confirm, that such men often behave masochistically towards women, displaying a positively dependent sexual attitude. The male only defends himself against passivity in relation to men, not against passivity in general. In other words, the 'male protest' is in fact nothing other than fear of castration.

Constructions in Analysis

I

A very well-respected researcher, for whom I have a high regard because he treated psychoanalysis fairly at a time when most people did not feel compelled to do so, none the less once made a comment about our analytical technique that was as hurtful as it was unjust. He said that when we present our interpretation to a patient we deal with him according to the infamous principle of *heads I win, tails you lose* [original in English]. That is to say that when he agrees with us, then we are in the right; but when he contradicts us, then that is just a sign of his resistance, so we are still in the right. In this way we are always right *vis-à-vis* the poor helpless person we are analysing, irrespective of his response to whatever ideas we impose on him. As it is quite true that a 'no' from our patient does not generally incline us to abandon our interpretation as incorrect, his exposure of our technique was very welcome to opponents of analysis. So it is worthwhile to set out in detail how we assess the 'yes' and 'no', the expression of their agreement or protest, of our patients during analytical treatment. Of course, the practising analyst will learn nothing from this justification that he does not know already.

It is well known that the object of analytical work is to bring the patient to the point of removing the repressions – in the widest sense of the term – of his early development, to replace them with reactions more in keeping with a state of psychological maturity. To do this he has to recall certain experiences and the emotional impulses they gave rise to, which he has now forgotten. We know that his present symptoms and inhibitions are the result of such repressions; in other words, they operate as surrogates for what he has forgotten. What kind of material does he make available to us that we can use to put him on the path to recovering his lost memories? A number of things: fragments of those memories in his dreams, of unique value in themselves, but usually badly distorted by all the factors involved in dream-formation; the thoughts that occur to him when he gives himself over to 'free association', from which we can discover allusions to the repressed experiences and derivatives of the repressed emotional impulses, as well as to his reactions against them; and, finally, indications of the recurrence of emotions attached to what has been repressed, in actions trivial or significant taking place both within and outside the situation of analysis. We have found the transference relationship established with the analyst particularly conducive to the recurrence of such emotional connections. From this raw material – so to speak – we have to produce what we want.

What we want is a reliable picture of the forgotten years of the patient's life, complete in all the essentials. But here we have to remember that this analytical work consists of two quite different parts, and that it takes place in two separate sites, involving two different people, each of them allocated a different task. For a moment you ask yourself why your attention was not drawn to this fundamental fact a long time ago, but you immediately tell yourself that nothing was being held back from you, that it is a matter of a universally known, you might say self-evident, fact that we are stressing and privileging here only for a particular purpose. We all know that the analysand is supposed to be induced to remember something he has experienced and suppressed. The dynamic conditions of this process are so interesting that the other part of the work, the analyst's contribution, fades into the background by comparison. The analyst has not experienced and not suppressed the things in question; it cannot be his job to remember anything. So what is his job? On the basis of the signs it has left behind, he has to guess what has been forgotten; or rather, more accurately, to construct it. What produces the link between both parts of the analytical work, between the analyst's share of it and the analysand's, is how and when and with what explanations he conveys his constructions to the analysand.

His work of construction or, if you prefer, of reconstruction, corresponds extensively to that of the archaeologist who excavates a ruined and buried settlement or an ancient building. It is in fact identical to it, except that the analyst works under better conditions, and has more material to help him, because he is dealing with something living, not a ruined object; and perhaps his objectives are different. But as the archaeologist builds up a picture of the shell of a building from remaining masonry, establishes the number and position of columns from depressions in the ground, and reconstructs the former decorations and pictures on the walls from remains found in the rubble, the analyst proceeds in exactly the same way when he draws his conclusions from fragments of memory and associations, and from comments volunteered by the analysand. Both are granted the right to reconstruct by piecing together and completing the existing remains. They also have many difficulties and potential mistakes in common. It is notorious that one of the most awkward tasks for the archaeologist is establishing the relative age of his finds, and when an object emerges at a particular level there is often a decision to be made whether this object belongs to that level or whether it has sunk down to it through some later disturbance of the site. It is not difficult to guess what corresponds to this doubt in the case of analytical construction.

As we have said, the analyst works under more favourable conditions than the archaeologist because he has material available for which there is no equivalent in an excavation; for example, the repetition of reactions dating from the early stage, and everything brought to light about these repetitions by the transference relationship. Moreover, we must consider that an excavation involves objects that have been destroyed, and that large and important fragments of these objects have quite certainly been lost, through mechanical force, fire and looting. No amount of effort can succeed in locating them in order to reunite them with the surviving remains. Interpretation depends simply and solely on reconstruction, which can therefore quite often claim at best only a certain degree of probability. The case is different with the psychological object whose previous history the analyst wants to establish. Something regularly

happens here that occurs only as a fortunate exception where archae-
ological objects are concerned, as with Pompeii and the tomb of
Tutankhamun. Everything essential is preserved; even things that
seem to have been totally forgotten are present somehow and somewhere, though buried and not accessible at the individual's will. As
is well known, we have reason to doubt whether any psychological
formation ever suffers really complete destruction. Whether or not
we will succeed in bringing the hidden object to light intact is simply
a question of analytical technique.

There are only two facts that run counter to the exceptionally
favoured situation of analytical work. The psychological object is
incomparably more complicated than the material ones of an excavation; and the state of our knowledge insufficiently prepares us for
what we will find, since the innermost structure of the psychological
object still contains so many mysteries. But this is where our comparison of the two types of work ends, for the main difference
between them is that, whereas for the archaeologist reconstruction
is the whole aim and the end of his efforts, for the analyst construction is only preparatory work.

II

The work is preparatory, however, not in the sense that it must be
entirely completed before the next stage can begin, as in building a
house, where the walls must all be standing and all the windows
fitted before one can go on to decorate the rooms. Every analyst
knows that things are not like that in analytical treatment; both types
of work go on concurrently, one running ahead, the other linking up
with it. The analyst completes a piece of reconstruction, communi-
cates it to the analysand so that it can have its effect upon him; then
he constructs a further piece from the new material that begins to
pour out, proceeds with it as before, and continues alternating in
this way to the end. If you hear very little about 'constructions' in
descriptions of analytical technique, that is because we talk instead
about 'interpretations' and their effect. But I believe that construc-

tion is a far more appropriate term. Interpretation relates to some
single element of the material, an idea, a mistake, etc., that you are
working on. But a construction means that you present the analysand
with a part of his forgotten early life-story, perhaps as follows: until
your *n*th year you saw yourself as the sole and undisputed proprietor
of your mother, then a second child came along, and with him
a serious disappointment. Your mother left you for a while, and
afterwards she never again devoted herself exclusively to you. Your
feelings for your mother became ambivalent, your father acquired
a new significance for you, and so forth.

In this paper our attention is exclusively centred upon work in
preparation for constructions. And this raises right from the start
the question of what guarantee we have, during the work on constructions, that we are not going wrong; are we putting the success
of the treatment in jeopardy by upholding an incorrect construction?
It may seem to us that there is no general answer to this question,
but before going on to discuss it, let us lend an ear to a comforting
piece of information gained from our experience of analysis. What
it teaches us is that it does no harm if we sometimes go wrong and
present the patient with an incorrect construction as the probable
historical truth. Naturally, it represents a waste of time; and if
somebody invariably relays mistaken constructions to the patient,
he will make a poor impression on him and not get far with the
treatment: but one such mistake is harmless. What actually happens
in such a case is that the patient appears to remain unaffected, and
responds with neither a yes nor a no. This might just mean that his
reaction is delayed; but if nothing else follows, then we can draw
the conclusion that we are wrong, and at some appropriate moment
we can tell the patient as much, without loss of authority. The
appropriate moment arises when new material comes to light, which
permits a better construction and thus the correction of the mistake.
The false construction falls away as though it had never been put
forward, and indeed in many cases you have the impression that, to
quote Polonius, 'your bait of falsehood takes this carp of truth'. The
danger of leading the patient astray by the power of suggestion, by
'talking him into' something you yourself believe in, but which he

would be wrong to accept, has surely been grossly exaggerated. For some mishap like this to befall him, the analyst must have behaved very incorrectly; above all he would have cause to reproach himself for not letting the patient have his say. Without vainglory, I can state that such an abuse of 'suggestion' has never once occurred throughout my career.

From the foregoing it will already be clear that we are not at all inclined to ignore the signals that are given out by the patient's reaction when we tell him about the construction. This is a point we would like to examine in detail. It is true that we do not accept the patient's 'no' at face value, but we are no more prepared to accept his 'yes', either; it is completely baseless to accuse us of converting his utterance into a confirmation in every case. Things are not so simple in reality, and we do not make the decision that easy for ourselves.

A direct 'yes' from the analysand is ambiguous. It can indeed show that he accepts the truth of the construction he has just heard, but equally it can be meaningless, or it can be what we may call 'hypocritical', in that it suits his resistance to go on covering up the truth he is hiding by agreeing with us. This 'yes' is only valuable if it is followed by indirect confirmations, if he produces new memories directly linked to his 'yes', which supplement and extend the construction. Only in that case do we recognize this 'yes' as fully settling the point in question.

The patient's 'no' is equally ambiguous, and in fact even less usable than his 'yes'. In rare cases it proves to be an expression of justified rejection; far more frequently it expresses a resistance that may be provoked by the content of the construction put forward, but can equally well derive from some other factor in the complex analytical situation. The patient's 'no' therefore proves nothing about the accuracy of the construction, but it is fully consistent with the possibility of accuracy. However, since every such construction is incomplete and contains only a small part of the forgotten events, we are at liberty to assume that the analysand is not actually denying what he has been told, but is basing his resistance on that part of the material that has not yet been revealed. He will usually only express agreement when he has learnt the whole truth, and the truth is often extremely far-reaching. So the only safe way to interpret his 'no' is as an indication of incompleteness; the construction has certainly not told him everything.

So it may turn out that you gain very few clues as to whether your guess is right or not from the direct comments of the patient after the construction has been put to him. It is all the more interesting that there are indirect kinds of confirmation that are completely reliable. One of them is an expression you hear in more or less unchanging form, as though by prior agreement, from the most varied people. It runs: I have never (would never have) thought (of) that. You can quite safely interpret this as: yes, in this case you have rightly identified what was unconscious. Unfortunately this formula, so welcome to the analyst, is heard more often after single, partial interpretations than after the presentation of an extensive construction. An equally valuable confirmation, this time expressed positively, is when the analysand responds with an association that contains something similar or analogous to the contents of the construction.

Instead of giving an example of this from an analysis, which would be easy to find but complicated to explain, I want to relate a little experience of mine that took place outside analysis, and conveys this kind of occurrence with almost comical vividness. It concerns a colleague who had selected me as a consultant – it was a long time ago – in his medical work. One day he brought his young wife to see me; she was upsetting him by using all sorts of excuses to refuse him sexual intercourse. He obviously expected me to explain to her the consequences of her unsuitable behaviour. I agreed to do so, and put it to her that her refusal would probably have unfortunate health consequences for her husband or lead him into temptations that could bring about the demise of their marriage. At this point he interrupted suddenly to say to me: 'The Englishman whom you diagnosed with a brain tumour has now died *as well*.' The comment at first seemed to make no sense, and the '*as well*' in the sentence was puzzling, since there had been no mention of anybody else dying. A little later it came to me. The man obviously wanted to back me up; he wanted to say 'Yes, you're absolutely right, and your diagnosis of that patient was vindicated.' It was the complete counterpart to the indirect confirmation through associations that we receive in analysis. I will not dispute that quite different thoughts, which he had thrust to one side, played a part in his comment.

Indirect confirmation through associations that fit into the content of the construction, and which bring this kind of 'as well' with them, provides valuable clues when we have to judge whether this construction is likely to be validated as analysis continues. It is particularly impressive when, thanks to a mistake, the confirmation insinuates itself into a direct contradiction on the part of the patient. I published a fine example of this kind of thing earlier in a different place. The name *Jauner*, which is common in Vienna, recurred frequently in the patient's dreams without any proper explanation in his associations. I then explored the interpretation that he must mean *Gauner* when he said *Jauner* [*Gauner*, '(audacious) crook', 'cunning devil'], and the patient promptly replied: 'that seems a little too daring to me'.[1] Or perhaps the patient uses the words 'ten dollars means nothing to me' while trying to refute the imputation that a particular payment seems to him too high, but in place of dollars he substitutes a less valuable currency and says 'ten schillings'.

If the analysis is under pressure from powerful factors that enforce a negative therapeutic reaction, such as a guilty conscience, a masochistic need to suffer, or resistance to the help the analyst is offering, the attitude of the patient after he has been told about the construction often makes the conclusion very easy for us to arrive at. If the construction is false, there is no change in the patient, but if it is correct or brings us nearer to the truth, he reacts with an unmistakable worsening of his symptoms and of his general well-being.

In summary, we can conclude that we do not deserve to be accused of contemptuously ignoring the analysand's attitude to our constructions. We note it and often gain valuable clues from it. But these reactions of the patient are usually ambiguous and permit no final decision. Only by continuing the analysis can we reach a decision about the rightness or uselessness of our construction. We do not claim that an individual construction is any more than a supposition that will eventually be investigated, confirmed or rejected. We do not claim any authority for it, do not demand any direct agreement with it from the patient, and do not discuss it with him if he initially contradicts it. In short, our model is that character in Nestroy, the porter who had one answer ready for every question and objection: 'Everything will become clear in the course of events.'

III

It is hardly worth relating how this happens in the further course of analysis, and by what means our supposition turns into conviction on the part of the patient; it is known to every analyst from his everyday experience and is not difficult to grasp. There is only one point about it that needs examination and explanation. The route whose point of departure is the analyst's construction should end in the patient's recall; but it does not always take us that far. Often enough it fails to lead the patient to recall what has been repressed. In lieu of that, through the correct conduct of the analysis we succeed in firmly convincing him of the truth of the construction, and therapeutically this achieves the same result as regaining a memory. Under what circumstances this occurs and how it is possible for an apparently incomplete substitution to have this full effect, is a topic for future research.

I want to close this short paper with a few remarks that open up a wider perspective. I have noticed in a few analyses that being presented with what was obviously an accurate construction had a surprising and at first incomprehensible effect on the analysands. They experienced vivid memories, which they themselves described as 'unusually clear', but what they recalled was not so much the event itself that formed the content of the construction, but details closely related to this content, for example, the unnaturally sharp features of the people who appeared in it, or the rooms in which something of that sort could have happened, or – a little less immediate – the furnishings of these rooms, of which the construction naturally could know nothing. This happened both in dreams immediately after the presentation, and in waking states, in a condition of heightened imagination. Nothing else followed in the wake of these memories; so it seemed reasonable to see them as the result of a compromise. An 'upsurge' of the repressed, activated by the narrating of the construction, wished to bring these important traces of memory up to the level of consciousness, but a resistance had succeeded, if not in blocking this movement, then in diverting it on to nearby, secondary objects.

You might have been able to call these memories hallucinations, if, in addition to their clarity, the patient also believed in their actual reality. But this analogy increased in significance for me when I noticed the occasional occurrence of true hallucinations in other cases that were definitely not psychotic in nature. My chain of ideas continued: perhaps it is a universal characteristic of hallucinations, not yet sufficiently recognized, that in them something returns that has been experienced at an early age and then forgotten, something the child heard or saw at a time when it was still incapable of speech, and that now imposes itself upon consciousness, probably distorted and displaced by the effects of the forces which oppose such a return. And with the close relationship of hallucinations to certain forms of psychosis, our chain of ideas can be extended even further. Perhaps the delusions in which we regularly find these hallucinations embedded are not so independent of the upsurge of the unconscious and the return of the repressed as we commonly assume. In the mechanism of a delusion we generally pick out just two factors; the turning away from the real world and its motives, on the one hand, and on the other the influence of wish-fulfilment on the contents of the delusion. But perhaps the dynamic of the process takes a course rather more like the following: turning away from reality gives the resurgent repression an opportunity to impose its content on consciousness. At the same time, the resistances aroused in this process, and the tendency to wish-fulfilment, are responsible respectively for the distortion and the displacement of what is recalled. This is, after all, what we know to be the mechanism of the dream, long ago equated with madness by the intuition of primitive man.

I do not believe that this conception of delusion is completely new, but it does emphasize a point of view that is not usually foregrounded. The essential thing about it is not just the assertion that madness has method in it, as the poet recognized, but that it also contains a certain historical truth, and we feel it is reasonable to assume that the compulsive conviction that delusions enjoy draws its power precisely from this infantile source. I have no fresh impressions at my command to demonstrate this theory, only reminiscences. It would probably be worthwhile to try studying relevant cases of illness in the light of the assumptions I have developed here and adapting the treatment accordingly. One would then give up the vain attempt to convince the sufferer of the insanity of his delusion and its contradiction of reality, and instead find common ground upon which therapeutic work can develop by recognizing the core of truth. The work would consist in freeing this piece of historical truth from its distortions and its dependence on the real present and shifting it back to the place in the past to which it belongs.

A shift from the forgotten past into the present or into expectations of the future is of course a regular occurrence with the neurotic, too. Often enough, when a state of anxiety gives him the feeling that something terrible is about to happen, he is simply under the influence of a repressed memory, which wishes to reach the conscious level but cannot, of something terrible really having taken place at that time. I believe that the therapeutic efforts to help psychotics that I have suggested can teach us valuable lessons, even when the therapy does not succeed for them.

I know it is not creditable to deal with such an important topic as casually as I have here. I was tempted into following an analogy. The delusions of the sick seem to me equivalent to the constructions that we build up in analytic treatment. They are attempts at explanation and recuperation, which, admittedly, under the conditions of psychosis, can only lead to our replacing the piece of reality which is being denied in the present, by another piece that the patient has already similarly denied in his early years. It becomes the aim of investigating individual cases to reveal the close relationship between the content of the current denial and that of the earlier one. Just as our construction can only work by retrieving a part of the patient's life-history that was previously lost, so a delusion owes its power of conviction to the segment of historical truth that it substitutes for the rejected reality. In this sense it would be appropriate to apply to delusion something I once said about hysteria: that the patient suffers from his reminiscences. With this brief formulation I had no intention, even at the time, of disputing the complex causes of illness or excluding the impact of so many other factors.

If you take mankind as a whole, and put it in the place of the individual human being, then you find that it too has developed delusions that are inaccessible to logical critique and that contradict reality. If these delusions none the less exert an extraordinary influence over people, investigation leads to the same conclusion as in the case of the single individual. They owe their strength to the measure of historical truth that they have extracted from the repression of forgotten past ages.

(1937)

Note

1. [In the original German the man says *jewagt* (for bold, audacious, daring) rather than *gewagt*, a form of the past participle that is not implausible, because the substitution of 'j' for 'g' occurs in the famous Berlin dialect. But the use of 'j' for 'g' unconsciously suggests confirmation of the validity of Freud's interpretation, at the very same time that the patient intends to contradict it. In other words, 'Jauner' really could easily suggest 'Gauner' to the patient, since he is familiar with the 'j'/'g' interchange.]